Blue & White

CHINESE PORCELAIN AROUND THE WORLD

Blue & White

CHINESE PORCELAIN AROUND THE WORLD

John Carswell

THE BRITISH MUSEUM PRESS

First published in 2000 by The British Museum Press
A division of The British Museum Company Ltd
38 Russell Square, London WC1B 3QQ
www.britishmuseum.co.uk

First published 2000
First published in paperback 2007

A catalogue record for this book is available
from the British Library

ISBN-13: 978-0-7141-2449-0
ISBN-10: 0-7141-2449-4

Designed by Gillian Greenwood and John Hawkins
Typeset in Palatino and Baskerville by Helen Robertson
Maps by Technical Art Services
Printed in Spain by Grafos

CONTENTS

For Sarah

&

Mr Christmas

ILLUSTRATIONS ON PREVIOUS PAGES:

1 Monochrome blue porcelain dish with a dragon in white relief. Yuan dynasty, mid 14th century. *D. 15.2 cm*
2 Blue and white porcelain dish. Yuan dynasty, mid 14th century. *D. 19 cm*
3 Detail of a vase (*meiping*) of blue and white porcelain. Yuan dynasty, 14th century. *H. (with lid) 44.5 cm*
4 Group of blue and white porcelain. Yuan and Ming dynasties, 14th/15th century. *H. (max.) 32.4 cm*

ACKNOWLEDGEMENTS

If I were to cite all those who have helped me over the years in the quest for blue and white, the list would be almost as long as the book itself. To every one who has helped me I extend my heartfelt thanks.

As far as this enterprise is concerned, I must warmly thank Emma Way and Nina Shandloff, whose idea it was in the first place and who, with their colleagues Nicola Denny and Antonia Brook at the British Museum Press, have shepherded it through from contract to completion. The fact that I was seldom in one spot – travelling to Spain, elsewhere in Europe and the United States – presented considerable logistical difficulties, all of which they cheerfully solved. At the British Museum itself, I am particularly grateful to Venetia Porter, Rachel Ward and Jane Portal for their sound advice and support.

I also owe an enormous debt to Julian Thompson, Colin Mackay and Henry Howard-Sneyd of the Chinese Department at Sotheby's, who allowed me to make use of their extraordinary archives of Chinese porcelain that has passed through the salerooms during the past twenty years. This has allowed me to illustrate the text with images of pieces which are often entirely novel, having been sold at such speed that I am sure many of my colleagues in the academic and museum world are as unaware of them as I myself was before delving into the archives. Nor could I have found my way among this material if it were not for the friendly and diligent help of the archivist, Katherine Gearon. In another context, I am profoundly grateful to the Chinese Department for allowing me to publish for the first time the two dozen pieces of Yuan porcelain found recently on a coral bank in the Red Sea. I must also thank my old friend and colleague Lucilla Phelps for her magnificent photographs of these new discoveries.

I have been very fortunate in having the helpful advice of Regina Krahl, who read two separate versions of the manuscript with scrupulous care. It was also scrutinized by my young friend Nicklas Cederqvist, who brought another most useful perspective, and in addition various sections were read by Julian Thompson, Henry Howard-Sneyd, Honor Frost, Jane Portal and Monique Crick. Needless to say, any remaining mistakes are entirely my own – the product of a creative imagination.

I was also most fortunate in being awarded Research Fellowships at both the School of Oriental and African Studies, London, and St Cross College, Oxford, which corresponded with a tricky moment in the assembly of all the material, and I am most grateful for the hospitality I received. In London, I am particularly grateful to Michael Rogers and Elizabeth Moore, and at Oxford to James Allan, Julian Raby and Michael Repp, the Master of St Cross, and Sue Robinson, the Assistant Bursar. I must also thank Victoria Leatham. The Larsson family in London have continued to be generous with access to their extraordinary collection of blue and white from Syria, to the extent of climbing up the wall to secure a missing measurement. Further afield, Aileen Lau kindly supplied photographs of Liu Xinyuan's discoveries at Jingdezhen. Dr Filiz Çagman, Director of the Topkapi Saray Museum in Istanbul, was also unfailingly helpful.

In the United States, I was warmly welcomed by Suzanne Valenstein at The Metropolitan Museum of Art, Eleanor Pearlstein and Stephen Little at The Art Institute of Chicago, and Robert Mowry and Michael Bass at the Sackler Museum at Harvard, as well as Wu Tung at the Museum of Fine Arts in Boston. I am also much indebted to Kimerley Rorschach and Richard Born of the David and Alfred Smart Museum, The University of Chicago, for locating the original plates used for the catalogue *Blue and White: Chinese porcelain and the Western World* (1984). The Chicago exhibition was in many ways the springboard for the present work.

I must single out for special thanks Mr Mohamad Reza Karlar, head of the National Museum of Iran in Tehran, Mrs Zohreh Roohfar, head of the Islamic Department, and Mr Safi, photographer at the same institution. Thanks to the intercession of my old friend Ali Afshar, they located an important Chinese dish in the Ardebil collection and had it photographed. I had already contacted Elizabeth Ettinghausen at Princeton, who took the original photos for Pope's monograph on the Ardebil collection in 1946, but neither she nor Louise Cort at the Freer Gallery could locate the negatives. It is nothing short of a miracle to be able to include a fine colour illustration.

In Portugal, I am specially grateful to Maria Antónia Pinto de Matos, Director of the Museum Dr Anastácio Gonçalves, Lisbon, for her assistance in obtaining photographs from Portuguese sources, as well as to Jorge Welsh, of Lisbon and London, who has been similarly helpful.

Closer to home, my thanks go to Theodora Izzard, for starting the index, and to my wife Peggy for undertaking the monumental task of finishing it. In fact, it is clear to all my friends that I would never finish *anything* were it not for Peggy's constant devotion and help, which I acknowledge here, with love.

INTRODUCTION

Many years ago, when I was a young man, Gerald Reitlinger once made the alarming remark over lunch that one day I would write *the* book on Chinese blue and white porcelain. As I was barely interested in the subject at that time, I was mystified by his statement. But I later learned to listen carefully to Gerald's pronouncements, for they were never as wayward as they seemed. I well remember telling him once that I was on my way to India to make a survey of the Coromandel coast. 'German stoneware!' he barked, and I wondered if he had gone mad. But sure enough, some months later, at a Dutch fort south of Mahabalipuram, that is exactly what I found – masses of it.

This book is certainly not the one that Gerald had in mind when he made his prophecy, but I think I can now see what he was getting at. He had already perceived that my fascination with Islamic ceramics would inevitably lead me to China, the fountainhead of so much influence in the Islamic world, let alone the rest of the world. What he could never have foreseen (nor I) was that in the late 1960s an enormous quantity of blue and white porcelain would come to light in Syria, where it had lain for centuries in a humble village on the outskirts of Damascus. I was fortunate enough at that time to be able to document it in detail, before it was dispersed worldwide. This inevitably led to a deeper interest as to how it ever came to be there in the first place. The present work really represents the answer to this question, and I like to think it might have appealed to Gerald Reitlinger, for it discusses many aspects of Chinese ceramics which also fascinated him.

At this point I should make it quite clear what this book is about, and what it is not. It has not been my intention to write a general survey of the evolution of Chinese blue and white, for there are already more than enough textbooks on that subject and it would be redundant to emulate them. Nor, lacking Chinese, can I quote from original sources in that language and my only references have depended on the good offices of friends more competent than myself, notably Regina Krahl and Stefan Polter. So this work is thin on direct knowledge of blue and white in China itself. But what does interest me profoundly is the movement of Chinese porcelain from its source, what stimulated this trade and what effect it had on the rest of the world. For me this culminates in the sixteenth century, when the whole world was encircled by blue and white, flowing westwards from its production centre at Jingdezhen by the traditional maritime routes, but also, more surprisingly, to the east across the Pacific Ocean to Mexico, then overland to Vera Cruz and finally across the Atlantic to Europe.

My own researches, which began quite fortuitously in Beirut forty years ago, have led me from Damascus throughout the Middle East, to the Indian subcontinent, Sri Lanka and the Maldive Islands, and more recently to Central Asia and Inner Mongolia. Almost every step was precipitated by a question provoked by a previous move. It has been a great adventure, and I have been extremely lucky in the friends and fellow scholars I have met along the way. The present work is probably just about as far as I can take my own contribution to the field, but, looking back in valedictory fashion, the long journey has an almost Proustian ring about it. I have ended up just about where I began – at the beginning, both in space and time.

John Carswell, MOYA, 2000

1 ORIGINS

The origins of blue and white in the Yuan dynasty

We reach the city of Sin Kalan [Guangzhou/Canton] *which is the city of Sin as-Sin. And in it is made the pottery* (al-fakhkhar as-sini) *and also in Zaitun* [Quanzhou] *... and it is among the largest of cities ... and among most beautiful of them for markets and among the largest of its markets is the potter's market* (suq al-fakhkharin) *and from it* [the pottery] *is carried to the other countries of China and to India and the Yemen ... it even reaches our country in the Maghreb* [Morocco]. *And it is the most marvellous of kinds of pottery.*[1]

IBN BATTUTA, *c.*1346

OPPOSITE
5 Dish of blue and white porcelain with a unique moulded *lingzhi* scroll on the rim and moulded peonies and leaves in the cavetto. Yuan dynasty, 14th century. *D. 48.2 cm.*

6 Stem cup of white porcelain. Tang dynasty (618–907). *H. 8.1 cm.*

During the Yuan dynasty (1279–1368) after the Mongol conquest of China, some time in the early fourteenth century an entirely new kind of porcelain appeared, painted in underglaze cobalt blue. With hardly any precedent, this blue and white porcelain sprang on to an empty stage, a platform which it was to dominate in the history of world ceramics for the next four hundred years.

The white porcelain body was a Chinese innovation, the last development in a long history of white glazed stoneware dating from at least as early as the Sui dynasty (581–618). By the early fourteenth century the body was made of white clay (kaolin) mixed with pulverized china stone (petuntse) and fired to a high temperature. The glaze consisted of similar elements and fused with it, so it is hard to tell where the body ends and the glaze begins. Floating between the two is the blue decoration, painted under a flawless transparent glaze. The blue was executed using cobalt initially imported from Persia, where it had been used for centuries for the decoration of Persian pottery. The impulse to use this new colour must have come from the Persian merchants who had been established on the coast of China almost from the beginning of Islam. The combination of dazzling white porcelain and brilliant cobalt blue created a product that was to fascinate the rest of the world to this day.

Because of the introspective nature of Chinese society and its lack of curiosity about or direct contact with the West, like so many Chinese inventions the true nature of the composition and manufacture of porcelain for centuries remained a secret. It was not until the early eighteenth century in Europe that Johann Friedrich Böttger, an alchemist, accidentally discovered its composition whilst

7 Dish of blue and white porcelain, with moulded flowers on the rim and in the cavetto. Yuan dynasty, 14th century. *D. 42 cm.*

8 a, b Bowl of blue and white porcelain with a foliate rim. Yuan dynasty, 14th century. *D. 40.5 cm.*

optimistically trying to turn base metal into gold.[2] This led to the foundation of the European porcelain industry at Meissen. Up till then, countless imitations of blue and white porcelain had been made in more humble low-fired earthenware, in Central Asia, Persia, Syria, Egypt and Turkey, further west in Italy and elsewhere in Europe, and even further afield in Mexico.[3]

From the very beginning Yuan blue and white, with its often massive forms and complex decoration, differed fundamentally from the slighter and more delicate wares of the preceding Song dynasty. It was held in great esteem all over Asia, and from the kilns at Jingdezhen in southern China it was carried westwards by both land and sea. Its archaeological trace can be observed in a trail of sherds from sites throughout Central and Southeast Asia, India, Sri Lanka, the Maldives, the Gulf and Red Sea and the coast of East Africa. Evidence of its ultimate destination can be found in the two famous collections of Chinese porcelain in the Near East which have survived: that of the Safavid Shahs of Persia, once housed in the Ardebil Shrine on the shores of the Caspian and now in Tehran, and that of

the Ottoman Sultans, now in the Topkapi Saray in Istanbul. This material is augmented by over six hundred pieces of porcelain found three decades ago in more humble households in Syria and retrieved more recently from a fourteenth-century wreck in the Red Sea, as well as masses of broken blue and white from the middens of Fustat (old Cairo), and fragments from Hama and elsewhere in Syria.

By the early fifteenth century a stylistic change can be detected in the blue and white and the porcelain becomes much more Chinese in appearance, with designs akin to other Chinese decorative arts. At the same time many of the shapes of the blue and white were influenced by Islamic forms, taken from Persian and Mamluk metalwork and even glass. Thus began a pattern of Chinese response to foreign stimuli that was to continue right up to the present day. It reached its peak during the period of Portuguese, Dutch and British colonial expansion into Asia, culminating in the eighteenth century and later with explicitly European – and American – designs sent to be executed in China.

The traditional export routes by sea across the Indian Ocean were supplemented from the sixteenth century by a new route eastwards across the Pacific. This was the result of the export to the Far East by the Spanish of enormous quantities of Mexican and South American silver, carried once a year by the Manila galleon sailing from Acapulco. It returned laden with products from China, India and the East in general, which were transported overland across Mexico to the port of Vera Cruz and then shipped across the Atlantic to Spain. Chinese porcelain figured largely in these shipments, and by the end of the century the export of blue and white encircled the world, the porcelain travelling either east or west from China until it reached its final European destination (see map, **10**, on p. 17). In the wake of European demand for other exotic products such as silks, paintings, lacquer and furniture, this led to a taste for *chinoiserie*. Special rooms were even created for the display of imported Chinese blue and white porcelain in England, France, Portugal, Sweden and Germany.

Although there are records showing the esteem in which porcelain was held by private individuals from at least as early as the sixteenth century, such as that of William Cecil, Lord Burghley's gift of a white bowl with gold mounts to Queen Elizabeth on New Year's Day 1587, the private collection of Chinese wares did not begin in earnest until the nineteenth century. Blue and white was part of the general vogue for *chinoiserie*, but it was appreciated for its aesthetic, Whistlerian qualities rather than for its historical context. The academic study of the history and development of blue and white has taken place largely in the past hundred years, and nowhere with greater enthusiasm and intensity than in England, where the Oriental Ceramic Society, founded in 1921, has played a major role. Originally a group of connoisseurs, collectors, museum officials and dealers, through its lectures, special exhibitions and publications the Society fostered the serious and detailed study of the subject.

To this were added the researches of scholars worldwide, most notably John A. Pope, whose pioneer work on the early evolution of blue and white remains a seminal contribution. In more recent years the investigation has broadened to include new evidence from archaeological excavations, surveys and particularly shipwrecks. Scientific enquiry now embraces sophisticated analysis of the actual ware and its manufacture and, most importantly, evidence provided by scholars within China itself. Its scope has been further broadened by incorporating material from other disciplines, such as history, economics and the study of international trade.

Blue and white has never ceased to exercise its phenomenal attraction, not only for collectors and the general public but also as a perennial source of inspiration for designers and craftsmen. The present work is an account of its invention, its technical and stylistic characteristics, its export and the influence it has exerted on the whole history of world ceramics and taste during the almost seven hundred years of its evolution.

The beginning

Most works on the history of blue and white porcelain acknowledge that whilst there appear to have been some earlier tentative experiments using cobalt blue, the real leap forward took place during the second quarter of the fourteenth century. It has also been pointed out that this development occurred during the Yuan dynasty (1279–1368), when the Mongol empire embraced not only China but most of Asia as well, invigorating the trade routes to the West following the old Silk Road. This seems to have had a catalytic effect on the potters at Jingdezhen, the major centre of the ceramic industry in south central China [**10**].

But what has been largely overlooked is the fact that the blue and white evolution took place a hundred years after the death of Genghis Khan in 1227, at a moment when the Mongol empire – the greatest empire the world has ever seen, before or since – had fragmented into four separate Khanates. Qubilai Khan, who founded the Yuan dynasty in 1260, had brought China under his yoke, but by the time he died in 1294 blue and white had barely been conceived. It was not until

9 Detail of a jar (*guan*) of blue and white porcelain. Yuan dynasty, 14th century. *H. 34.6 cm.*

10 The distribution of Yuan blue and white
From its production centre at Jingdezhen in southern China, blue and white circulated widely, not only in China itself, but throughout Asia as far as the Mediterranean.

The sites indicated are those where such porcelain has been found, their distribution showing clearly how it was exported, by both land and sea.

The maritime routes followed those already well established, from Chinese ports throughout Southeast Asia, through the Malacca Straits to India, the Maldives, the Persian Gulf, the Red Sea and East Africa.

The land route is less well defined, but from Dadu (Beijing) in the north it can be traced to Liaoning and westwards through Mongol territory to the garrison city of Kharakhoto in the Gobi desert, to Almalik, capital of the Chaghatai khanate, on to Samarkand and Tabriz, and ultimately down into Syria.

In schematic form, this map illustrates the present state of our knowledge, but more evidence may well be found in the future.

more than thirty years later, during the latter half of the Yuan period, that the new ware really took off.

It is generally accepted that the production of blue and white began in earnest on a large scale some time shortly after 1325. The main evidence for this is its complete absence from a cargo of Chinese ceramics salvaged from a wreck off the coast of Sinan in South Korea. Among more than 18,000 vessels so far recovered, 5,000 are from Jingdezhen, but there is not a single piece of blue and white. The date of the vessel is secure, as a number of inscribed wooden tags have also been found, one of which is dated the 1st of June of the third year of Zhizhi – that is, AD 1323.

It has been widely asserted that the introduction of blue and white is attributable to Moslem influence in China, the Persian merchants who brought the cobalt having played a leading role. This is a convincing premise and may well be true. It does, however, leave out the fact that this occurred under Mongol rule. Although the large dishes, bowls and vases predominate, there are also slighter and finer wares, such as spouted bowls with loop handles, stem cups and dishes, which got no further in the north than Mongol territory. This implies that from the

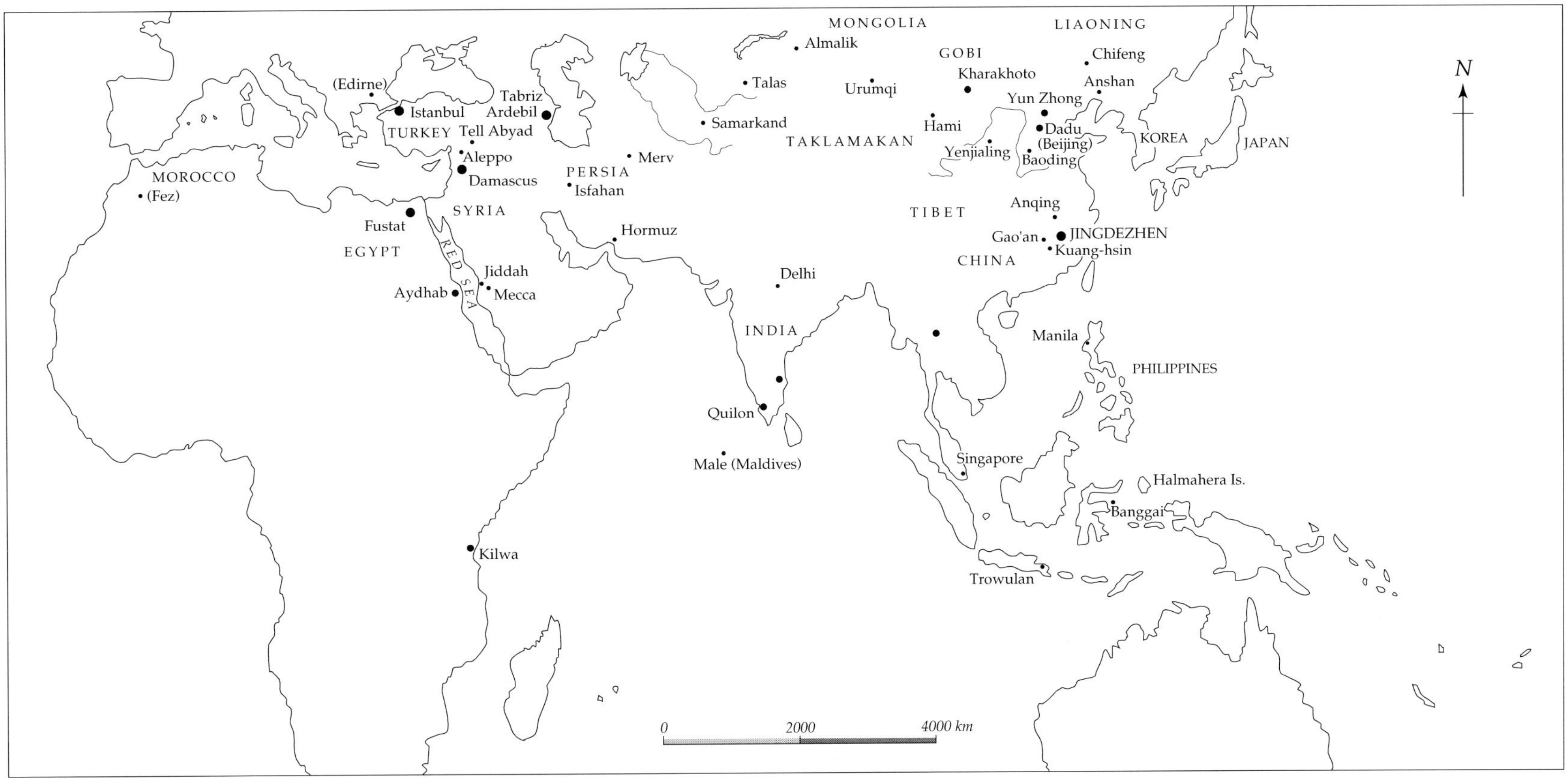

very start there were a number of quite different patrons to be supplied, an assumption corroborated by recent excavations at Jingdezhen itself, where wares of superior quality have been found mixed up with others meant for a less sophisticated market.

Since the collapse of the Soviet Union and the accessibility of Central Asia to foreign researchers, coupled with greater freedom to travel within China itself, some new evidence has come to light for the movement of blue and white during this early evolutionary period. Besides following the traditional sea route to the West that had been in use since at least the Tang period, it is now evident that Yuan porcelain also travelled northwards and then west by land, following the ancient routes through Central Asia.

The qualities of porcelain

The name 'porcelain' has a curious etymology. It was first used as a ceramic term by Marco Polo. Here it should be noted that Marco Polo did not actually write his description of his travels to China, but dictated it to one Rustichello of Pisa, who shared a dungeon with him when he was in prison in Genoa in 1298. Rustichello was from Languedoc and therefore wrote his account not in Italian but in the *langue d'oc*. Although his original manuscript has not survived, the oldest known copy of his work is in this Italianate French,[4] and in it Marco Polo's reference is to *porcelaine*. But what he would have dictated was *porcellana*, and this is the clue to the origin of the term.

'Porcellana' is the feminine diminutive of *porcus* (pig) and simply means 'little female piglet'. The first recorded use of the term in Europe is in the maritime code of Barcelona, *c.*1250, where the Spanish word *porcelanas* refers to cowry shells (*cypræa moneta*) in a list of products imported from Alexandria. The shells, with their snouts and humped backs, do indeed look like little piglets. Their feminine attribution can only refer to the vulva-like opening on the underside [**11**].[5]

What is intriguing is that Marco Polo uses the same word to describe two completely different commodities that he encountered on his travels in China. When he was in the southern province of Yunnan he used *porcellana* in its original sense, referring to the cowry shells that served locally as a kind of small change, a usage which has a long history throughout the Indian subcontinent, Southeast Asia and China. But his second reference to *porcellana* describes the fine ceramics that he saw being manufactured at Tingiu, near the southern port of Zaytun (Quanzhou). As Marco Polo would have been there in the 1280s, what is

11 Cowry shells in a lacquer box, from the Maldive Islands.

12 Vase *(meiping)* of *qingbai* porcelain, with loosely carved lotus panels. Song dynasty. *H. 32 cm.*

interesting is his reference to 'bowls … of the colour of azure, and very shining and beautiful beyond measure'. This is a fair description of *qingbai* porcelain, the immediate predecessor of blue and white. Recent investigations in China have shown that *qingbai* was indeed being made in that area.[6]

Why should he have used the term *porcellana* for ceramics? Simply because the analogy between shells and porcelain with its shell-like appearance is obvious. Indeed, when porcelain breaks it has a shell-like conchoidal fracture. And later on in the medieval period it was even speculated that it was actually made of ground-up shells.

13 White *qingbai* porcelain bowls from Allaippidy, in northern Sri Lanka. Song dynasty, early 12th century.

Composition

Until relatively recently it had been generally thought that porcelain was a combination of two basic materials: kaolin (white china clay) and petuntse (pulverized porcelain stone). This was based on the observations of a French Jesuit, Père d'Entrecolles, who visited Jingdezhen in the early eighteenth century.[7] Both materials derive from granite and when fired at a high temperature (around 1280°C) fuse to form a hard, vitrified body. To state this in simple terms, it is as if the materials which originally derived from decomposed granite were then reassembled and by the use of fire turned back into stone again. The contrast between this high-fired ware and ordinary earthenware with its low-fired and friable body is really the essential difference between the Chinese invention and the whole history of ceramics elsewhere in the world.

Two decades or so ago it began to be questioned whether the kaolin/petuntse combination was true, and a series of international conferences on ceramic technology in China have concluded that the formula is far more complex, not only varying at different periods and kiln sites but more recently being revealed to have a major divide between north and south China, based on the ultimately different prehistoric geological structure of the two regions. Nigel Wood, who has made a fundamental contribution to this new research over the past twenty-five years, and who has approached the subject from the ideal perspective of being not only a scientist but also a practising potter, has made some extremely pertinent observations.[8] First, that wares which superficially appear to be similar, such as Ding and *blanc de Chine*, are of completely different composition, namely clay and pulverized volcanic rock, respectively. Second, that wares which appear to be totally different, such as the Xian terracotta warriors and black-glazed Yaozhou wares, have, in fact, near identical material composition.

According to Wood, the great divide occurred some 200 million years ago, when the Indian tectonic fault raised the Tibetan plateau and created the Siberian and Mongolian block. The freezing and heating of the igneous rocks of the Gobi Desert combined with high winds produced the fine-grained loess distributed all over the southeast of the area. This loess and local refractory clays provided the raw material for wares as varied as northern Neolithic pottery, the moulds for Shang bronzes, the terracotta warriors, Han green-glazed pottery, black-glazed stonewares and even the bricks used in the Great Wall.

By contrast, in southern China the volcanic mass 140 million years ago was subjected to a warm and wet climate, producing a crumbly mass of quartz, mica, clay and feldspar easily levigated to produce a fine stoneware clay. This was used for some Neolithic wares by the Shang dynasty, with the firing temperatures being raised and natural glazes appearing. By the tenth century porcelain stone had begun to be exploited, producing a white-firing body, and one of the earliest sites to use it was Jingdezhen. The final advance was the addition of kaolin in the thirteenth/fourteenth centuries, but only in small quantities, at which its utility is somewhat debatable. It is not until the seventeenth century that the kaolin content rises to 40–50 per cent.

Nigel Wood would dispute the accepted view that the kaolin was used as an additive to give greater plasticity to the large-scale wares of the Yuan dynasty, and points out that in the larger dishes greater plasticity would actually be a disadvantage. The evidence is far from clear cut, and the transition from the Song *qingbai* composed of kaolinized porcelain stone to the enigmatic *shufu* ware to Yuan porcelain is uncertain. But whatever empirical methods were used in its evolution, there is no doubt that the porcelain of the early fourteenth century, with its sparkling glaze, provided the perfect vehicle for painting in cobalt blue.

Underglaze blue

Although there is evidence of the use of cobalt blue in the Tang dynasty for the decoration of *sancai* wares and very occasionally white stonewares, this was not pursued in later periods and its appearance in Yuan ceramics was a striking innovation. There is a further difference in the type of cobalt used in the Ming dynasty.

It has been generally accepted that the cobalt was imported from Persia, probably in the form of smalt, at the instance of the Persian merchants who had been established on the coast of China since the earliest Islamic period. An important treatise on the manufacture of ceramics by Abū ʻl-Qāsim Kashani,[9] written about AD 1300, mentions the source of cobalt ore (*lajvard*) from the mountains near Kashan in Persia, and the use of cobalt blue to decorate pottery in the Near East and Mediterranean area predates its use in China by centuries.

Whilst cobalt was used in the Tang period as a glaze colourant for monochrome blue and *sancai* (three-coloured) ware, like the amber and green it was relatively difficult to control [**14**]. It tended to diffuse in the glaze, its decorative effect thus being limited to areas where it could be contained by incised outlines or moulded details, or where general staining was appropriate. It is of note that when underglaze cobalt blue was used many centuries later in the Safavid period, the

14 Pottery jar decorated in *sancai* colours, including cobalt blue. Tang dynasty (618–907).

potters experienced a similar difficulty in controlling the pigment. In this instance they solved the problem by using a more stable black outline.

In China during the Yuan dynasty the designs were often sharply outlined with darker blue. The only defect was that when the cobalt ore was thickly applied, the iron impurities in it tended to fire to metallic blackish spots. Indeed, one large dish in Topkapi Saray is so affected by this spotting that it gives the appearance of suffering from some sort of contagious disease [**15**].

In the fifteenth century the disparity between the lighter and more heavily applied areas of cobalt blue continued, producing an effect which the Chinese christened 'heaped and piled' [**95**, **98**, **104**]. During the Ming dynasty the hue and intensity of the blue changes, a mutation that must to a certain extent have been brought about by the discovery of local cobalt and its admixture to the imported Persian blue, and by the gradual switch to the indigenous material from the

16 Bowl of blue and white porcelain. Jiajing mark and period (1522–66). *D. 28.5 cm.* The outside is decorated with strange grotesque marks, for which an Italian Renaissance source has been suggested.

17 Ewer of blue and white porcelain. Transitional period, mid-17th century. *H. 26 cm.* On one side, three boys playing in a landscape; on the other, three seated figures, one with a book. On the neck is a symmetrical spray of tulip-like flowers.

LEFT
15 Dish of blue and white porcelain. Yuan dynasty, 14th century. *D. 45 cm.* The dish has misfired, the cobalt blue heavily speckled.

middle of the fifteenth century. By the reign of Jiajing (1522–66) the blue had attained an almost violet intensity [**15**, **196**]. In the mid-seventeenth century, in the 'Transitional' period, finely graded washes of cobalt blue were used to great effect and melting shades of blue became a characteristic by which porcelain of this period can be easily identified [**16**]. This striking use of washes of cobalt blue of diminishing intensity was a mannerism picked up by the Persian potters of the Safavid period, who produced some quite convincing imitations of Chinese ware [**175**, **176**]. In the reign of Kangxi (1662–1722) the blue has a controlled dark intensity of glacial perfection. Fastidiously applied, it no longer exhibits the spontaneity of the brushwork of the earlier periods.

Form and construction

Although the earliest blue and white immediately brings to mind the large-scale dishes and vessels of the Yuan dynasty, there are also a number of smaller pieces which complement them. It is useful to study these two groups separately and come to some conclusion about this diversity.

THE LARGER WARES

The massive forms of Yuan blue and white are in radical contrast to the slighter wares of the preceding Song period. The most striking feature of the new ware is its sheer scale, with great dishes, bowls and jars that imply a complete change in culinary habits. Whilst Chinese cuisine depends on numerous individual dishes and bowls, under the Mongols large vessels were in demand for communal feasting. One has only to read travellers' accounts, such as de Clavijo's description of the court of the Great Khan at Karakorum,[10] or to look at the depictions in Persian miniatures, to see what a central role these massive pieces played [**18**]. This change has been largely ascribed to the influence of the Western Islamic world, which created the demand for these new forms, with their equally novel blue and white decoration.

18 Persian painting, late 16th century. A landscape with figures preparing food, using Chinese blue and white bowls and other utensils. *H. 22.4 cm.*

However, recent research into the culinary history of the Mongols suggests that the issue is not quite as simple as it might seem. Until the Mongol empire embraced the whole of Asia from China to the Mediterranean, the Mongols had sustained themselves on an unrelenting diet of meat, milk products, game and occasional fish. But their incursion into the lands of the Near East led to a new exposure to the spices, condiments and recipes of Central and Western Asia.[11] This fundamentally changed Mongol court cuisine, introducing all sorts of new dishes. A key document is an imperial dietary manual, *Yin-shan cheng-yao* ('Good and Essential Things for the Emperor's Food and Drink'), presented at court in 1330.[12] Many recipes are given in great detail, using Turkicized forms of Persian words, and the soups, stews and sweetmeats described are easily correlated with the food tradition of Western Asia. Indeed, many of the recipes can be found in Turkey and Syria to this day, for example boiled mutton and wheat (*qarisa*, Leb. *hreesi*), spiced ground mutton (*kogurma*, Leb. *qawwarma*, Tk. *qavurma*), fruit drinks (*sharbat*, Ar./Pers. *sherbet*) and stuffed flaky pastry (*pirak*, Tk. *borek*; *yuvqa*, Tk. *yufqa*). Condiments used in Mongolian cuisine included cardamom, cinnamon, mastaki, fennel, ginger, coriander and fenugreek; novel ingredients were ghee, chick peas, walnuts, pine nuts and almonds, bitter orange peel and *makdunis* (parsley). But it was the marriage of these new ingredients and techniques of preparation to the existing Mongolian food tradition that created what has been described as the first truly world cuisine.

It follows that the Mongol zest for this new cuisine must have been an important reason for the sudden production of large-scale blue and white, and not simply the potters at Jingdezhen supplying the demands of a far-flung Islamic market. If this is so, it should be pointed out that the decoration of these vessels is usually a mixture of Buddhist, Daoist and other symbolism, with motifs that were hardly likely to have been understood by Moslem patrons [**36**, **56**]. Nor should one overlook the fact that examples of these large wares have been found within Mongol territory both in China and elsewhere.

Of the massive forms, those that make the most immediate impression are the dishes, in a great variety of designs. For the majority no two pieces are exactly the same, although some designs, such as the lotus pond, are constantly repeated. Over a hundred examples of these dishes have survived in the Near East, Central Asia and India, and it is this corpus which forms the basis of the general analysis below, drawn from the collections of the Topkapi Saray (twenty dishes) and the Ardebil Shrine (nineteen), from excavations in Delhi (forty-four, all in fragmentary form), from a recently discovered shipwreck in the Red Sea (fourteen),[13] from Damascus (nine), from the Hutian kilns at Jingdezhen (four), and from Inner Mongolia (one). There are, of course, many more from other collections worldwide.

Most of the dishes were made upside down on moulds, and were sufficiently thick that the foot ring could later be carved from the body with a sharp knife on a wheel. A dish from Damascus on which a small area at the centre was accidentally left unglazed shows the impression of a fine cloth; two more, from Delhi, show the same feature under the glaze.[14] This cloth must have been inserted between the

19 Dish of blue and white porcelain, with moulded flowers on the rim and fruit in the cavetto, including peaches, pomegranates, plums and citrons. Yuan dynasty, 14th century. *D. 42.5 cm.*

20 Dish of blue and white porcelain, with moulded flowers on the rim and in the cavetto. Yuan dynasty, 14th century. *D. 46.3 cm.*

body and the mould to lessen the adhesion of the dish when it was finally lifted off. A later eighteenth-century commentator, the Jesuit priest Père d'Entrecolles, describes the use of such moulds and also notes that the pieces were gently heated to aid their removal from the mould.[15] Almost all the dishes have gently curved cavettos, with a slight ridge at the junction with the centre of the dish. The flat rims are often carved with a foliate edge, sometimes with a raised profile. The rims are also occasionally decorated with moulded rosettes and sometimes waves, and moulded decoration in the cavetto is not uncommon, further enhancing the painted designs [**5**, **19**]. The foot ring is sharply carved from the body of the dish, and like the base itself is unglazed on the bottom and the inner side. Because of the iron content of the ware, the unglazed areas tend to fire orange.

Of the 111 dishes from the seven provenances listed above, 49 have foliate rims, 43 are plain and 19 are too fragmentary to determine. This almost equal division between foliate and plain rims, and the fact that both are represented in the Red Sea group, which must surely represent contemporary wares, would imply that there is no chronological distinction between the two types. Nor does there appear to be any connection between the type of rim and the central design, for although eight dishes painted with fish show a predilection for plain rims, a ninth example from Delhi has a foliate rim. The smallest dish, also from Delhi, is 27.4 cm in diameter, but the majority are in the 40–46 cm diameter range, and one extraordinary dish in the Ardebil collection (24.49) [**47**] is a colossal 57.5 cm in diameter. This superbly executed dish also has the distinction of a Persian inscription beneath the rim, discussed below.

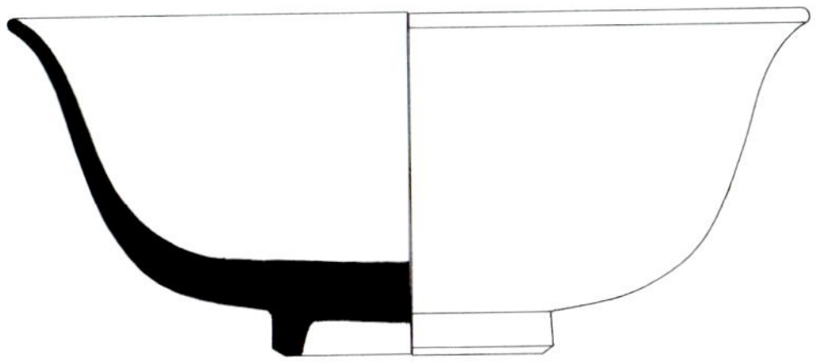

21 a, b Bowl of blue and white porcelain, from Syria. Yuan dynasty, 14th century. *D. 30.6 cm.*

The thirty-three bowls from the same locations of medium size range from 20 cm to 30 cm in diameter. The majority have sturdy, sharply cut foot rings and also appear to have been made with abnormally thick lower sections from which the foot ring could be carved. On several examples from Damascus and the Red Sea, where it has been possible to measure the section, it is clear that when the bowl was upside down on the wheel for finishing, the potter had no idea how to relate the inner profile to the outer one, so that the lower body is as much as 2 cm or more thick [**21b**, **206 d, f**]. This is immediately apparent when you lift the bowls, which are abnormally heavy. All these bowls have curved sides with slightly flaring plain rims. The most common design found on bowls of this type is a lotus pond, with or without a pair of connubial ducks. Mention should also be made of two fragmentary smaller bowls from Fustat (old Cairo), one 16 cm in diameter, of the lotus pond type [**61**]. There are a few larger bowls known,

OPPOSITE, CLOCKWISE FROM LEFT

22 Double-gourd shaped vase of blue and white porcelain. Yuan dynasty, 14th century. *H. 60.5 cm.*

23 Jar (*guan*) of blue and white porcelain. Yuan dynasty, 14th century. *H. 40 cm.*

24 a, b Bowl with inverted rim of blue and white porcelain. Yuan dynasty, 14th century. Painted on the outside with the 'Three Friends': pine, prunus and bamboo. *D. 36 cm.*

ABOVE, FROM LEFT

25 Vase (*meiping*) of blue and white porcelain. Yuan dynasty, 14th century. *H. 42 cm.*

26 Vase *(meiping)* and cover of blue and white porcelain. Yuan dynasty, 14th century. Painted with scenes from a Yuan drama. *H. 27.8 cm.*

27 Vase *(meiping)* of blue and white porcelain. Yuan dynasty, 14th century. *H. 41.3 cm.*

including one fine example with a foliate rim in Topkapi Saray (TKS 15/1422) [**8**]. Others have inverted rims, suggesting a metal prototype of Islamic origin [**24**].[16]

Besides the bowls and dishes, there are also very large jars (*guan*), often with moulded animal heads on the shoulder pierced for metal ring handles. There are also elegant vases (*meiping*), the swelling bodies surmounted by tiny rimmed necks, some with a raised neck and flanged mouth. Although not many survive, both *guan* and *meiping* originally had covers. Impressive double-gourd vases are more than 60 cm high, some with octagonal sections. Most striking of all are the large flasks of rectangular section, which have rounded shoulders with twin loop handles; these have a short neck and rim. Bottles (*yuhuchun*) have spherical or octagonal bodies and flaring trumpet-shaped necks, sometimes faceted. A silver example of exactly the same size and profile as a porcelain bottle (both are in the Hohhot Museum in Inner Mongolia) clearly shows its affinity with the *yuhuchun* shape [**134 a, b**]. There are also faceted ewers with lids of similar but more angular form [**2**].

Finally, mention must be made of the site of Kharakhoto, the Mongol garrison city in the middle of the Gobi Desert that was abandoned shortly after the advent of the Ming dynasty in 1368. Hundreds of sherds of blue and white have been recovered from the site, the majority of which are in the Hermitage in St Petersburg and the Ethnographic Museum in Stockholm, from the Kozlov and Hedin expeditions respectively.[17] These include fragments of large vases (*guan*) and other vessels, and numerous examples of the slighter wares discussed below.

THE SMALLER WARES

One of the most distinctive shapes of the Yuan group is the pouring bowl, with an angular spout and a tiny suspension loop below [**28**]. Here there is no doubt of the metallic origin of the form. Mongolian gold cups also have rings for suspension below their flanged handles. It has been suggested that these bowls were for drinking *kumiss* (fermented mare's milk), the Mongolian national beverage. The form is certainly an innovation in porcelain, unknown before the fourteenth century. That it existed before blue and white can be deduced from a celadon example decorated with iron brown spots (Japanese *tobi-seiji* 'spotted celadon') found on the Sinan wreck, before AD 1323 [**29**]. Other examples are decorated in white slip on a blue ground, and a plain blue pouring bowl with gold decoration was amongst a hoard discovered at Baoding, south of Dadu (Beijing), which also contained Yuan blue and white; the hoard has been assigned to the first half of the fourteenth century.

31 Flask of blue and white porcelain with faceted sides. Yuan dynasty, 14th century. *H. 22.5 cm (neck missing).*

32 Small jar of blue and white porcelain. Yuan dynasty, 14th century. *H. 7.8 cm, D. 9.5 cm.*

OPPOSITE
28 Pouring bowl of blue and white porcelain. Yuan dynasty, 14th century. *L. 15.9 cm.*

29 Pouring bowl of celadon with brown spots. Yuan dynasty, before 1323. *L. 20.4 cm.*

30 Stem cup of blue and white porcelain. Inside, a moulded medallion within a wreath of peonies and chrysanthemum, with a flaming pearl superimposed; outside, a three-clawed dragon pursuing a pearl. Yuan dynasty, 14th century. *H. 10.4 cm.*

Stem cups share many of the same features and northern distribution as the spouted bowls, decorated not only in blue and white but also copper red [**30**]. Fragments of stem cups, now in the Freer Gallery in Washington, were found by John Pope in Beijing in 1946, close to the walls of the Forbidden City; these date from the period when it was the Yuan capital, Dadu. A complete stem cup, which once belonged to Pope, is now in the Dayton Art Institute and is an excellent representative of the type.[18] More stem cups have been found in Inner Mongolia, two from a hoard northeast of Chifeng, as well as many fragmentary examples from Kharakhoto. Again the form is of metal origin, probably copying a silver shape from Central Asia, and its popularity persisted into the Ming dynasty. The *Ge gu yao lan*, a Chinese collectors' handbook, states that neither 'stem wine cups (*ba bei*) with tray … nor the bowls (*yu*) with lips were known in the wares of the Song dynasty'.[19] All of which would make it reasonable to assume that both stem cups and spouted bowls were introduced in direct response to Mongol taste.

In terms of function, less explicable are the small flasks with flaring necks, often with faceted sides, examples of which have again been found in the north, at Kharakhoto. They probably contained some sort of liquor, and the *Yin-shan cheng-yao*, the Mongol dietary text of 1300, refers to beer (*boza*), liquor (*suma*) and wine (*tngri*). Also from Kharakhoto are extremely finely potted and painted small bowls.

33 Water-dropper of blue and white porcelain, the spout in the form of a phoenix and its tail as a handle, the base pierced for filling. Yuan dynasty, 14th century. *L. 12.8 cm.*

Finally, mention must be made of a quite different category of small vessels, common to many sites in Southeast Asia for which they appear to have been expressly made. These are simply decorated in blue and white with sketchily drawn flowers including chrysanthemums with cross-hatched centres and trails of little hook-shaped leaves **[32]**. They are slighter versions of the more sophisticated ware from Jingdezhen and include bowls, little vases and bottles with loop handles, jars of cuboid shape, and even little figurines and model boats. Although some scholars have assigned these wares to later in the Yuan dynasty, a key piece is a fragmentary blue and white bowl found at Fustat, of which a near-identical sherd has been excavated at the Hutian site in Jingdezhen, in association with other Yuan sherds.[20] Typical decoration of this kind is here painted over the moulded decoration and radiating panels at the centre, and such moulded bowls without painted decoration are known in *shufu* ware **[35]**.[21] Again, these simple export wares are also embellished with relief beaded trails, linking them to the Fonthill vase, *c.*1300 **[201]**. This would argue that this style of decoration dates from the very earliest introduction of blue and white, though it may well have had a long life. That the type also permeated northwards can again be seen in a bowl from Kharakhoto, and in other sherds with the same hooked leaf motif. What is interesting is that the circulation of these slighter wares appears to have been confined to Mongol territory and Southeast Asia, as they have not been found further west.

OPPOSITE

34 a, b Fragment of a blue and white bowl, from Fustat. Yuan dynasty, 14th century. *Depth of foot ring: 6.4 cm.* The central design of a chrysanthemum with sketchy leaves is painted *over* the moulded ribs, like those on the *shufu* bowl below (**35**).

35 Bowl of *shufu* porcelain with moulded ribs. Yuan dynasty, 14th century. *D. 17.3 cm.*

2 PATTERN AND PERCEPTION

Blue and white porcelain and its perception

The particular fascination of blue and white during the Yuan dynasty is the way in which the colour was used. It is not only that the complex designs were executed with consummate skill and assurance – for in painting ceramics there is no going back, no possibility of correcting a mistake – but the awareness of the subtle play between contrasting areas of blue and white [**36**]. The artists had hit upon the so-called 'Albers effect', centuries before it was codified.[1] Joseph Albers, scion of the Bauhaus, discovered that all colours are radically affected, even totally changed, by the colours that surround them [**37a**]. Furthermore, their tonal value can be altered totally by the light or dark areas around them [**37b**]. It was this latter proposition that the Yuan artists exploited with such phenomenal success.

For instance, on a well-known jar depicting scenes from a Yuan drama, a cloud and a waterfall both have their intrinsic 'whiteness' heightened by the surrounding areas of darker blue [**38**]. By similar means, many pieces are not only

OPPOSITE
36 Dish of blue and white porcelain. Yuan dynasty, 14th century. *D. 45.5 cm.*

RIGHT
The Albers effect:
37a The two blue squares above and below the centre line are identical, but because of the surrounding colours they appear to be different.
37b The grey frame appears to be lighter at the top, but is a uniform tone.

38 a, b Jar (*guan*) of blue and white porcelain. Yuan dynasty, 14th century. *H. 27.6 cm.* The scenes are from a Yuan drama, the *Sangu Caolu* ('The Three Visits to the Thatched Hut'), possibly from the *Sanguozhi pinghua* ('Plain Narrative on the History of the Three Kingdoms'), relating events during the 3rd century AD.

painted in different shades of cobalt blue, but also appear to display different shades of white [**44**, **55**]. The white is further enhanced by key elements of the designs being moulded in relief [**5**, **7**, **19**]. At the same time the use of thick and thin outlines to frame decorative panels, and concentric rings separated by a plain band on many of the dishes, create the illusion of relief [**39**]. This interplay of contrasting light and dark areas and the manipulation of tonal values seems to have been an empirical discovery and does not appear to have any immediate parallel in the other arts in China, such as painting.

39 Dish of blue and white porcelain. Yuan dynasty, 14th century. *D. 46.7 cm.*

40 Pair of vases of blue and white porcelain, inscribed and dated 1351. Yuan dynasty. *H. 63.6 cm*. The inscriptions state that they were presented to a Daoist temple in Yushan district, 120 km southeast of Jingdezhen.

In listing the numerous decorative elements in the painter's repertoire, John Pope's study of fourteenth-century blue and white porcelain in the Topkapi Saray museum is the fundamental text.[2] In this seminal work he includes a catalogue of all of the different flora and fauna and other miscellaneous designs. Besides their identification, he gives the correct Chinese term and transcription, and for the flora a botanical definition.

However, there are two pieces – the twin vases in the Percival David collection **[40]** – which, because of their dedicatory inscription dated 1351, play an exceptional role. They are a keystone in Pope's definition of the fourteenth-century style and, as he rightly observes, must mark its peak, being neither tentative experiments nor witness of impending decadence. Following his classification, the designs on the vases may be listed as follows:

Flora:	chrysanthemum, fern/plantain, peony, lotus, spiked lobed leaves
Fauna:	dragons (four-clawed), elephants, phoenixes
Miscellaneous:	auspicious objects, cloud scrolls, flames, lotus panels, serpentine waves

The vases, unlike so many Yuan pieces, do not have contrasting panels with white or blue grounds, but the enhanced white effect can be observed in the breaking serpentine waves, so heavily outlined that they appear to be almost in relief. Discussing the lotus, Pope remarks on the strange spiked lobed leaf that often accompanies it, which seems to have no parallel in the natural world **[41]**. Although it appears in debased form in later Ming wares, it is synonymous with Yuan porcelain, as indeed is the chrysanthemum with a cross-hatched centre. The importance of the David vases is that the motifs they display were fully developed by the time of their manufacture, and were used in conjunction with many other designs on other pieces. If it is admitted that blue and white only began to be produced in significant quantities after 1325 or thereabouts, then it came to maturity in the relatively short time of a quarter of a century.

41 A spiked lobed leaf, characteristic of Yuan blue and white porcelain.

What of the decorative schemes on the other wares of the period? On the large dishes there is a bewildering series of themes, and – with the exception of the popular motifs of a lotus pond and ducks and of fish among waterplants – no two pieces are exactly alike. This is, of course, not true for the wreaths of floral and other motifs that encircle the central panel, nor the various treatments of the rim and underside of the dishes, which are much more repetitive. This suggests not so much mass production as a division of labour. The central design was reserved for the artist/potter and the rest usually carried out by subsidiary painters. This may not have always been the rule, for certain dishes, such as the great one in the Ardebil collection with a Persian inscription (29.49) **[47]**, must surely be the work of a single hand. And the cavetto of a dish in Topkapi Saray (TKS 15/1420) is painted with the same masterly touch, with the central design of a *qilin* leaping over rocks **[44]**. Although they are very rare, the blue-ground dishes show very little painterly skill **[42]**. The background is filled in a perfunctory manner and follows the contours of the moulded flower sprays and flying phoenixes with little sensitivity. There is no attempt to echo the intrinsic rhythms of the images and they become instead rather static cut-outs.

On the dishes the most popular designs include dragons, phoenixes (usually in pairs), pheasants (again often paired, one swooping down on its partner perched on a parapet), *qilin* of leonine and equine types, white egrets stalking around a lotus pond, elaborate landscapes with rocky outcrops and stands of

OPPOSITE
44 Dish of blue and white porcelain. Yuan dynasty, 14th century. *D. 46.5 cm.*

BELOW, FROM LEFT
42 Dish of blue porcelain with white slip decoration in reserve. Yuan dynasty, 14th century. *D. 41.5 cm.*

43 Dish of blue and white porcelain, with Arabic/Persian inscription on the base. Yuan dynasty, 14th century. *D. 45.4 cm.*

45 Dish of blue and white porcelain. Yuan dynasty, 14th century. *D. 40 cm.*

plantain, ferns and bamboo, morning glory, grapes, melons and other flowers and insects, and fish swimming through a background of swirling eelgrass [**5**, **19**, **43**, **46**]. A large group of dishes have radial designs which combine cloud-collar panels filled with different ground patterns and rings of lotus panels, each with an auspicious object.

Yet another distinctive feature of Yuan blue and white is the treatment of the lotus panels, each framed with a thick and thin outline [**23**, **24**, **26**]. The pointed

OPPOSITE
46 Dish of blue and white porcelain. Yuan dynasty, 14th century. *D. 46.7 cm.*

lobed leaf within the frame usually has a blue ring below, but there are many variants. Rim patterns include serpentine waves, diamond diaper bands, classic scrolls, crapemyrtle and blackberry-lily wreaths, concentric waves and marble-like trefoils. The rosettes, often applied in relief, are very similar to those unglazed rosettes, fired red, that are applied to the rims of contemporary celadon dishes [**7**, **19**, **113**].

47 Large dish of blue and white porcelain from the Ardebil Shrine. Yuan dynasty, 14th century. *D. 57.5 cm.*

Any discussion of Yuan dishes should include the largest known example, 57.5 cm in diameter, in the Ardebil collection (29.49), mentioned above [**47**]. It has a raised foliate rim with breaking serpentine waves, which Pope aptly describes as springing forward with the energy of a striking serpent. The waves break to the left and on the spray is a triangle of three dots. At the centre of the dish is a bracketed medallion with eight points, with a single white lotus surrounded by spiked leaves, the twin lobes having knobbed edges. A ring of eight lotus panels contains auspicious objects on a blue ground. A second wide white ring separates the central design from four phoenixes which circle the dish, two with feathery tails (*luan*) and two spiralling (*fenghuang*), on a field of chrysanthemums, reserved again on a blue ground. Another ring of serpentine waves, this time breaking to the right, is framed with two white bands. Finally, in the cavetto there is a delicately painted wreath of nine peonies, five in profile, on a leafy stem with smaller buds, also on a blue ground. On the underside of the dish is a lotus wreath with spiked lobed leaves and at the foot an unusual ring of large and small pointed leaves with shaded tips.

48 Inscription in underglaze blue on the underside of the dish from the Ardebil Shrine (**47**).

The base of this dish is typically unglazed; on it are inked two tiny Persian words and there is a drilled mark. But apart from its size, what makes the dish unique is a Persian inscription painted in underglaze blue just below the rim [**48**]. This has been variously read, *Hosein/harim/Mohammed* being suggested for the first word and *haqq/be-juft/marhum/Mohammed* for the second. Possible combinations are *Hosein haqq* ('Hosein is truth'), *Hosein be-juft* ('Hosein is peerless') and *Hosein ibn Mohammed* ('Hosein, son of Mohammed').[3] The reference to Hosein, the Shi'ah saint and grandson of the prophet, would be entirely appropriate if the dish was commissioned by a Persian; and the illiteracy of the inscription and peculiar formation of the Persian characters are consistent with the work of a Chinese artist who had no idea what he was copying. But there is no doubt of the grandeur and scale of the dish, nor the mastery and and complexity of the design. These qualities, added to its unique inscription, make it one of the most important of this series of dishes, a landmark in Yuan blue and white equal in its own way to the David vases. It also has an impeccable pedigree, for the *vaqfnameh* of Shah Abbas is engraved on its underside. Of the 805 still surviving from the Persian monarch's original gift of 1162 porcelains to the Ardebil Shrine in 1611, this *vaqfnameh* is to be found on all but 31 of the pieces.

However, this is not the only fourteenth-century dish with an underglaze inscription. A second example, once in the Richard Hobart collection, is now in

49a Dish of blue and white porcelain, with an inscribed panel in the cavetto. Yuan dynasty, 14th century.
D. 48.8 cm.

49b The inscription on the Hobart dish (**49a**).

the Arthur M. Sackler Museum at Harvard [**49**]. Hobart had acquired it from the Cummings collection, which had been formed in India between 1864 and 1883. The Persian inscription is reserved in white on a panel in the cavetto; it has been variously read, and John Ayers suggested that the first word might be *chin* ('China'), with the first letter the Persian *ch*.[4] A fragment of a similar dish with moulded panels in the cavetto has been found in East Java, with the same inscription, this time painted in blue on white.[5] Jane Beamish notes that the inscription could conceivably be in *Java Pegon* (Arab Indonesian). Finally, pieces of Yuan blue and white have been found in Fustat and Syria with Arabic/Persian inscriptions inked on the unglazed bases,[6] and a celadon dish from Syria is similarly marked on the unglazed base ring, this time bearing a Chinese cyclical date (see p. 113, **120**).

50 Dish of blue and white porcelain. Yuan dynasty, 14th century. *D. 46.7 cm.*

The decoration of other forms presented the painters with different problems, for the three-dimensional surfaces meant that there was no single focus. As far as the bowls are concerned, the central area, as on the dishes, presents a 'right' way of looking at them by indicating a vertical axis – most obviously with the lotus pond designs [**24a**], but even with the more decorative schemes in which a single lotus is placed in profile, or a four-armed cross (double *vajra*) at the centre. The large jars (*guan*) with twin handles present the spectator with two alternative views, with the main design on the shoulder, such as *qilin*, phoenix or cloud-collar panels, symmetrically disposed between them [**56**]. Curiously, the broad floral band that frequently encircles the main body below is often slightly out of kilter with the designs on the shoulder, perhaps once more suggesting a division of labour.

51 Double-gourd vase of blue and white porcelain. Yuan dynasty, 14th century. *H. 60.5 cm.*

This is not so with the vases (*meiping*), where the different panels are totally integrated with classic scroll, diaper and plain horizontal bands and lotus panels. A double-gourd vase in Topkapi Saray (TKS 15/1453) is indisputably the work of a single artist and has a brilliant floral design with neither vertical nor horizontal

52 Flask of blue and white porcelain. Yuan dynasty, 14th century. The twin handles and neck are missing, the latter replaced with a Turkish silver-gilt mount. *H. 39.5 cm.*

53 Flask of blue and white porcelain. Yuan dynasty, 14th century. *H. 39 cm.*

bands to interrupt. The floral elements seem to expand and contract in scale with the form. It is almost as if a Yuan textile had been specially woven to fit the vase. Other large double-gourd vases and *meiping* in the same collection are octagonal in section, presenting eight or even sixteen different surfaces to decorate. One of these is a masterpiece and again certainly the work of a single artist (TKS 15/1471) **[22]**. The upper panels are filled with different combinations of fruit and flowers: peonies, chrysanthemums, pomegranates, peaches, grapes and melons. The larger panels below are painted with elaborate compositions of flowers or fruit, in which are poised pheasants or where lurk such creatures as a praying mantis, a frog, a cockerel, butterflies and insects. On a second faceted vase **[51]** the painter has straddled the panels on the lower half with pointed and lobed cloud-collar medallions, which ingeniously frame asymmetrical designs of flowers, fruit and insects. Even the lotus panels on these vases are filled with auspicious objects and floral designs of unusual imagination and virtuosity.

The large double-handled flasks are decorated in the same vein. The two separate sides present the opportunity for phoenix and pheasants, dragons and *qilin* to sport against a floral background, with cloud-collar panels above and breaking waves below [**52**, **53**]. The narrow sides are painted with lotus or chrysanthemum within a panel with a trefoil top, rather like a bookmark. The short necks have necklaces of tiny flowers and leaves. Whatever purpose these flasks may originally have been intended for, they have been transformed into splendid decorative objects to be admired for their own sake; they would have been inordinately clumsy, put to practical use.

The smaller forms that were destined for the Philippines, Indonesia and Southeast Asia are decorated with simpler but no less elegant designs [**32**, **33**]. Indeed, the small scale led to a sprightliness and freedom of brush, so much easier to execute than the decoration of porcelain on a grand scale. All of these tiny bottles, vases and other pieces have simple floral designs, with characteristic trails of hooked leaves. Nor are the forms of limited repertoire, for they include tiny ewers, some of double-gourd shape, and even model ships.[7]

Finally, mention should be made of the decoration of the stem cups, which, as we have seen, held a particular attraction for the Mongols in the north. These are frequently decorated with dragons chasing the elusive pearl amongst flaming cloud scrolls, both within and without the vessels [**30**]. Inside, the painted blue decoration is often combined with less visible slip ornament, usually floral, which provides a subtle counterpoint. Some stem cups and saucers have a flaming pearl motif painted in blue at the centre. The form it takes could easily be read as 'Allah', but this may be a mere coincidence.

Perceptions

Such a radical change occurred in porcelain production during the Yuan period that it not unnaturally elicited comment. Although the texts, whether Chinese or by foreign travellers, are few, they are important. In China itself an account of the manufacture of porcelain at Jingdezhen in 1322 was composed by Jiang Qi; in his *Tao qi lue* he describes the ware of pure white colour, prepared from stone (pulverized china stone), the finest of which came from Jingdezhen.[8] Red clay (earthenware) was used only for making saggars (containers within which the pieces were fired) and moulds. Brushwood was collected from the hills of Yushan, to be used in the preparation of glaze ash. He also lists a variety of different forms. The pieces were thrown on a wheel, and further refined by shaping with a knife. Decoration was applied by moulding, painting or carving. There was a division of labour between the potters, those who prepared the basic material and those who made the saggars.

By this time at Jingdezhen the industry was carefully controlled and the revenue from the kilns heavily (but not always successfully) taxed. The potters were unpaid and instead given land in the area, their services being levied when needed. This meant that fluctuations in the harvest had an immediate effect on the productivity of the kilns. The date of Jiang Qi's account (1322) indicates that he was describing the white wares such as *qingbai* and *shufu*. Although he does mention painting as one of the decorative techniques, his account refers to porcelain production immediately before the introduction of painting in cobalt blue on a large scale. What Jiang Qi does make quite clear is that at this stage the industry was sufficiently well organized that it would have provided the perfect base for such an innovation.

Precisely four hundred years later a French Jesuit priest, Père François Xavier d'Entrecolles, gave detailed descriptions of the porcelain industry at Jingdezhen in two letters, dated 1712 and 1722.[9] These dovetail surprisingly well with the

54 Chinese artist's illustration, *c.*1790, of firing beehive kilns and discarding the sherds – one stage in the production of porcelain at Jingdezhen.

earlier account, and serve both to corroborate and to amplify Jiang Qi's remarks. By the eighteenth century kaolin (*gaolin*) had become a major component of the ware along with petuntse (*baidunci*). The china stone was broken up with hammers (of the water-powered trip hammer variety), pulverized and then washed free of impurities. It was then moulded into bricks of white paste. The kaolin (decomposed feldspar of granitic origin) was mined, and both substances were brought some distance to the potteries at Jingdezhen. The glaze derived from the same source as the petuntse, to which was added shihkao (*shigao*), 'a mineral like alum', as a flux and glaze ash made from burning ferns with lime. By this time the petuntse and kaolin were used in equal proportions, and were further refined by kneading. The vessels were then fashioned on the wheel and finished with a polishing knife. Père d'Entrecolles describes exactly how the base was cut:

> A cup, when it first comes off the wheel, is very imperfectly shaped, like the top of a hat before it has been put on the shaping mould. The foot is only a piece of clay of the diameter that it is intended to have ultimately, and it is not excavated with the knife until all the other operations are finished.[10]

A different workman was employed for each stage and d'Entrecolles was told that a vase would have gone through the hands of seventy workers. Large pieces were made in sections luted together with slip, and moulded details applied separately in the same manner. Individual pieces were held near a fire for a moment to facilitate their removal from the mould.

The painted decoration was applied by workmen whose status was no greater than that of any other of the labourers, and each painter was responsible for different parts of the same design. The cobalt blue itself was prepared by burying it in the gravel floor of the kilns and roasting it for twenty-four hours; it was then ground to a powder in a porcelain mortar, the bottom of which was unglazed, as was the head of the pestle. Père d'Entrecolles also described the manufacture of underglaze red, and how enamel colours and gold were applied during a second firing. He gives details of the construction and firing of the kilns, how they were stacked, and the use of saggars.

The value of d'Entrecolles' account lies in its details of the pottery industry at Jingdezhen, which in no way conflict with the early fourteenth-century account, showing a surprisingly consistent use of materials and their preparation. There are also two earlier references to porcelain in China by foreigners, which although sometimes enigmatic are worth examining in detail.

The first is by the Venetian traveller, Marco Polo. Mention has already been made of Marco Polo's singular contribution as the initiator of the term 'porcelain', used throughout the world ever since – though not, one might add, by the Chinese themselves, who refer to it as *ci*. Nor, in similar vein, do they call their country 'China', but *Zhongguo*, 'The Middle Kingdom'; we owe 'China' to the Persians and Arabs, who called it *sin*. This led in turn to the transference of 'China' to china, a name for the ware that is still in use to this day.

Marco Polo was in China around 1290 and, leaving aside the controversy about exactly where and when the events he described took place and his own precise role, his descriptions of everyday manners and customs are sufficiently detailed to have the ring of truth, even if some of his information was harvested at second hand.[11] In southern China, describing the great port of Zaytun (Quanzhou), he says:

> And again I tell you the most beautiful vessels and plates of porcelain, large and small, that one could describe are made in great quantity in this aforesaid province [Figiu/Fujian] in a city which is called Tingiu, more beautiful than can be found in any other city. And on all sides they are much valued, for none of them are made in another place but in this city, and from there they are carried to many places throughout the world. And there is plenty there and a great sale, so great that for one Venetian groat you would actually have three bowls so beautiful that none would know how to devise them better. And these bowls are made in this way, as he was told, of this kind of earth; namely, that those of the city gather as from a mine mud and rotten earth and make great mounds of it, and leave them thus in the wind, in the rain, and in the sun for thirty and forty years that they do not move the mounds. And then in this space of time the said earth being so long a time in those mounds is so worked up that the bowls made of it have the colour of azure, and they are very shining and beautiful beyond measure. And you must know that when a man gathers that earth he gathers for his sons and grandsons. It is clear that owing to the long time that it must lie quiet for its working up he does not hope to gain profit from it nor put it into use, but the son who will survive him will reap the fruit of it.

Comments can be made on several aspects of Polo's text above. First, the identity of Tingiu: previous scholars have tried to equate it with other ceramic sites, but the answer is quite simple: Marco Polo meant what he said. If *Figiu* is Fujian, then *Tingiu* is Tingian, i.e. Tong'an, which is close to Quanzhou; recent excavations have produced *qingbai*, a perfect candidate for his 'bowls the colour of azure'.[12] His description of the preparation of the raw material is interesting, for apart from the china stone being mined, it would certainly have had to be finely washed and levigated, and exposure to the elements may well have helped. Interesting too is his statement that the clay reserves passed from one generation to the next, for such a stockpile would have been the family's investment.

The second traveller was not a European but an Arab, Ibn Battuta. Born in Tangiers in 1304, he left his native land in 1324 on a pilgrimage to Mecca, which then extended into his travels throughout Asia and finally China, from which he did not return home until 1350. He is in many ways a far greater traveller than Marco Polo, providing us with more detailed information on the countries he visited. That he is less well known to the general public is perhaps attributable to the fact that whilst a French translation of his writings has been available since 1859, the complete work only became available in English in 1994.[13] Ibn Battuta was in China in 1345, and discusses ceramics on three separate occasions in his account:

> The mention of Chinese pottery (*al-fakhkhar as-sini*). As for Chinese pottery none of it is made except at the city of Zaytun [Quanzhou] and Sin Kalan [Canton/Guangzhou]. And it is of the earth of the mountains there in which the fire ignites like charcoal, we will describe this later. And they add to it stones which they have there and they apply the fire to it three days and then pour water on it so that the whole returns to earth. Then they ferment it [the earth] and the best of it is that which is fermented a whole month but no more than that, and the lesser [quality] is that which is fermented ten days and it has a price there equivalent to pottery in our country or [even] cheaper. And it is carried to India and to the other climes so that it even reaches our country in the Maghreb. And it is the most marvellous of kinds of pottery.

His description of firing the material would seem to confuse the firing of ferns and lime to make glaze ash with the preparation of china stone, but he repeats Polo's statement that the longer the raw material is kept ('fermented'), the better the quality. His remark that it was exported to India can now be corroborated from recent finds; as for Morocco, this is tantalizing but certainly feasible, in view of the sophistication of trans-Mediterranean sea trade from Egypt and Syria in the fourteenth century.

His second description is more concerned with a combustible earth which is reduced to ashes and then kneaded to make a raw material for ceramics, and 'they

55 Dish of blue and white porcelain, with moulded flowers in the cavetto. Found in Damascus. Yuan dynasty, 14th century. *D. 43 cm.*

add to it other stones as we have mentioned'. This would also seem to refer to the production of glaze ash. His third account, written towards the end of his time in China, is a description of Sin Kalan (Canton/Guangzhou), where he states that, as in Zaytun (Quanzhou), pottery is manufactured. There is a pottery market (*suq al-fakhkhar*) 'and from it [the pottery] is carried to the other countries of China and to India and to Yemen.' Here the 'other countries' might well refer to Mongol territory in the north, and spectacular proof of its export to the Red Sea – and, by implication, to Yemen – long sought but until now never found, is included in the present work.

But before we leave Ibn Battuta, there is another incident concerning porcelain during his travels which also deserves mention. He visited Damascus twice – once on his way to Mecca in 1326, when he spent some time studying and acquiring the knowledge of Islamic theology and jurisprudence that was to give him such status during his subsequent travels throughout the Islamic world, and again in 1348 after he had been to China.[14] In his first description of the city he includes material that can only have come from his second trip, for instance an 'anecdote' about the Great Plague (Black Death), which he witnessed in July 1348. A few paragraphs further on is a second 'anecdote':

> As I went one day along a lane in Damascus, I saw in it a young slave-boy out of whose hand there had just fallen a Chinese porcelain dish (*sahfatan min al-fakhkhari-l-siniyyi*, 'dish of Chinese pottery') which they call by the name of *sahn* [the dialectical term for what Ibn Battuta would call a *sahfat*] and had broken to bits. A crowd gathered round him and one of them said, 'Pick up the pieces and take them with you to the custodian of the endowment for utensils' (*al-sahibu 'awqaf fil 'awani*). So he picked them up, and the man went with him to the custodian, to whom the slave showed the broken pieces and thereupon received from him enough to buy a similar platter. This endowment is one of the best of good works, for the boy's master would undoubtedly have beaten him for breaking the dish, or at least have scolded him, while he too would have been heartbroken and upset because of that. The benefaction is thus indeed a mender of hearts – May God well reward him whose charitable zeal rose to the height of such an action.

Ibn Battuta was interested in the incident as an illustration of the sophistication of a charitable institution (*waqf*) in Damascus – indeed who would not be, even today? – and his story comes in the middle of a general description of pious endowments. But we have no knowledge of whether the events of this tale happened during his first or second visit to Damascus.

If it was in 1326, it is just possible that it could have been a blue and white dish, though it was more probably a celadon one. If it was in 1348, it could have been a blue and white one at the peak period of production during the Yuan dynasty; after all, this was just three years before the David vases were made in 1351. Adding credence to the later date is the fact that he was so clear that it was a Chinese dish; would he have been so specific, as a young man of twenty-two? Also, the story comes within the context of a general description of Damascus and its institutions, which certainly draws on his later experiences, such as witnessing the Black Death.

It will perhaps strain the credibility of the reader if the writer recounts a personal tale relating to a broken dish of exactly this period, which could conceivably even be the one that Ibn Battuta saw. But in 1968, whilst wandering around the old city of Damascus, I found a fourteenth-century dish – broken – underneath a pair of trousers in a second-hand clothes shop just off the Suq al-Hamadiyeh. For 1326, it was too soon; but for 1348 it was just right, exhibiting all the features one would expect from a blue and white dish at that time: serpentine waves, moulded flowers and an elegant depiction of a lotus pond. For good measure it had an inked Arabic/Persian inscription on the unglazed base. Like so many pieces of porcelain from the Near East, after it had been broken it was deemed valuable enough to be riveted back together again.[15]

This leads me to a further personal anecdote, for surely twentieth-century perceptions are also valid? When I embarked on the laborious task of recording all the blue and white that was coming on to the marketplace in Syria between 1968 and 1970 I found myself in the apartment of the Belgian consul, who had bought a small collection. That morning he left for his office, leaving my wife and myself taking photographs on the balcony. In the zest to complete our task, a sixteenth-century bowl slipped and smashed on the marble below.

What to do? We picked up the fragments and took them to the Syrian dealer who had sold the piece to the diplomat in the first place. He laughed and said he would have it mended immediately. At lunch we had to confess to the crestfallen diplomat what had happened. When we returned to the dealer at five o'clock, he had not only expertly mended the broken bowl, but also found an intact exact replica. So we were able to present the owner with both.

3 DESTINY

Asia, Africa, Syria and Egypt

If the Persian merchants on the China coast were indeed responsible for the suggestion that the potters at Jingdezhen should use cobalt blue for painting porcelain, then they must also surely have had a market in mind. The Moslem community had been established since the first century of Islam, having settled at the end of a lengthy system of maritime connections with the central Islamic heartland, which had existed since at least the Tang dynasty and was built on the trading networks established by the pre-Islamic Arabs. The discovery of the pattern of the annual monsoon winds in the first century AD allowed ships to sail directly across the Indian Ocean from the coast of Arabia, and thence to the Straits of Malacca and across the China Sea.[1] This opened up a direct connection between the Mediterranean and the Pacific. At the western end any goods that filtered through as far as Alexandria could be easily dispersed throughout the Mediterranean, to Italy, Greece, North Africa and the Iberian peninsula. All these connections were well established by the Roman period, with luxury goods from south Arabia and the Indian subcontinent transported to Rome, and Roman bronzes, ceramics, glass and coinage moving eastwards in the opposite direction.[2]

By the early eleventh century at least three major societies were interacting with each other economically: the Song dynasty in China, the Chola kingdom in south India and the Fatimids in Egypt. The conditions were propitious for the import and export of a wide variety of goods to and from all three of these sectors. In China, porcelain was one of the export commodities, and the lucrative trade was actively encouraged by the ruling power. As an early twelfth-century Chinese text describes the ships at that time: 'The greater part of the cargo consists of pottery, the small pieces packed in the larger, till there is not a crevice left.'[3]

Nor was this a one-way street. Even during the Tang dynasty, Abbasid pottery imitations of Tang white wares were being exported from Mesopotamia as far as Sri Lanka, where excavations at Mantai and the inland capital at Anuradhapura have shown that they co-existed with the Tang stoneware which had inspired them.'[4] Even more widely distributed was the turquoise-glazed pottery of the Sasanian/Islamic type, which reached as far as China itself. Large storage vessels of this type have been found in the tomb of Lia Hua (d. AD 930), near Fuzhou in

56 Jar (*guan*) of blue and white porcelain, with a Turkish silver-gilt mount. Yuan dynasty, 14th century. *H. 48 cm.*

Fujian province, and fragments excavated at Yangzhou in Jiangsu.[5] Such brilliantly coloured pottery was outside the usual Chinese repertoire and it is interesting that Cizhou ware painted under a turquoise glaze appears in the thirteenth century, which might well have paved the way for the introduction of cobalt blue as a foreign novelty in the early fourteenth century. Be that as it may, when blue and white began to be produced on a commercial scale it quickly found markets abroad, not only along the traditional maritime routes to the Mediterranean and Africa, but also within China itself and following the overland trade routes to Central Asia and the West.

The slighter blue and white wares discovered all over Southeast Asia have already been mentioned, but the more classical larger pieces were also exported. A fine example is the large *guan* spotted by Schuyler Camman in a crypt of the Wat Mahathat in Thailand, published by John Pope.[6] In the general disposition of its various registers, and even more so in its style of painting, it is very close to a *guan* in the British Museum.[7] Particularly striking is the similarity between the peony scrolls and the two bands of lotus panels filled with unusually elaborate auspicious objects, in both of which the upper panels have foliate frames. The British Museum vase, with a similar diamond diaper pattern on the rim, acquired a Turkish (or possibly Indian) silver mount at some stage in its history. A third related *guan* was once in the Cummings collection, which had been formed in India between 1864 and 1883. And a fourth similar *guan* in the British Museum was excavated from a tomb in Anhui dated to the Hongwu period (1368–98).

In Vietnam the numerous fifteenth-century underglaze blue stoneware imitations show that fourteenth-century Chinese blue and white, including large porcelain dishes, also made its way there. There are Vietnamese jars which quite faithfully copy dragons chasing flaming pearls, breaking waves, lotus panels with auspicious emblems and cloud-collar panels from blue and white porcelain. The large dishes replicate the Chinese designs even more carefully, particularly fish advancing through swirling water-weeds. The date of the first Vietnamese blue and white has yet to be precisely determined. It probably developed in the late fourteenth century from the earlier wares painted in underglaze iron-brown, of which sherds have been found in Japan that date to as early as 1330. It has been suggested that the production of blue and white received a special stimulus during the brief period when the country was under direct Chinese rule between 1407 and 1427.[8] This could imply that the earlier Yuan blue and white was brought

57 Vase *(meiping)* of blue and white stoneware. Vietnamese, 15th century. *H. 38 cm.*

58 Jar of blue and white stoneware, with three lions chasing brocaded balls. Vietnamese, 15th century. *H. 52.5 cm.*

59 Dish of blue and white stoneware, found in Syria. Vietnamese, 15th century. *D. 42.9 cm.*

in as a model, but it is more likely that it was already familiar in Vietnam. The Yuan traveller Wang Dayuan in 1349, in his *Dao Yi Zhi Lue* ('A Brief Description of the Island Foreigners'), lists forty-five countries which sought Chinese wares including Vietnam, though he does not list it as one of the countries that preferred blue and white as opposed to celadon and other types.[9]

Like the Chinese ware, Vietnamese blue and white also had its own export market. Dishes and other forms have been found in Turkey and Syria, and fragments show that it even reached East Africa, where pieces have been recovered from the island of Kilwa in Tanzania.[10] The most famous example of Vietnamese ware is the great flask in the Topkapi Saray collection in Istanbul, which is dated 1450. Of massive form, it has a spherical body and a tall, slightly tapering cylindrical neck. The Vietnamese inscription, in Chinese characters, reads:

> Painted for pleasure by the craftswoman Bui of Nam-sach-chau
> in the eighth year of Thai-hoa [i.e. 1450].

Apart from the fact that the painter was a woman and she regarded her work as agreeable, Nam-sach-chau is about 50 km east of Hanoi and presumably the kiln site.[11] The flask has a deep recessed base coloured chocolate brown, a typical feature of Vietnamese ware and perhaps an attempt with brown dressing to copy the unglazed bases of Yuan ware, which, as we have seen above, accidentally fired orange. In the same Turkish collection there is a faceted bottle with Vietnamese inscriptions in Chinese characters, this time a welcoming poem, but with no date. Like the flask, it once more picks up several distinctively Yuan motifs. A third piece, also in Topkapi Saray, is a *kendi*, the body broadly decorated with lotus flowers and cloud scrolls on a blue ground.[12]

Jane Beamish has pointed out that besides the prevalence of minor wares of the Yuan dynasty throughout Southeast Asia, there is enough evidence to show that the finer large vessels made at Jingdezhen were also exported.[13] These include examples of a *guan* from the Philippines; four more from Thailand, one with a lid from the crypt of the Wat Mahathat; a spectacularly well painted large flask of rectangular section with two pairs of handles on each shoulder, found in Indonesia and now in the Idemitsu Museum, Tokyo; an equally well painted large dish from Halmahera Island, Maluku, now in the National Museum in Jakarta; and fragments of blue and white and white on blue dishes, as well as a large *meiping*, all from East Java. As already noted, the blue and white sherd has the same underglaze inscription as that on the Hobart dish at Harvard. Probably a name, it is written in Arabic characters in Persian cursive style (*nastaliq*); it has been suggested that it is in Arab Indonesian (*Java Pegon*), allowing the intriguing possibility that these dishes were specially ordered for a Javanese client. The two dish fragments with white dragons reserved on a blue ground are of the very rare type of Yuan porcelain. The large vase (*meiping*) reconstructed from fragments believed to have been found at Trowulan, the Majapahit capital, is painted with a unique design, including an interior with a man seated writing at a table and an ogival window behind him.

The eighteen countries specifically listed by Wang Dayuan in 1349 as desiring blue and white are the Philippines, Tanjongpura (?southwest Borneo), Champa, Tambralinga and Patani (Thailand), Treganu and Kelantan (Malaysia), Java, Lamuri (northwest Sumatra), Kain Colam, India, Bengal, Orissa and Comari, Mecca, Borneo, Su-luo-ga (?) and Jai-li-na (?).[14] Even allowing for the imprecise identification of some of the place names, the broad spectrum is corroborated by the facts: Yuan blue and white has indeed been found in the Philippines, throughout Southeast Asia and in India, and the recent discovery of a wreck in the Red Sea with fourteenth-century porcelain aboard makes Mecca not quite so unlikely a destination as it might at first appear.

Moving westwards to India, fourteenth-century material has been found by the Japanese scholar Professor N. Karashima at various sites in the south on the Coromandel and Malabar coasts, such as Periyapattinaman (which he believes is Fattan, mentioned by Ibn Battuta) and Quilon, as well as earlier celadon ware.[15] No early blue and white has so far been recovered from Sri Lanka, though it must doubtless have reached the island. A thirteenth-century celadon bowl [**115**] was found at Yapahuwa in 1911 along with two white Ding ware bowls.[16] Yapahuwa had a short life from the early thirteenth century until it was destroyed in 1284, confirming the date of this well-known type, of which an identical example is the earliest piece of celadon in the Topkapi Saray [**60**]. As for the celadon bowl from Yapahuwa, William Willetts suggested that this might be the historic Bowl Relic, the alms-bowl of Buddha, which disappeared around that date. He maintained that it fits very well with Marco Polo's description of the bowl as being of 'very beautiful green porphyry'.[17] Further south in the Indian Ocean, two sherds of Yuan blue and white have been found on Male, the capital island of the Maldives, which was an important stopover for all maritime traffic moving westwards from the Straits of Malacca to the Indian subcontinent, the Persian Gulf, the Red Sea and the East African coast.[18]

60 Celadon bowl with lotus petals carved on the outside. Song/Yuan dynasty, 13th/14th century. *D. 22.5 cm.*

In East Africa fourteenth-century blue and white has been found at both Kilwa and Manda, and Chinese wares at Gedi and sites further south, including Madagascar and the Comoros islands.[19] Whether this material arrived directly across the Indian Ocean we do not know, but it is more probable that it was part of the transit trade with the Persian Gulf, with which the African merchants had strong ties. Further evidence for this is the amount of Persian fifteenth-century blue and white pottery that has been recovered with the Chinese porcelain. In turn, Kilwa was the main port of call from Aden to the Comoros and Madagascar, its rise and supremacy from the early thirteenth century being brought about by the monopoly it had on the gold trade from Sofala. Fourteenth-century fragments recovered from Kilwa include not only the slighter wares so common in Southeast Asia, but also sherds from larger, finely painted jars (*guan*) with motifs including a dragon, a phoenix, a peony with shaded petals, a chrysanthemum, and cloud-collar and lotus panels with thick and thin blue outlines. There are also contemporary celadon sherds and one that can be paralleled with a bowl from the Sinan wreck, *c*.1323.[20]

In the Gulf itself, fine quality Yuan blue and white and celadon has been found at Hormuz.[21] The blue and white includes fragments of large dishes with typical spiked lobed leaves, some in white reserved on a blue ground, and sherds of faceted vases. There are also examples of early fifteenth-century blue and white, one of which has been riveted, indicating that it was valuable enough to merit repair when broken. The celadon is typical of the thirteenth/fourteenth-century spectrum. From Bahrain, a fourteenth-century sherd is painted with a lotus and a spiked lobed leaf, and there are also fragments of Ding ware and celadon.[22] Celadon is also common at other Gulf sites, such as Sohar, Julfar, Ra's al-Khayma, Qays, Shenas, Kung and Bahrain, and along the South Arabian coast.[23]

In the Red Sea area, on the west coast Aydhab was particularly important as the landfall for merchandise to be trans-shipped across the desert and down the Nile. As early as the 1920s blue and white was found there, although it was not identified at the time as Yuan.[24] Because of the prevailing north wind, it was difficult for shipping to proceed northwards; indeed, the invention of tacking (*takkiyah*) was one solution to the problem. This led to the importance of Aydhab, and Jeddah on the opposite coast, from where much merchandise continued on northwards by land. The two ports were further linked by the *hajj*; they were used by Moslem pilgrims from Egypt, and from Morocco and West Africa, travelling either by the Mediterranean coastal route or the sub-Saharan land route. It is feasible that the blue and white in Morocco referred to by Ibn Battuta could have travelled either way, and it is interesting that his first attempt to visit Mecca was aborted at Aydhab, all the local shipping having been sunk by the Mamluks.[25] The Aydhab sherds are in the British Museum and include sketchily painted blue and white, one piece with a lotus spray. There is also part of a celadon bowl with a moulded fish, and another celadon fragment has an incised Pagspa character. Pagspa (1235–80) was a Tibetan lama who invented the script, which, for a brief span during the Yuan dynasty, was in official use. A celadon dish in the Topkapi Saray collection also has a moulded Pagspa character at the centre of a peony spray.[26] Celadon has also been found further north on the Red Sea at Qusayr, and at al-Qaraw east of Aden.[27]

In Egypt masses of Yuan blue and white excavated from Fustat (old Cairo) make it clear that this was a major destination for Chinese export ware, as it had been since the Tang dynasty. Fustat was first excavated by Ali Baghat Bey in 1912, and since the Egyptian authorities' decision to clear the area for redevelopment in 1963, Egyptian, American and Japanese archaeologists have worked there intensively.[28] It has been estimated that over half a million Chinese sherds have so far been recovered, ranging from the ninth to the fifteenth century. Only a selection of them has been published and it is regrettable that no comprehensive catalogue has ever been attempted. Amongst the blue and white the lotus pond design predominates, as it also does among the numerous Egyptian pottery imitations of Chinese ware. The Chinese imports represent an almost continuous sequence over five hundred years, so it is hardly surprising that local imitations are common, not only of blue and white but also of celadon and the earlier wares. It can be no coincidence that one Fustat fragment [**34**, **35**] is a *qingbai* copy of a *shufu* moulded bone, with the radial panels then overpainted with an underglaze blue design.[29] At Fustat the Chinese sherds are intermingled with Islamic material, and as the site was used as a city dump in post-medieval Cairo, all archaeologists who have tackled it agree that it is a stratigrapher's nightmare. But the mere existence of such a vast quantity of Chinese imports makes Fustat

61 Chinese blue and white porcelain *(centre)* and local copies, from Fustat. 14th/15th century.

62 Syrian blue and white pottery, found near Bab es-Sharqi, Damascus. 15th century.

63 Street scene in Douma, near Damascus, Syria.

hugely important, even if the material is in no easily discernible chronological sequence.

How did such a vast quantity of material ever get to Fustat from the Far East? Its journey along the maritime routes is not difficult to ascertain, but once it reached the Red Sea the final stage is more difficult to trace. The evidence from Aydhab and Qusayr is scanty, and we do not know whether the porcelain was then carried across the desert and shipped down the Nile, or landed farther north at some port yet to be determined.

Much of the porcelain that finally ended up in Topkapi Saray was booty, brought back from Egypt and Syria in the early sixteenth century after the successful campaigns of Sultan Selim I. A number of intact examples which have survived in Turkey must have come from Egypt, unlike the broken porcelain that ended up on the rubbish dumps of Fustat. In Syria a similar situation pertained and there was the same attempt by local potters to copy Chinese blue and white designs. If the existence of Chinese porcelain had previously only been implied by these imitations, the situation changed radically in the late 1960s, when a huge quantity of Chinese blue and white came to light in Damascus.[30]

More than six hundred pieces of blue and white and celadon were discovered in Syria, most of it from Douma, a small town on the northern fringe of the *ghuta*, or gardens of Damascus. The porcelain belonged to local families and only emerged when they moved from their traditional mud-brick houses into modern apartments by courtesy of President Hafez al-Assad, who also blessed them with a new post office and a two-lane highway linking Douma directly to Damascus. The new apartments were considerably less spacious than the old houses, and, having no idea of the antiquity of their family porcelain (unlike pottery, it shows no sign of age), people had no hesitation in selling it off to local dealers. Indeed, I saw my first piece of blue and white in the Singer shop just off the Suq al-Hamadiyeh in Damascus, where it had been offered in part exchange for a new sewing machine, and I was not convinced that it was really so old. Nor are the people of Douma humble peasants, for they have always been entrepreneurs, managing the gardens and crops of the *ghuta* for the Damascene landlords and taking to this day 40 per cent of the annual profit. Over centuries they have become wealthy, though the town shows no evidence of prosperity. The inhabitants of Douma wear mud-coloured clothes and lived in mud houses, and are renowned for their reticence and general inconspicuousness. Indeed, it is well known in Syria that if you are a politician and your star has fallen, Douma is the place to retire to until better times.

The Syrian porcelain ranges in date from the fourteenth century right through to the nineteenth. Of the earliest Yuan material several pieces are of outstanding quality. A superbly painted dish with two pheasants from Damascus is now in the Art Institute of Chicago **[43]**. Other dishes are equally original in the treatment of their subjects, including one bearing a pheasant, with wings outstretched, perched on the trunk of a peony bush, and another with two ducks and a posse of seven ducklings, both formerly in the Larsson collection.[31] Bowls with lotus pond designs are more conventional. A large jar (*guan*) has a finely painted floral design **[66]**; this came from Aleppo, where recent excavations on the citadel have turned up a number of blue and white sherds.[32] Another Yuan blue and white base sherd came from Tell Abyad in northeast Syria, and it is highly probable that more material will turn up in the future.

A fine example of Syrian blue and white pottery imitating Chinese porcelain is a large dish painted with a lotus pond design, now in the National Museum at Damascus.[33] It was found at Hama, on the River Orontes; this town was totally destroyed by Timur during his Syrian campaign of 1401, thus giving a secure *terminus ante quem* for the dish. An example of a Chinese lotus pond dish found in Damascus has already been mentioned **[55]**. A number of other Syrian blue and white pottery dishes and bowls are known, including more sherds from Hama.[34] Fragments and kiln wasters have been recovered from a site near Bab es-Sharqi outside the eastern walls of Damascus; they are now in the museum of the American University of Beirut.[35] In Beirut itself, a base sherd of blue and white pottery with a floral design was found during recent excavations at the centre of the city.[36] Again in Damascus, the mausoleum and adjacent mosque of Ghars ad-Din al-Khalili al-Tawrizi (d. 1423) are decorated with hundreds of blue and white hexagonal tiles interspersed with turquoise triangles, largely inspired by Chinese designs. There are also a number of other buildings in the city with fifteenth-century *chinoiserie* tiles.[37]

Whilst Syria and Egypt were the destinations for much of the Yuan blue and white found in the Near East, some of which may have been transported to Istanbul in later centuries, it is clear that fourteenth-century porcelain reached the Ottoman heartland at least as early as the first half of the fifteenth century. Here the evidence again rests on its local imitation, in this case the Turkish hexagonal tiles that line the *mihrab* and the flanking walls of the Murad II mosque at Edirne. The mosque was dedicated in 1435/6, and whilst there is some doubt as to whether the tiles were installed then or brought later from another building,

64 Interior of a shop in Douma, on the outskirts of Damascus.

65 A transaction takes place; a Syrian lady in Douma negotiates the sale of her Chinese dish.

66 Jar (*guan*) of blue and white porcelain, found in Syria. Yuan dynasty, 14th century.

there is no doubt about their early date, as the tiled *mihrab*, like the mosque, is dedicated to Sultan Murad II (1421–51). The tiles are painted in underglaze blue and turquoise, and used in conjunction with moulded tiles executed in *cuerda seca*. The latter is a typically Persian technique used earlier by the same band of craftsmen for the decoration of the Green Mosque (*Yesil Cami*) and Green Tomb (*Yesil Turbe*) in Bursa, *c.*1419–21.[38]

Bursa was the first Ottoman capital; the Turks then moved to Edirne on the European mainland in the fifteenth century, before Mehmet the Conqueror captured Constantinople from the Byzantines in 1453 and established Istanbul as the final capital of the expanding empire. The salient point about the Edirne tiles is that their designs include both Yuan motifs, such as the spiked lobed leaf, and floral patterns from early fifteenth-century porcelain. In order for it to have inspired the potters, this presupposes the existence of actual Chinese porcelain at Edirne, a couple of decades before the court moved to Istanbul. Further evidence can be found in a Turkish miniature of *c.*1450–60, which shows a prince enthroned and flanked by janissaries, with pieces of blue and white in the foreground **[67]**.[39] Although schematic, they depict in stylized fashion typical Yuan lotus panels with their emphatic outlines.

Having traced the movement of early blue and white by sea from China to Southeast Asia, India, Africa and the Middle East, what was happening in China itself during the latter half of Mongol rule? Until relatively recently the apparent paucity of Yuan porcelain in China itself led to the mistaken belief that it was really just an export ware, of no great interest to the Chinese themselves. Support for this view came from an early Ming text (1387) describing Yuan wares: 'There were blue-and-white and five-colour wares but they were very vulgar.'[40] Quite apart from the evidence to the contrary provided by the David vases, which were made in 1351 for a temple not far from Jingdezhen itself, in recent years increasing quantities of Yuan blue and white have been surfacing in China. Much of this has reached the West via Hong Kong and the international art market. A good number of the pieces have come from Buddhist and Daoist contexts, such as temples, and other unspecified sources. These have been supplemented by pieces found in datable tombs, and from archaeological excavations in China. Quite apart from Jingdezhen itself, where the Hutian site and other kilns have yielded Yuan and early Ming sherds,[41] excavations in Dadu (Beijing), the Mongol capital, have produced further material, both from the vicinity of the Yuan palace and from the surrounding city.[42]

Nor was Dadu the furthermost point north for the movement of Yuan blue and white from its production centre at Jingdezhen. Quite apart from a large *guan*, a dish, vases (*yuhuchun*) and stem cups found in Inner Mongolia over the past few decades,[43] there is the evidence from Kharakhoto (*Heicheng*, 'Black City'), the Mongol walled city in the middle of the Gobi Desert **[68]**. Kharakhoto was discovered by the Russian explorer Count Kozlov in 1908 and subsequently visited by Sir Aurel Stein in 1914, by the American Langdon Warner in 1923 and by the Swedish explorer Sven Hedin during his major expedition to Central Asia in 1930–33.[44] Since then, because of travel restrictions imposed by the Communist regime in China and the site's proximity to the modern frontier with Outer Mongolia, it has been virtually out of bounds. However, in the 1980s expeditions were organized by the Inner Mongolia Institute of Archaeology, as well as by Fu Nin, Curator at the Inner Mongolia Museum in Hohhot; I myself made a brief visit in 1997.[45]

All of these investigations produced sherds of blue and white porcelain, which are worth examining collectively in order to clarify the kind of material the Mongols

67 *The Sultan and His Court* (detail), from al-Katibi, *Divan*, *c.*1450–60. It depicts the Sultan with his janissaries, with several pieces of blue and white in front of him.

68 Kharakhoto, in the Gobi Desert. The city was abandoned in the late 14th century, with the end of the Yuan dynasty.

LEFT: *The southwest angle of the city, looking east.*
RIGHT: *The western ramparts, looking north.*

themselves wanted. It should be stressed that blue and white was not the only kind of ceramics found at Kharakhoto, and such sherds were in the minority compared to the masses of Jun, Cizhou, celadon, Northern Song, Liao and other types.

But first a word about the geographical location of Kharakhoto and its strategic importance. The city is located approximately 25 km southeast of Etzina, the oasis at the terminal point of the Etsin Gol river where it finally drains into the Gobi Desert. The river has its origin in the mighty range of the Qilian Shan, not far from the source of the Yellow River. But unlike the Yellow River, which flows eastwards towards the Pacific, the Etsin Gol runs north into the desert. The Gobi is an extremely inhospitable place, but the river never fails. In winter, it continues to flow under black ice, and in summer it is fed by melting snow. Along its course there are dozens of settlements from the Han dynasty onwards, and a branch of the river is believed to have once watered Kharakhoto.

Strategically Kharakhoto not only lies astride the east–west caravan route across the Gobi but is also on the north–south route from the Mongol capital at Karakorum to China. Founded at the end of the eleventh century by the Tanguts, it was devastated in 1226 when captured by the Mongols, who then held it until 1380. It would certainly have played an important role as a garrison city for

Qubilai Khan's conquest of China and the establishment of the Yuan dynasty in 1260. After the capture of Dadu in 1368 by the Ming, it became the capital of the Later Yuan dynasty until this was finally subdued in 1380. It was never inhabited again. Nor is Kharakhoto the only site in the area, for there are a number of monastic complexes nearby with basically a similar range of Yuan material.[46] As in ancient Egypt, the desert climate is conducive to the preservation of organic material such as textiles, wood, leather, paper and paintings, which was the primary attraction for explorers in the twentieth century. Count Kozlov, who discoverered Kharakhoto in 1908, visited the site again in 1909 and for a third time in 1926. The material from all three Russian expeditions is in St Petersburg. About ten thousand books and manuscripts, mostly written in Tangut but also in Chinese, Tibetan, Mongolian, Uighur, Arabic and Syriac, are kept in the Institute of Oriental Studies. The rest of the material is in the Hermitage and includes about three hundred Buddhist paintings and a hundred sculptures. There are also almost two thousand sherds, of which more than five hundred are of blue and white porcelain. In Dr Lubo-Lesnichenko's preliminary study of this material he illustrates seventy-seven pieces. He notes that most are small-scale, though there are some larger pieces with more complex decoration. Many of them have hooked leaves of the type so common in Southeast Asia, and he remarks on the similarity between the two types.[47]

Sir Aurel Stein's expedition to Kharakhoto in 1912 was aimed more at finding paintings and manuscripts than collecting ceramics.[48] Langdon Warner visited Kharakhoto in 1923 and remarks in his 1926 account of the expedition that 'my pockets were bulging with pottery fragments and remained so during the rest of our stay, though they were emptied a dozen times a day into baskets'. This is tantalizing, but so far it has been impossible to locate any such fragments, though they may perhaps some day turn up in a storeroom at Harvard, where he was a curator at the Fogg Museum.

The material from Sven Hedin's expedition in 1930–33 – the importance of which John Pope was quick to realize, publishing a selection of the blue and white sherds Hedin found as an appendix to his *Ardebil* publication in 1958[49] – at one time appeared to have suffered a similar fate. Published by Sommarström in 1956–8 in his two carefully documented and well-illustrated volumes, they too seemed to have disappeared. However, thanks to Dr Håkan Wahlqvist the sherds were finally located in the basement of the Ethnographic Museum in Stockholm. Now being studied and definitively published by a young Swedish scholar,

Nicklas Cederqvist, they include many pieces of fine quality, including fragments of both blue and white and copper red. There are also numerous examples of other types of ware from Kharakhoto.

The excavations by the Inner Mongolia Institute of Archaeology in the 1980s produced examples of at least two large pieces of blue and white of superior quality: a large bottle with pendant cloud-collar panels on the body alternating with cloud bands above a key-fret band and lotus panels, and another fragmentary vessel, probably a *guan*, with a four-clawed dragon on the neck, a peony wreath on the body between diaper and classic scroll bands, and pendant lotus panels filled with spiky lotuses. Among the smaller wares was a small cup with floral and hooked leaf patterns.[50]

Finally, sherds recovered by Fu Nin, and later by myself, from Kharakhoto and also from monastic sites north and south of the city include parts of blue and white bowls, a faceted flask and a stem cup, many of which are extremely finely painted. All of these sherds are now in the study collection of the Hohhot Museum.[51] My perception was that the other Yuan wares far outnumbered the blue and white, but this may simply be the result of the site having been thoroughly scoured of the more decorative sherds by previous visitors.

Besides the material from Kharakhoto, a number of important finds have been made elsewhere in Inner Mongolia.[52] A magnificent large dish with radiating cloud-collar panels was found at Yun Zhong, at the centre of this enormous city dating back to Han times and reused in the Mongol period. This dish can be directly related to other pieces of similar design from Damascus, Topkapi Saray, Delhi, and from the Hutian kiln site at Jingdezhen. A large *guan* was recovered from Yanjialing, another reoccupied Han site, and further east blue and white vases (*yuhuchun*) have been unearthed in the Chifeng region, as well as five stem cups with dragons or phoenixes painted on the outside and with moulded designs within. These are very close in style to the stem cup at the Dayton Art Institute, which once belonged to John Pope, and to the material he himself found in Dadu/Beijing.[53] Such evidence from northern China makes it easy to begin to track the northern and westward movement of blue and white during the fourteenth century. But much remains still to be discovered.

Moving westwards along the most northern branch of the Silk Road, the next point of reference is in the western province of Xinjiang, at Almalik (Huocheng), the capital of the Chaghatai Khanate. Here again, Chinese archaeologists have unearthed Yuan blue and white, *qingbai* and celadon, as well as Islamic coins dating from the first half of the fourteenth century and Persian inlaid metalwork.[54] From then onwards the route would have skirted the Tianshan and continued on to present-day Kazakhstan and the great cities of Central Asia, Samarkand and Bukhara. In Samarkand sherds of Chinese porcelain have indeed been found, one of which, in the reserve collection of the Samarkand Museum, shows part of a prancing deer that might have been painted by the same hand as a sherd picked up by John Pope in Beijing, now in the Freer Gallery.[55] As in Syria and Turkey, much can be learned here about the import of Chinese porcelain from its local imitations, in this case Timurid blue and white pottery. A bowl in the Bishkek Museum excavated at Talas is a fairly faithful imitation of a Yuan bowl of the lotus pond type. Sherds from Samarkand clearly demonstrate the influence of fourteenth- and early fifteenth-century Chinese designs, for example two dishes with floral and bird designs in the museum of the Ulugh Beg observatory.[56] The influence of Chinese patterns can also be easily detected in the mosaic tilework in the major monuments of Samarkand, particularly the Shah-I Zindeh cemetery with its use of lotus and peony motifs. Down into Persia and westwards through Tabriz, the westward trail is clear.

How was the Chinese porcelain transported across Central Asia? Extraordinary though it might seem, there is a painting which shows precisely that [**71**]. It is part of an album in the Topkapi Saray Library (H.2153), the date, origin and iconography of which have been the subject of much scholarly debate.[57]

This particular painting shows a cart full of blue and white being hauled across a rocky landscape by a donkey. The carter clutches the donkey's saddle and casts an anxious look backwards at his precarious load. In front is a second donkey, ridden by a lady in a state of fatigue who is supported by a young man attempting to prevent her from falling off her mount. There are various other figures, including two who exchange covered metal bowls, one of them being dressed in European costume. A winsome lady also casts an apprehensive glance over her shoulder at the loaded cart. Two more ladies and a man with a topknot are further spectators, while a white-bearded old man tipples from a spouted ewer in a state of happy inebriation. Crouching behind rocky outcrops are grotesque figures making faces at each other and a black man proffers a covered blue and white box to a young woman who is preoccupied watching two more men peering over the wall of an enclosure at a *ger*-like domed structure.

What can all this mean, if anything? One possible interpretation is that the central scene is a wedding procession, with the exhausted bride and her dowry –

69 Tankard of blue and white porcelain. Xuande mark and period (1426–35). *H. 13.3 cm.*

70 In the Gobi Desert, between Jiayuguan and Jinta. Note the similarity to the background in the painting below.

71 Album painting from Samarkand or Tabriz, 15th century. *25 × 48 cm*. It depicts a procession through the desert with a cart full of blue and white porcelain.

a sort of upmarket *batterie de cuisine*. Some of the figures are Chinese, others are not. The setting is an accurate depiction of desert landscape, such as the Gobi with its volcanic rocks. withered tamarisk and oasis-like patches of green [70]. But it is the blue and white that provides a clue to the painting's date. The large *guan* with snarling dragons separated by a lotus suggests a fourteenth-century model, but the arcading on the neck as well as on the two smaller covered jars is more in early fifteenth-century style. So is the spouted ewer, and the covered box. The lower half of an almost identical box, along with a jug bearing similar designs to those of the ewer, have recently been excavated at Jingdezhen itself.[58] Both have Xuande reign marks (1426–35). As this was the period when the last of the trading missions initiated by the previous emperor, Yongle, took place, the painting can be read as a highly appropriate, if allegorical, illustration of the westward movement of blue and white. Where it was painted we do not know; Samarkand or Tabriz have been suggested. The eclecticism and mixture of Chinese and Central Asian elements is typical of the other paintings and drawings in the album, whose compilation is also a mystery.

One final feature of the procession remains to be explained. How on earth would one ever transport fragile blue and white porcelain in an open cart across such uneven terrain? The cart has two large central wheels and four smaller ones at the corners, as a kind of shock absorber. But the idea of an open cart is lunatic, and can only be explained by the exigencies of the artist who was obliged to depict the valuable cargo.

That the reality was rather different we know, for the merchandise that travelled east and west across Central Asia was carried by caravans of Bactrian camels. This would appear to be almost as dangerous as an open cart for goods as fragile as Chinese porcelain, and for this reason alone it has been argued that the bulk of Chinese export ware must always have been carried by sea. But we know from the increasing evidence of shipwrecks (and in one instance an abandoned cargo of Song porcelain on the shores of Sri Lanka) that even the maritime routes were not without hazard.

However, thanks to Professor Li Zhiyan, citing a Chinese text, we now know how porcelain could be safely transported by land.[59] First you place it in a container, which you then fill with a mixture of sand, earth, soya bean and wheat. This is then sprinkled with water and the mass sets rock hard. On the container's arrival at its destination, say in Damascus or Istanbul, you sprinkle the mixture with water once again and it dissolves, leaving an intact vessel. This is sound professional practice in any modern museum, where delicate objects are packed as rigidly as possible within their containers, trucks and planes being the contemporary equivalent of the Bactrian camels.

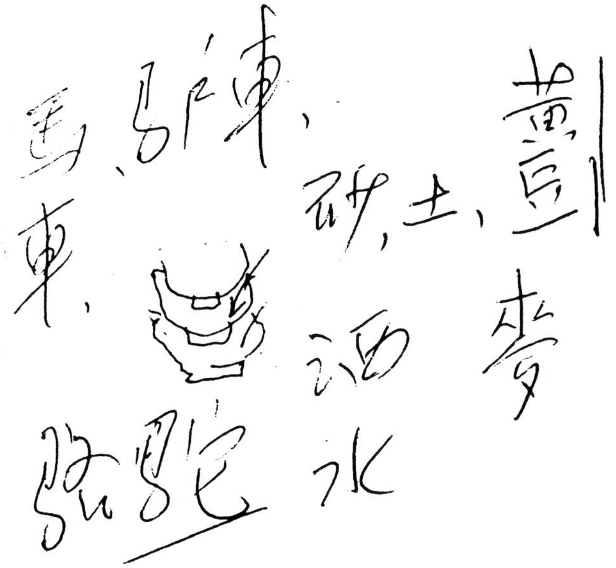

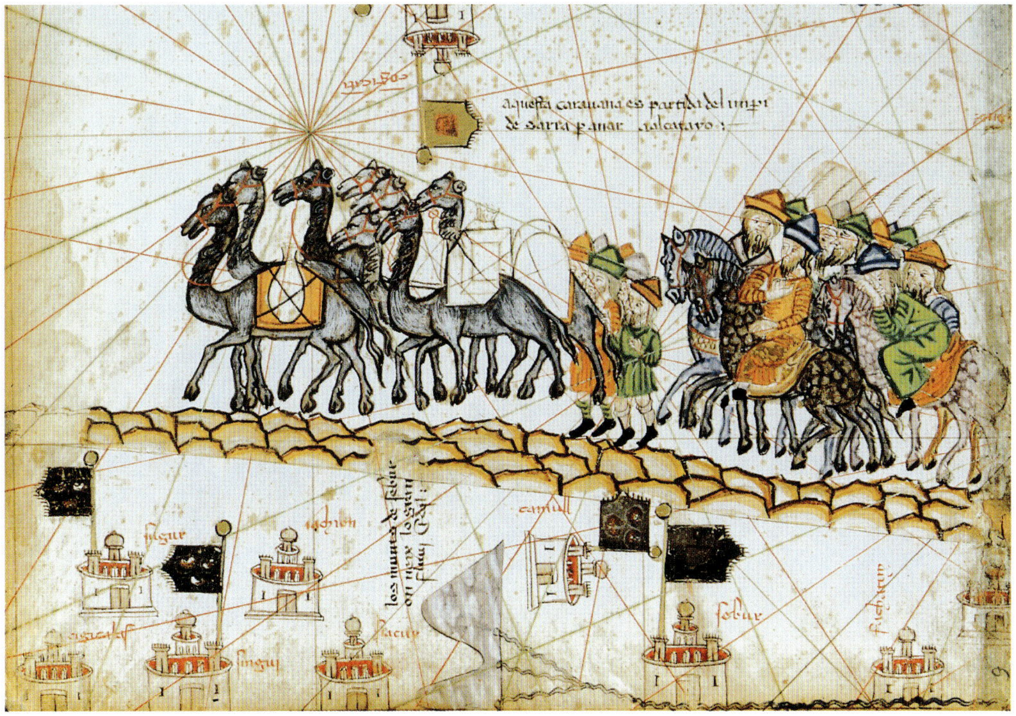

72 Professor Li Zhiyan's explanation of how to pack and transport porcelain.

73 The Great Wall near Jiayuguan.

74 Detail from the *Catalan Atlas*, *c.*1380. It shows a caravan of Bactrian camels on its way eastwards to the Chaghatai Khanate, the camels laden with square boxes. The legend reads: 'This caravan has left the empire of Sareas [the Kipchak Khanate] to go to Cathay.'

4 CHANGE

The decline of the Mongols and the early Ming dynasty

With the rise of the Ming dynasty and the overthrow of the Yuan regime, the potteries at Jingdezhen suffered a temporary reverse. The new emperor, Hongwu (1368–98), established his capital at Nanjing, and the northern retreat of the Mongols meant that the land routes to the west that had been such a vigorous feature of their administration were in abeyance. Nor was Hongwu interested in free trade, issuing a series of decrees throughout his reign that it should cease. Paradoxically, at the same time he was responsible for a series of exploratory missions bearing gifts to Southeast Asia to proclaim his sovereignty, one of which in 1383 included 13,000 pieces of porcelain.

During his reign, the character of the porcelain produced at Jingdezhen changed considerably. The designs became distinctly more sinicized, breaking with the richly decorated Yuan wares and subscribing to a more Chinese taste. The porcelain of this period is painted in a slate-like blue with conventional floral designs and the Yuan motifs become more attenuated. The vigorous serpentine waves are transformed into a ring of surf, and the lotus and cloud-collar panels no longer stress contrasting thick and thin outlines. Floral sprays float on a white ground, like carelessly thrown bouquets. Peonies and other carefully painted flowers with thinly outlined petals alternate with simple chrysanthemums. Key-fret bands often play an important part in the designs, as do overlapping vertical plantain leaves. A vase and a ewer illustrate many of these characteristics [**76**, **77**], as does a chunky little bowl [**79**]. The vase has the 'Three Friends' – pine, bamboo and prunus – disposed so that their upper parts disappear behind a ring of pendant trefoils. There are also underglaze red vessels in this linear, attenuated style, of which those that survive actually outnumber those in blue and white. A difficult colour to manage, the red frequently fires a dark brown, or even mutates to a greyish tone. The red vessels are discussed separately in chapter 5.

The difficulty with this period of ceramic history is that whilst all the pieces cited form a stylistically coherent group, there is no absolute date for any of them, and opinions have varied wildly in the past as to where they might fall between the final years of the Yuan dynasty and the early fifteenth century, when we are

75 Large flask (*bianhu*) of blue and white porcelain. Yongle period, early 15th century. *H. 47.2 cm, D. 41.3 cm.* Inspired by an Islamic metal prototype, the unglazed flat underside has a countersunk centre.

77 Ewer of blue and white porcelain. Hongwu period, (1368–99). *H. 32 cm.*

78 The 'Porcelain Pagoda' in Nanjing. Detail of a 19th-century painting by J.-J.-J. Defer.

79 Bowl of blue and white porcelain. Hongwu period. *D. 21.4 cm.*

OPPOSITE
76 Vase (*yuhuchun ping*) painted with the 'Three Friends'. Hongwu period. *H. 32 cm.*

on more secure chronological ground. What can be said with certainty is that there is an evident change of style from Yuan to early Ming wares.

The advent of Yongle in 1403 and the necessity for him to prove his legitimacy after ousting Hongwu's rightful successor, Jianwen (1399–1402), led to yet another change of taste. Public display of his respect for his father, Hongwu, included the construction of a porcelain pagoda in Nanjing, built with white porcelain bricks from Jingdezhen [**78**]. White wares were also a conspicuous feature of Yongle's reign, including so-called 'monk's cap' ewers testifying to a direct connection with Tibetan Buddhism, which was politically important for the emperor in reinforcing his position.

Even more surprising are white wares directly modelled on Persian and Islamic metalware. A number of these have been found and reconstructed from excavations at the Zhushan site in Jingdezhen. They include ewers, angular candlesticks of octagonal section, three-legged ewers with filters, pilgrim flasks with twin loop handles, basins with everted rims, small jugs with a pronounced convex moulding at the juncture between spherical body and fluted cylindrical neck, and even a faithful copy of a Mamluk brass stand with flaring foot and rim [**80**]. Why these white copies of foreign metal forms were made is uncertain, but what is fascinating is that during the reign of Yongle's successor, Xuande (1426–35), these forms were made and decorated in blue and white, bearing Xuande reign marks.

a

b

c
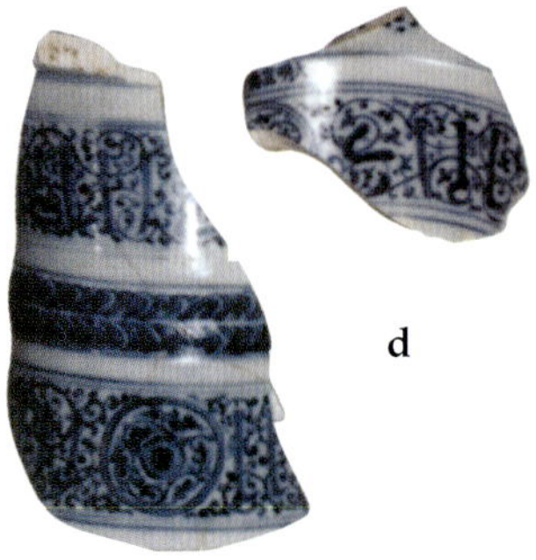
d

e

f

g

h

i

j

k

l

m

81 a, b Stand of blue and white porcelain, imitating an inlaid Mamluk metal stand. Xuande period (1426–35). *H. 17.2 cm.*

OPPOSITE:
80 Chinese porcelain excavated at Jingdezhen:

- **a** Yongle white candlestick
- **b** Xuande blue and white candlestick, marked on the edge
- **c** Yongle white stand
- **d** Fragments of blue and white stand, with Xuande mark below the rim
- **e** Yongle white ewer
- **f** Xuande blue and white ewer
- **g** Yongle white basin
- **h** Xuande blue and white basin, marked below the rim
- **i** Yongle white tankard
- **j** Xuande blue and white tankard
- **k** Yongle white pilgrim flask
- **l** Yongle blue and white pilgrim flask
- **m** Xuande blue and white pilgrim flask, marked below the rim

The context of their production can be explained by the fact that during Yongle's reign his predecessor Hongwu's introspective policy was sharply reversed. Yongle initiated a series of maritime missions to the West, which suggests that some of these Persian- and Near Eastern-inspired vessels must have been intended as diplomatic presents in return for tributary gifts. Indeed, a blue and white stand belonging to this category, now in the British Museum, was found in Damascus **[81]**.[1] The stand is decorated almost entirely with painted interpretations of Mamluk engraved metal ornament, with even an unsuccessful attempt at copying Arabic benedictory inscriptions. The only Chinese element is the rosettes almost hidden under the rim, and identical rosettes are on two rare marked Yongle cups.[2] Not all such stands were exported, as a similar one, which never left China, is in the Tianjin Municipal Museum, and fragments of a third stand have been excavated from Jingdezhen.[3] This third example is unique in that it bears part of a Xuande reign mark just below the rim. So, too, do a number of the other pieces found at the Zhushan site, confirming the dating of many of the decorated pieces of this group to the Xuande period.

Unmarked examples of these Islamic-inspired forms are in the Topkapi Saray and Ardebil collections. The most prominent are ewers copying Persian or Central Asian shapes, with tall cylindrical necks, angular spouts and scalloped panels on the shoulder replicating details of the metal prototypes.[4] But whilst the floral decoration is in early fifteenth-century style, on some ewers **[83]** the lotus panels, blackberry lily and crapemyrtle scrolls, and the vertical panels with bracketed corners, are somewhat anomalous, being more usually associated with the early fourteenth-century Yuan style.

The most spectacular of this group are three very large flasks, of which the best-known example is in the Freer Gallery in Washington, where it is displayed with an inlaid metal Islamic prototype of equally impressive scale.[5] The porcelain flasks are by no means straightforward copies of the metal forms, which have strap handles and recessed panels at the centre. Both the Freer flask and the one illustrated here **[75]** have ring handles, are convex on one side with a raised boss at the centre, and are flat and unglazed beneath. The decoration is eclectic, with breaking waves and floral spirals contrasting with an eight-pointed star on the boss, of Islamic inspiration.

Other smaller examples are the moon flasks, with flattened circular bodies, strap handles and bulbous mouths. Again Yongle and Xuande blue and white flasks have been excavated at Jingdezhen, and whole unmarked specimens are in

OPPOSITE, FROM LEFT

82 Ewer of blue and white porcelain, inspired by an earlier Persian metal ewer. Early 15th century. *H. 32.4 cm.*

83 Ewer of blue and white porcelain, inspired by an Islamic metal prototype. Yongle period, early 15th century. *H. 36.5 cm.*

RIGHT

84 Moon flask (*bianhu*) of blue and white porcelain. Yongle period, early 15th century. *H. 24.7 cm.*

86 Basin with everted rim of blue and white porcelain. Early 15th century. *D. 30.5 cm.*

85 Detail of flask (*bianhu*) of blue and white porcelain, with dancing figures. Early 15th century. *H. 30 cm.*

the Topkapi Saray and Ardebil collections.[6] While some have formal radiating patterns at the centre, others are painted with floral sprays. One extraordinary flask in Istanbul depicts five dancing figures and musicians in a landscape **[85]**.[7] Their belted tunics, floppy sleeves and short boots suggest that these figures are Turkic or Uighur. The round drum and trumpet point to Central Asia and the landscape itself, featuring mountains, trees and running water, brings to mind a Shamanist ritual dance.

A blue and white basin with a flaring rim has been reconstructed from the Zhushan sherds, once more copying a Mamluk metal or glass prototype. A complete example is in Istanbul, and another with a Xuande mark is in Japan.[8] A third is in the Avery Brundage collection in San Francisco **[86]**.[9] Here the decoration is Chinese, rather than Islamic, and represents the early fifteenth-century style at its finest. An odd motif on the inner rim is a squiggle repeated between the flowers. It has been suggested that it could be interpreted as an illiterate attempt to render 'Allah', but cursive Arabic is not a feature of Mamluk engraved decoration.

All these examples of Yongle/Xuande porcelain inspired by Islamic models can be easily explained in terms of Yongle's unusual interest in the outside world, culminating in the six maritime expeditions initiated by him from 1405 onwards, with a seventh and final expedition dispatched by Xuande in 1431:

1405–07 Fleet of 317 ships, 27,870 men; to Java, Semudera, Lambri, Ceylon, Calicut

1407–09 249 ships; to Thailand, Java, Aru, Lambri, Coimbatore, Kayal, Cochin and Calicut, where the Commander erected an inscription to commemorate the relations between China and India.

1409–11 48 ships, 30,000 men; to Champa, Java, Malacca, Semudera, Ceylon, Quilon, Cochin and Calicut. In Ceylon Zheng He set up a commemorative inscription in Galle carved in Chinese, Tamil and Persian mentioning gifts in gratitude to the Buddha for his successful first expedition. On his return trip he had an altercation with the ruler Alagakkonara, whom he captured and took back to China.

1413–15 63 ships, 28,560 men; to Champa, Kelantan, Pahang, Java, Palembang, Malacca, Aru, Semudera, Lambri, Ceylon, Kayal, the Maldives, Cochin, Calicut and Hormuz. In Semudera Zheng He captured the usurper to the throne and took him back to China, where he was executed.

1417–19 To return ambassadors to China.; to Champa, Pahang, Java, Palembang, Malacca, Semudera, Lambri, Ceylon, the Maldives, Cochin, Calicut, Cannanore(?) Hormuz, La'sa (near Mukalla), Aden, Mogadishu, Brava and Malindi. The first expedition to reach East Africa.

1421–22 41 ships, again with returning envoys; to Malacca, Aru, Semudera, Lambri, Coimbatore, Kayal, Ceylon, the Maldives, Cochin, Calicut, Hormuz, Dhufar, La'sa, Aden, Mogadishu, Brava and Thailand on return.

87 *The Trilingual Inscription* (detail)
Carved in Chinese, Tamil and Persian, and set up by Zheng He in Galle, on the southern tip of Ceylon. Dated 15 February 1409, it commemorates gifts by Zheng He to a Buddhist temple in the name of Yongle, in thanks to the Buddha for the success of his first expedition in 1405–7.

1431–33 More than 100 ships with 27,550 men; to Champa, Java, Palembang, Malacca, Semudera, Ceylon, Calicut, Hormuz, as well as emissaries to Thailand, Aru, Nagur, Lide, Lambri, Nicobar islands, Bengal, Quilon, Cochin, Coimbatore, the Maldives, Dhufar, La'sa, Aden, Mogadishu and Brava, and to Mecca.

All seven were under the command of the Muslim admiral Zheng He, who had found favour under Yongle and been appointed superintendent of the office of eunuchs. A detailed account of the expeditions exists in a chronicle (*c.*1433) by Ma Huan, who was appointed as Zheng He's official translator.[10] Converted to Islam, at some stage Ma Huan had acquired a working knowledge of Arabic and Persian, sufficent to give authentic descriptions of the manners and customs of the countries he visited. He is to be compared in some ways to Ibn Battuta, and in many respects outdistances him in the detail of his accounts. It is not without interest that, like Marco Polo and Ibn Battuta, Ma Huan also had a collaborator. This was Guo Zhongli, who was on three of Zheng He's expeditions and whose notes amplified Ma Huan's in the compilation of the final text.[11] The chronicle consists of twenty chapters, each devoted to a particular country: Champa (central Vietnam), Java, Palembang, Thailand, Malacca, Deli, Semudera (Lho Seumawe), Nagur (Peudada), Lide (Meureudu), Lambri (Atjeh), Ceylon, Quilon, Cochin, Calicut, Maldive and Laccadive Islands, Dhufar, Aden, Bengal, Hormuz and Mecca (which Ma Huan charmingly calls *tian fang* – 'The Heavenly Square', i.e. the Ka'ba).

In the case of five of these countries blue and white porcelain is mentioned among the lists of goods traded and products of interest to the Chinese. The first such country is Champa, ten days' sailing from Fu chou:

> They very much like the dishes, bowls and other kinds of blue porcelain articles, the hemp-silk, silk-gauze, beads and other such things from the Central Country. They constantly bring rhinoceros' horns, elephants' teeth, *qie lan* incense, and other such things, and present them as tribute to the Central Country.

In Java, the large vessels sailed to Surabaja at the east end of the island, goods being then trans-shipped in smaller vessels and overland to the capital at Majapahit:

> The people of the country are very fond of the blue patterned porcelain-ware of the Central Country, also of the musk, gold-flecked hemp-silks, and beads. They buy these things in exchange for copper coins.

In Ceylon the Chinese ships moored at Pieh-lo-li (Beruwala), where local products included gemstones and pearls:

> The musk, hemp-silk, coloured silk-taffeta, blue porcelain dishes and bowls, copper coins and camphor of the Central Country are very much liked; and so they take precious stones and pearls to give in exchange.

Further west across the Indian Ocean, at Dhufar:

> When the treasure-ships of the Central Country arrived there, after the reading of the imperial will and the conferment of presents was finished, the king sent chiefs everywhere to issue instructions to the people of the country and they took such things as frankincense, dragon's-blood, aloes, myrrh, benzoin, liquid storax, and *mu biezi*, and came to barter them for hemp-silk, porcelain-ware and other such articles.

Finally, Ma Huan describes Mecca, and as he was a Muslim there is no reason to doubt that this is a first-hand account. The expedition divided at Calicut and seven emissaries proceeded to Jiddah in 1432 then travelled a day to Mecca; a detailed description is given. The embassy was sent from India:

> with a load of musk, porcelain articles and other such things … it took them one year to go and return. They bought all kinds of unusual commodities, and rare valuables, *qilin*, lions, 'camel-fowls' [ostriches], and other such things; in addition they painted an accurate representation of the 'Heavenly Hall' and they returned to the capital [Beijing].

88 The shore at Calicut, with the reefs out to sea on which the Chinese junk in which Ibn Battuta had intended to sail was wrecked in 1342.

The scale of the operation was extraordinary, the first expedition alone, in 1405–7, consisting of 317 ships and 27,870 men. Ambitious though they were, these expeditions did nothing to establish permanent commercial relations between China and the West. The actual survival of early fifteenth-century blue and white in the lands specifically mentioned by Ma Huan as desiring blue and white porcelain are disappointing. For Champa (central Vietnam) and Java nothing is known that can be directly linked to the expeditions, though in the case of Vietnam there is the indirect testimony of local imitations of Chinese imports.[12] The well-known design of two birds perched on a branch **[89]** is copied in spritely fashion in Vietnamese blue and white, as is the lotus bouquet (TKS 15/1454).[13]

In Java there are three pieces of Vietnamese blue and white in the Museum Pusat in Jakarta, which are of the fourteenth/early fifteenth century. A splendid dish, *c*.1400, with a foliate rim painted with surfing waves, sixteen bouquets in the bracket-moulded cavetto and a peony tree at the centre, is closely related to a dish in Istanbul (TKS 15/1389). It came from Padangsidempuan, Tapanuli, north Sumatra. There is also a dragon jar (*guan*) from the north Celebes, and a ewer from Halmahera, east Indonesia, which appear from the catalogue illustrations to be early fifteenth century.[14]

As for Ceylon, there is a curious lacuna, considering Zheng He's deep involvement in local politics. On his outward voyage in 1409 he had erected a trilingual inscription **[87]** evoking his benevolent visit in 1406,[15] but on his return trip in 1411 he had a violent altercation with the ruler, Alagakkonara, to the extent of taking the king and his family and entourage captive and removing them to

89 Dish of blue and white porcelain. Ming dynasty, early 15th century. *D. 55 cm.*

90 The foundations of the city wall of Kotte, capital of Ceylon, in the early 15th century.

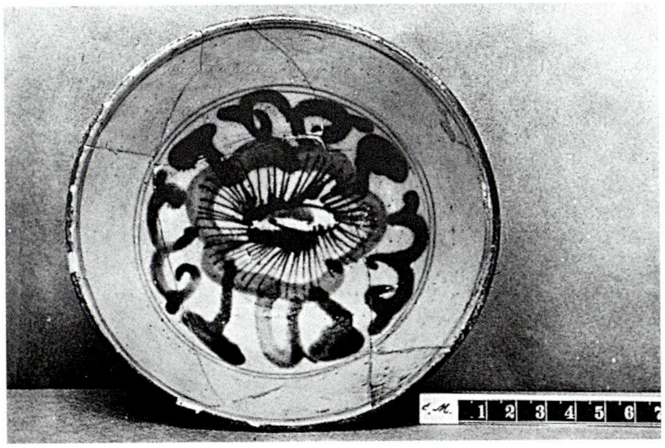

91 a, b Bowl of blue and white porcelain excavated at Dhlo-Dhlo, near Great Zimbabwe, in 1929. 16th century. Photographed by Kathleen Kenyon.

China, only to be returned later, after being released by the emperor. It is recorded that the mission landed at Beruwela, and the capital at that time was at Kotte [**90**], a few miles inland from Colombo. But a diligent search at both sites for any trace of fifteenth-century porcelain has so far proved negative, nor do any examples appear to have survived in monastic or private hands.

Although porcelain is not mentioned, the last four of Zheng He's expeditions all visited Hormuz, and Ma Huan devotes a whole chaper to the island and its inhabitants. Half a dozen fragments of unmistakably early fifteenth-century blue and white have been picked up there.[16] As for Dhufar and Arabia in general, nothing has so far come to light, although a survey of the contents of old houses in Mecca, and those of the traditional wealthy merchants at Jiddah, might well prove fruitful. If this seems far-fetched, it should be remembered that more than six hundred pieces of Chinese porcelain lay undiscovered in private houses in Syria until the late 1960s.

Zheng He's expeditions reached as far as East Africa, and in this context one might note the case of a later Chinese bowl that played an important part in dating a previously elusive civilization. This was at Zimbabwe, where the excavation of a sixteenth-century blue and white bowl at Dhlo-Dhlo, a related site approximately a hundred miles to the west, helped establish the period of that culture, formerly dated anywhere from the 1100 BC to the late Middle Ages.[17] Gertrude Caton-Thompson successfully identified Zimbabwe as an Iron Age settlement, probably the largest south of the Sahara. With a population of 12–20,000, it controlled the export of gold and ivory to the coast, where these commodities were bartered for porcelain, glass and cloth. The photograph of this bowl [**91**] was taken in 1929 by Caton-Thompson's young assistant, Kathleen Kenyon, later to become one of the most distinguished archaeologists of the twentieth century, and who was quite proud that her career should have started with blue and white.

The Topkapi Saray collection reflects a hiatus between the Yuan and Ming dynasties, with a mere half-dozen pieces representing the late fourteenth century. One of these, a broken dish [**93**], was discovered in storage by Regina Krahl, who remembers that it was so dirty that she was not sure at the time whether it was blue and white or celadon. A closely related dish has the same foliate rim with a formal classic scroll in fourteenth-century style, combined with a naturalistic spray of gardenia at the centre [**92**]. These dishes represent the transition to the fifteenth century, like one in the Ardebil collection (29.68) with a pair of peonies at the centre and a classic scroll on the rim, while others in the same collection are painted with separate floral sprays on the rim or cavetto.

When the new naturalistic style finally developed, the effect was stunning. This is illustrated by ten massive dishes in Istanbul, some of which are over 60 cm in diameter (TKS 15/1374, 1407, 1372, 1384). Five of them are painted with a pair of birds cheekily perched on a branch of peach blossom **[89]**. Two more have a rocky landscape as their main subject, with rippling water below and trailing clouds above **[96]**. Even more impressive are the eight elaborate floral sprays in the cavetto, all different and springing from leafy tufts, and similar sprays are painted on the backs of the dishes **[97, 98]**. Smaller dishes and bowls are decorated with lotus bouquets, and single flowers surrounded by five more on wiry, spiral stems, bunches of grapes, melons and pomegranates, and an angular bowl depicts the 'Three Friends'. There are also a number of early fifteenth-century

CLOCKWISE FROM LEFT

92 Dish of blue and white porcelain. Hongwu period (1368–99). *D. 36.5 cm.*

93 Dish of blue and white porcelain. Ming dynasty, *c.*1400. *D. 36.5 cm.*

94 Bowl of blue and white porcelain. Ming dynasty, *c.*1400. *D. 42 cm.*

OPPOSITE

95 Dish of blue and white porcelain. Early 15th century. *D. 40.3 cm.*

96 Dish of blue and white porcelain. Ming dynasty, early 15th century. *D. 64 cm.*

97 Dish of blue and white porcelain. Ming dynasty, early 15th century. *D. 63.5 cm.*

plain white bowls, dishes, *meiping* and ewers. One elegant ewer incised with faintly discernible hollyhocks and a *lingzhi* scroll is splendidly set off by an Ottoman gold cap studded with rubies and a turquoise [**103**]. None of these plain white pieces is marked.

In the Ardebil collection Pope assigned five small dishes to the Hongwu period, but they could as easily be Yongle.[18] The early fifteenth-century wares from Ardebil largely mirror those in Istanbul – the massive landscape dishes and preponderance of smaller dishes with lotus bouquets, flowers on thin spiral stems, and bunches of grapes. And from Syria only one bowl is a candidate for the late

98 Details of the fruit and floral sprays on the reverse of the dish illustrated below left (**97**), including peach, pomegranate, persimmon, peony, chrysanthemum and camellia.

fourteenth century. This is a large bowl, probably of copper red, which had misfired to an appealing shade of grey [**105**].[19] It was found in rather odd circumstances, under the sink in the kitchen of the Sursock Museum in Beirut, where it was being used as a receptacle for dirty dishcloths. When it was pointed out to the Director that it deserved a less lowly fate, he took due note. Alas, instead

99 Dish of blue and white porcelain, the cavetto moulded with twelve bracketed panels each with a floral spray. Yongle period, early 15th century. *D. 37.5 cm.*

ABOVE (BOTH PICTURES)
100 Bowl of blue and white porcelain.
Ming dynasty, early 15th century. *D. 34 cm.*

ABOVE
101 Dish of blue and white porcelain.
Ming dynasty, early 15th century. *D. 43 cm.*

102 Dish of blue and white porcelain.
Ming dynasty, early 15th century. *D. 31 cm.*

RIGHT
103 Ewer of white porcelain, incised with hollyhock, lotus scrolls, chrysanthemum, *lingzhi* scroll and other motifs, with an Ottoman gold cover inlaid with rubies and a turquoise finial. Early 15th century. *H. 33 cm.*

of becoming part of the permanent collection on display, it turned up some months later for sale in London. Its present whereabouts are unknown.

Only three pieces found in Syria definitely belong to the early fifteenth century. The first is the Xuande stand in the British Museum [**81**]. This belonged to Dr Aractingi, who had a small but interesting collection of blue and white in his apartment in Damascus, collected over a number of years. After the stand was published, some months later, like the Sursock bowl, it turned up in England. Apparently, after the owner's death his nephew put the stand in a suitcase and flew to London, where it was acquired by Basil Gray for the museum. The second piece is a dish once in the collection of H.E. Henri Pharaon in Beirut (its whereabouts now unknown), finely painted with the 'Three Friends' – pine, prunus and bamboo – and twelve flowers in the cavetto, no two of which are exactly the same [**106**]. An almost identical dish is in the Ardebil collection (29.35). The third fifteenth-century piece is a vase (*guan*) once in the Larsson collection and now in the Cincinnati Art Museum [**104**]. The body is painted with a peony wreath, and on the shoulder are four sprays of cherry, grape, litchi and persimmon. The base has an unusual arcade of shaded panels, with a lotus

105 a, b Porcelain bowl decorated in copper red but misfired grey. Once in the Sursock Museum in Beirut, present whereabouts unknown. Hongwu period (1368–99).

104 Jar (*guan*) of blue and white porcelain, from Syria. Early 15th century.

106 Dish of blue and white porcelain, found in Damascus and then in the collection of H.E. Henri Pharaon in Beirut. Decorated with the 'Three Friends': pine, prunus and bamboo. Early 15th century. *D. 34 cm.*

107 a, b Bowl of blue and white porcelain. Early 15th century. *D. 31.6 cm.*

flanked by symmetrical leaves; one is immediately reminded of the frieze of pointed panels round the neck of the large vase on the crazy cart in the Istanbul painting [**71**].

There is a fourth and more enigmatic piece which might also be a candidate for the fifteenth century. It is a bowl, once in the Pharaon collection and still in a private collection in Beirut [**107**]. Inside there is a band of serpentine waves and spirals at the rim, a peony at the centre and four different floral sprays in the cavetto. On the exterior is an aquatic panorama with four different kinds of fish. The composition suggests the early fifteenth century, while the loose style of painting could even place it in the mid-century Interregnum.

Considering the Chinese interest in western Asia in the first half of the fifteenth century, it is surprising that so few pieces – only three or four – have turned up in Syria amongst the six hundred or so porcelains of the Yuan and Ming dynasty. But this is easily explicable in Syrian terms. As a result of Timur's devastating campaign in 1400, and the sack of Damascus and other major Syrian cities, Mamluk trade suffered a reverse. It did not essentially recover its momentum until the end of the century, when the importation of blue and white picked up substantially.

The early fifteenth-century blue and white in the Topkapi Saray and Ardebil collections and from Syria offers no clue as to how the porcelain reached its final destination [**110**]. For instance, if the blue and white in Istanbul was carried by sea as far as the Red Sea, we have no idea whether it then travelled overland through Syria and Turkey or was shipped directly across the eastern Mediterranean from Egypt. In the case of Ardebil, it must surely have travelled north by land from the Gulf, although there is always the possibility that some may have come via Central Asia. There are numerous sherds of Timurid blue and white pottery in the Samarkand museum, and even two complete dishes, one imitating the twin-peony type and a second with a bird on a branch in early fifteenth-century style.[20]
A recent study of Timurid imitations of Chinese blue and white has thrown up an enormous bulk of new material.[21] On the basis of analysis of the petrofabric, suggested production centres range as far afield as Samarkand, Bukhara, Tabriz and Nishapur. Whilst many of the designs are of Yuan origin, others can only have been inspired by fifteenth-century motifs. The whole corpus suggests the dispersal of blue and white porcelain over a wide area in Central Asia and northern Iran.

In Istanbul the situation changes radically in the mid-fifteenth century. Regina Krahl lists forty-one pieces in the Topkapi Saray collection belonging to the earlier

108, 109 Timurid blue and white pottery in the Ulugh Bey Observatory museum, Samarkand. 15th century.

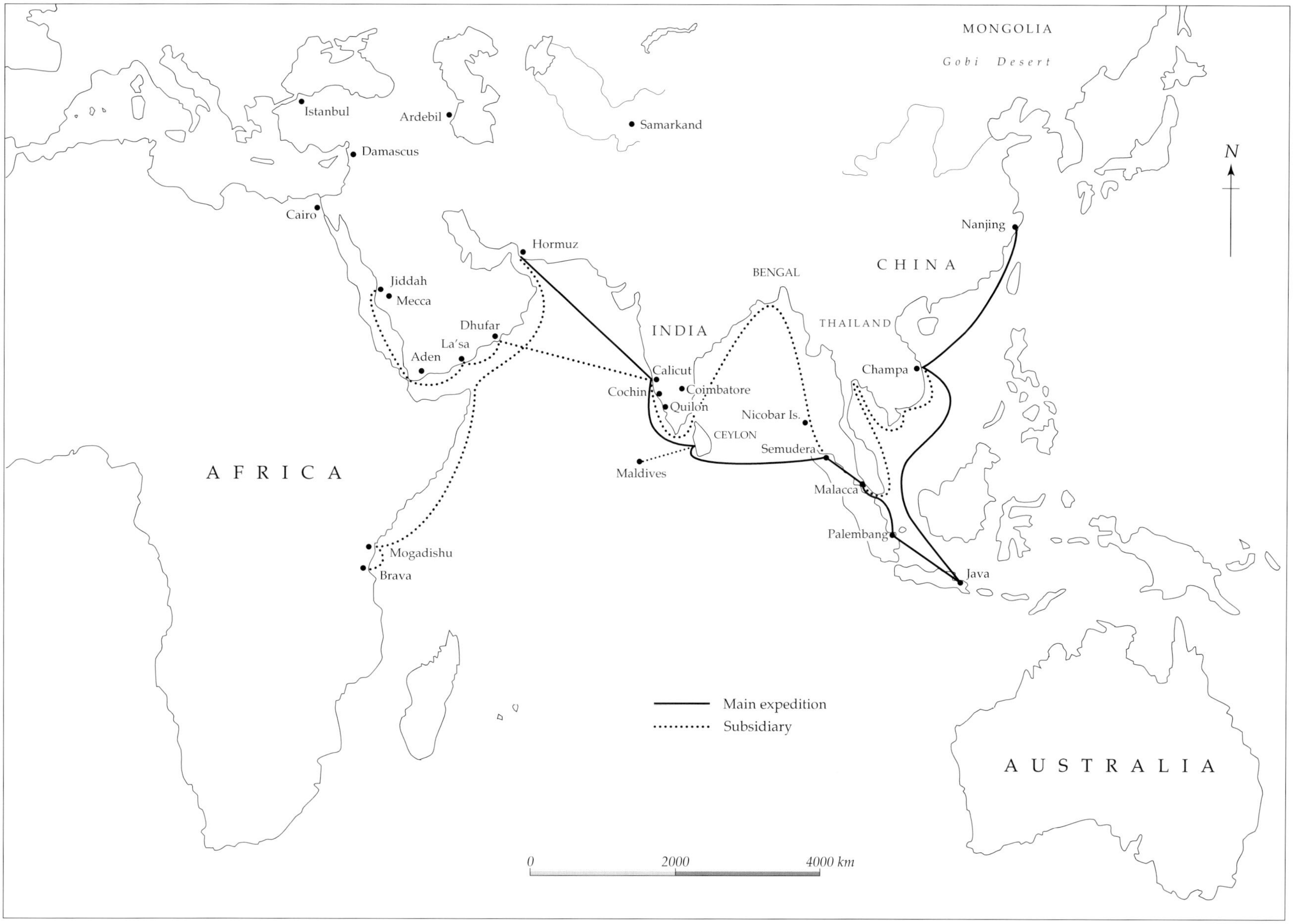

110 Map of Zheng He's last expedition, 1431–3, ordered by the Xuande emperor.

part of the century, including some of the largest and most spectacular pieces from this period in the world. From the mid-fifteenth century she notes only a dozen, and they look forward stylistically to almost a hundred pieces of late fifteenth-/early sixteenth-century date, of which over two hundred more are known from Syria alone.

It was during the Xuande period that the use of six-character reign marks written on the vessels became common practice, although there are instances of Yongle porcelain marked with four characters (*Yongle nian zhi* – 'made in the years of Yongle') in seal script. From the Xuande period onwards, the six characters for each reign follow a regular sequence, for instance *ta Ming Xuande nian zhi*, literally 'great Ming Xuande period made'. This formula was used throughout the Ming and Qing dynasties, and although it would seem to clarify the period of any piece so marked, it is not as simple as that. First of all, the reigns themselves were of different duration, and the shift of political power from one emperor to the next was not necessarily reflected in an immediate change in design at Jingdezhen. Second, reign marks from earlier periods of porcelain production such as Xuande and Chenghua were often used in later times, particularly in the sixteenth century. This was not done spuriously, but rather through Chinese reverence for the past, marking blue and white with reigns of much-admired earlier periods.

This brings up the whole question of dating blue and white, celadon and Chinese wares in general. There are exceptional pieces, like the David vases, which are fully inscribed and dated. Occasionally other pieces are also specifically dated, sometimes with cyclical marks. The latter offer a range of cyclical dates at sixty-year intervals, so which one is the right one must be clarified by other criteria. This is the case with a celadon dish from Damascus (see p. 113). Porcelain found in datable tombs would also seem to be secure, but the tomb only gives a *terminus ante quem* and the contents may well include heirlooms. A perfect example of this is the celebrated vase from the tomb of Mu Ying (d. 1369),[22] illustrated with multiple views by Addis in his catalogue of material from datable contexts. But Addis again issues a caveat that from the Ming period onwards one must be wary. He notes that Mu Ying was the adopted son, or favourite, of Hongwu, and this blue and white *meiping*, depicting superbly painted episodes from a Yuan drama, a measure of Mu Ying's importance; it was also the only piece of porcelain in his tomb. However, in style it surely dates a good deal earlier than 1369, the year after the defeat of the Mongols. Shipwrecks present a similar problem to the tombs, which may include wares of various periods, as will be discussed later. So does the depiction of blue and white in paintings, whether European works of art or Persian and other miniature illustrations. Finally, material from an archaeological context presents its own set of difficulties, its validity being dependent on the accurate interpretation of the stratigraphic evidence.

To sum up, with very rare exceptions all of these criteria have to be handled with caution and reinforced by a supplementary study of technique, style and decoration. This is both the frustration and the fascination of attempting to establish an orderly chronological sequence for blue and white manufactured at

Jingdezhen. However individual and versatile the potters may have been, they were not artists producing work for its own sake, but craftsmen with the ultimate client firmly in mind. Unlike those of some of the craftsmen in the Islamic world, their works were never signed.

This is never more true than in the Xuande period, when extremely fine blue and white was marked intentionally for the emperor's use, as epitomized by an elegant bowl with a six-character mark just below the rim [**111**]. With the end of Xuande's reign in 1435 there is a gap in the production of marked imperial wares until the Chenghua period (1465–87), when political strife in China, famine and government policy had an adverse effect on production at Jingdezhen. It would be difficult to place blue and white in the Interregnum with any certainty were it not for pieces from dated tombs nearby, and one important inscribed and dated temple jar, now in the Art Institute of Chicago [**112**]. The inscription on the base reads *da Ming Zhengtong er nian zheng yue ji dan dizi Cheng Jin*(?) *gongfeng* – 'given in offering by the disciple Cheng Jin(?) on an auspicious day in the fifth month of the second year of the Zhengtong period of the great Ming' (i.e. 1437). Although presumably the best the potters were able to produce, its static decoration is fairly pedestrian, relying on an overall richness of pattern for effect.

111 Bowl of blue and white porcelain. Xuande mark and period (1426–35). *D. 28.9 cm.*

112 Jar (*guan*) of blue and white porcelain. Zhengtong period (1436–49), dated 1437. The inscription on the base reads: *da Ming Zhengtong er nian zheng yue ji dan dizi Cheng Jin gongfeng* ('given in offering by the disciple Cheng Jin on an auspicious day in the fifth month of the second year of the Zhengtong period of the Great Ming').

With the reign of Chenghua it is as if the potters woke up after a long sleep. Not only blue and white but enamelled wares were produced for the emperor, and in particular for his entourage, dominated by the concubine Wan Guifei. Seventeen years older than Chenghua, she consolidated her family's position and was largely responsible for the extravagances of the Imperial Palace. Our knowledge of the specially commissioned porcelain has been infinitely extended during the past few years by Liu Xinyuan's controlled excavation of the Zhushan kilns, which contain thousands of fragments of every conceivable type, deliberately smashed as the pieces were not up to the standard required by the kiln superintendents. Two major exhibitions, first in Hong Kong and then in London, and their accompanying catalogues have revolutionized our knowledge of these fine wares.[23] To complement the researches of the Chinese scholars, Julian Thompson has produced a *catalogue raisonné* of all known pieces of marked Chenghua ware around the world. Surprisingly, two marked pieces are in the Ardebil collection, one a plain white dish (26.657) and the other plain inside, with blue designs of fish and water-weed under a turquoise enamelled glaze on the outside.[24] A similar dish has been excavated at Zhushan.[25] How these rare marked pieces came to Persia is a mystery, but perhaps it was as a direct present from the Chinese court.

5 CELADON AND COPPER RED

Parallel developments in Chinese ceramics

It is perhaps ridiculous to write about blue and white porcelain alone. Although it was one of the world's great innovations, it can only be understood in the context of China's ceramic industry as a whole. It shone like a star but it was always part of the general picture, which included not only the immediate past but the continuing production during the Yuan and Ming dynasties of all kinds of parallel developments in underglaze polychrome and enamelled wares. This is the moment to consider two of them – celadon and underglaze copper red – which are so closely linked to the evolution of blue and white that they cannot be ignored.

First of all, celadon. The Chinese term is *qingci* (in Japanese, *seiji*), used to describe green-glazed stoneware, such as that made in the Longquan district of Zhejiang province. The word 'celadon' is of French origin and derives from a character in a work by Honoré d'Urfé, *L'Astrée*, who wore a greyish-green costume. The term 'celadon' has gained universal currency in the West, and whilst some scholars have translated *qingci* as 'green glazed wares', believing this to be more accurate than celadon, a convincing case has been made that this is not so and only adds to confusion and that it is wiser to use the generally accepted term.[1]

Longquan is a city situated on the Xi river, southeast of Jingdezhen and about halfway to the coast. Hundreds of kilns in the area, particularly in the southern part of the province, produced celadon. Although the stoneware body varies, it is generally a light grey in colour. This is a suitable ground for the opaque greyish-green glaze. The glaze contains iron oxide and careful control of temperature and of the reduction process in firing produces different tones of green. Where the body is unglazed, as a wide ring on the base of the majority of the dishes, the iron content fires orange-red. This unglazed ring was for a supporting stand, so that the wide base of the large dishes would not sag. Sprigged decoration and moulded panels were also often left unglazed, so that when fired they became pinkish-red, contrasting with the green glaze. The celadon was placed in saggars and fired in 'dragon' kilns, a series of linked chambers ascending a slope with the firebox at the bottom.

Longquan celadon has its ancestry in the wares of the Tang dynasty, such as Yue. From the thirteenth century onwards it was produced in increasingly large

114 A group of celadon from Syria. Yuan and Ming dynasty, 14–15th century.

OPPOSITE
113 Celadon dish with dragon and details in applied biscuit red. Yuan dynasty, 14th century. *D. 41.5 cm.*

quantities and gained popularity as an export ware. The celadon can be divided into two categories: those which copied archaic bronze forms such as tripod incense burners, and large bowls, dishes, vases and ewers that have direct parallels in Yuan and Ming blue and white. As with the blue and white, precise dating is a problem, but a number of pieces at least give a clue to the chronological development of celadon.

Once more the Sinan wreck of 1323 provides a *terminus ante quem*. This cargo, probably bound for Japan, contained a wide variety of wares, including the archaic forms and more utilitarian bowls and dishes.[2] One characteristic of the Sinan celadon is the loosely carved designs with a freedom of execution very much in the style of the earlier incised Song *qingbai*. On a number of dishes, with either plain or foliate rims, the lively treatment of incised floral motifs in the cavetto is often combined with central designs of moulded dragons or pairs of fish, or stamped patterns of chrysanthemum and other flora. Another typical motif is a sort of simplified key fret, with incised lines below the outer rim intersected at intervals by diagonal strokes. Large jars (*guan*) have ribbed sides and lids to match, with wavy rims. There are lotus bowls with carved petals, identical to the Yapahuwa bowl in Sri Lanka [**115c**], which is dated before 1284, when the site was

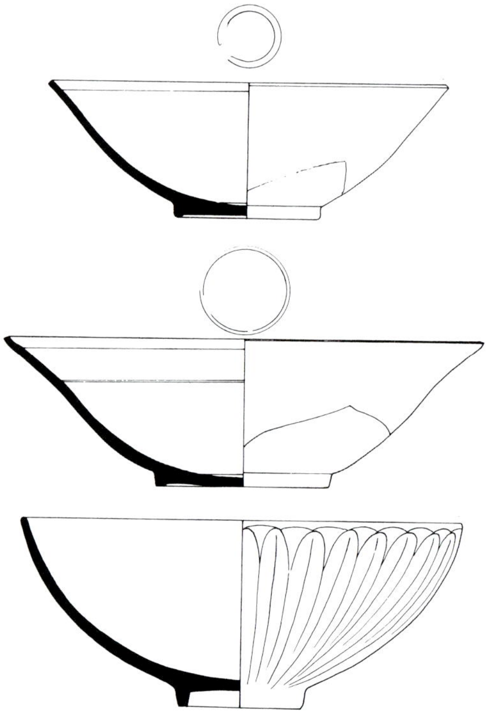

116 Celadon jar (*guan*) with cover and vertical ribbing. Yuan dynasty, 14th century. *H. 30.5 cm.*

OPPOSITE
115 Celadon bowl and two white-ware bowls, from Yapahuwa, Ceylon. Before 1284.
a, b White-ware bowls, *D. 19.2 cm, 23 cm.*
c Celadon bowl, *D. 21 cm.*

abandoned. There are also examples of *tobi seiji*, or brown-spotted celadon, where large iron-rich brown spots are used to decorate the green glaze.

Very similar to the Sinan corpus is celadon from another wreck as yet unexcavated, lying just off the east coast of Sri Lanka (discussed in chapter 8). Sherds of celadon washed up on the shore have the same simplified key fret below the outer rim and must be more or less contemporary with those from the Sinan wreck. Further parallels are evident in part of a large dish with a moulded dragon **[202]**, stamped designs and moulded details. Finally, a large base sherd of a bowl has a complicated design of moulded flowers inside **[117 a, b]**. It is very similar to a rare moulded bowl in Topkapi Saray (TKS 15/691), and also a fragmentary bowl found half a century ago down a well in Aleppo, Syria **[118]**. A fourth example was excavated from the Dayaoshan kiln sites near Anfu, to the east of Longquan.[3] In short, the Sri Lankan ship must have been carrying

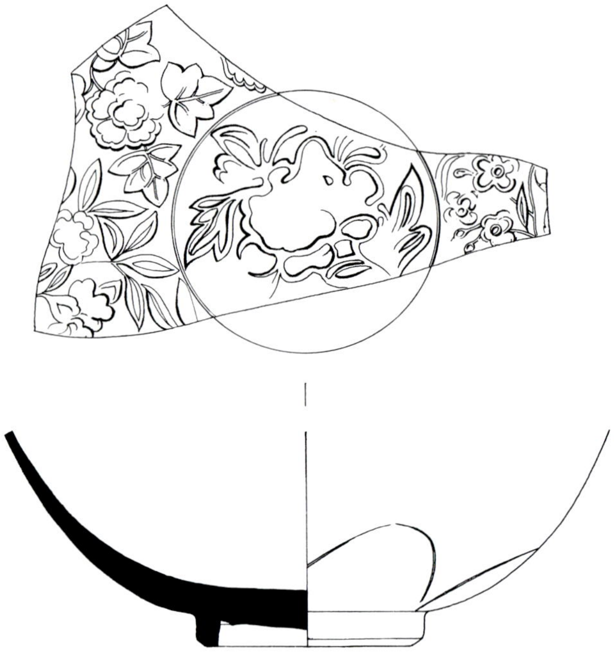

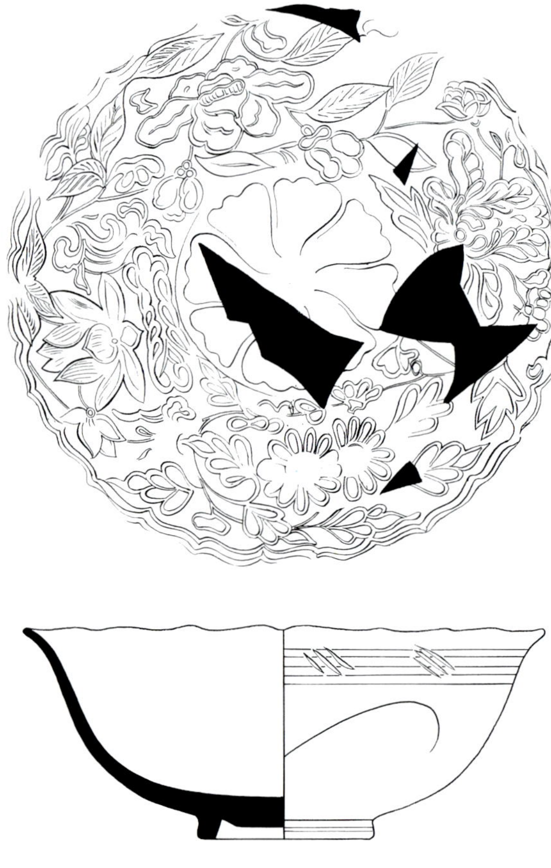

Longquan celadon further west, the immediate precursor of the blue and white that was to follow closely in its wake.

Celadon sherds have been found at almost every site of the early medieval period connected with maritime trade from China. The Sinan vessel is believed to have been on its way to Japan, and in Japan itself lotus bowls have been excavated at Fukuoka, Izumo and Kamakura.[4] A number of fine pieces of celadon that have survived intact have pedigrees linking them to distinguished Japanese families and can be traced back to the sixteenth century and earlier. Indeed, one Song dynasty celadon bowl has a legendary history as a Chinese gift to a Japanese benefactor of a Buddhist temple in China in 1175 . The bowl was broken in the fifteenth century and sent back to China for replacement, but instead it was returned, repaired with an iron clamp. It was in the collection of the shogun Yoshimasa (1435–90) and its history since then is well documented, the bowl having been passed on from one generation to the next until finally entering the Tokyo National Museum in 1970.[5]

Longquan celadons and their provincial imitations are found all over the Far East.[6] Further west, in south India, celadon sherds abound at Kayalpattinam, Marco Polo's *Cail*, a port directly associated with the import of horses from Arabia. Sherds have also been found at Quilon on the Malabar coast.[7] Five pieces of celadon supplement the important collection of fourteenth-century blue and white recovered from the garden of the Kotla Firuzshah palace in Delhi.[8] Two of the excavated dishes have plain rims and loosely carved floral motifs, and two more have ribbed cavettos, with stamped floral designs at the centre; one has *matbah-i khas* ('the royal kitchen') drilled on its base. A small bowl with an everted rim is incised with a flower. The palace was built by the nephew of Sultan Muhammad ibn Tughluq, who became Ibn Battuta's patron when he arrived in Delhi in 1334. It was Muhammad ibn Tughluq who sent Ibn Battuta on a mission to China in 1341, in response to a delegation of ambassadors from the Yuan emperor.

As for whole pieces of celadon that survived in India, the Cummings collection, made by an engineer on the Bombay–Calcutta railway in the nineteenth century, contained thirty-four specimens. Almost all of these were illustrated by Basil Gray in his pioneer article in 1964 on Chinese porcelain in India.[9] He cites a letter written by Cummings in Cawnpore in 1883, in which he states that many of the pieces in his collection – which also included blue and white – came from the Kings of Oudh, but otherwise there is no more detailed evidence of its provenance.

OPPOSITE
117 a, b, c Sherd of celadon bowl with moulded interior, from the Nilaveli wreck in Sri Lanka. Yuan dynasty, 14th century.

118 a, b, c Celadon bowl with moulded decoration, found in a well in Aleppo, Syria. Yuan dynasty, 14th century. *D. 20 cm.*

A second collection, also spotted by Basil Gray, was made by N.T. Williams, a solicitor in Calcutta between 1920 and 1950. This contained thirty-two pieces of celadon, which Gray dated no earlier than 1500. According to Williams these were mostly from the Nawabs of Murshidabad. Finally, the S. Berkeley Smith collection in the Cheltenham Art Gallery also had an Indian provenance and contains numerous pieces of celadon.[10] Smith was an active collector in India at the beginning of the twentieth century and donated his collection of more than eight hundred pieces, then stored in Calcutta, to the gallery in 1922. The celadon includes fourteenth- and early fifteenth-century dishes.

In the Indian Ocean region a number of celadon sherds were picked up on Male, the capital island of the Maldives.[11] These include parts of bowls and dishes with moulded designs. Further west, the coastal sites of the Persian Gulf are littered with celadon, at Ra's al Kaimeh and round the coast of Oman, and in particular at Hormuz.[12] It is also commonly found on the East African coast, for instance at Kilwa, Gedi and elsewhere.[13] In the Red Sea there is the evidence from the fourteenth-century wreck **[203g]**, and from Fustat/old Cairo in Egypt, where masses of celadon have been recovered.[14]

Moving north, a chance find in 1968 was a single celadon sherd of a dish picked up in the sandy forecourt of the Monastery of St Catherine in Sinai. Of excellent quality, it clearly demonstrated that the Greek Orthodox monks were affluent enough in the fourteenth century to afford distinguished tableware. And further north a similar sherd was found on the *glacis* of Saladin's castle at Kerak in Transjordan.

In Syria there is celadon from Palmyra, on one of the main overland routes from the east; indeed, the indefatigable Ibn Battuta passed through Tadmur/Palmyra on his way home from China across the desert from Baghdad to Damascus in 1348. As the traveller remarked, 'Tadmur, the city of the Prophet of God Sulaiman … which the jinns built for him, as Nabigha [a famous pre-Islamic poet] said, "they built [it] with flagstones and columns".'[15] Another sherd from northern Syria is of a large bowl, the interior carved with radiating petals and at the centre a moulded, glazed plaque covering a hole in the base. This is a feature of a well-known type of celadon bowl, of which there are many examples in the Topkapi Saray collection, and in section the fragment shows exactly how the plaque was glazed in place, which is corroborated by the Red Sea bowl **[203g]**. A number of pieces of celadon came to light between 1968 and 1971 in Syria, including jars, lids, dishes and bowls. The moulded bowl from Aleppo has

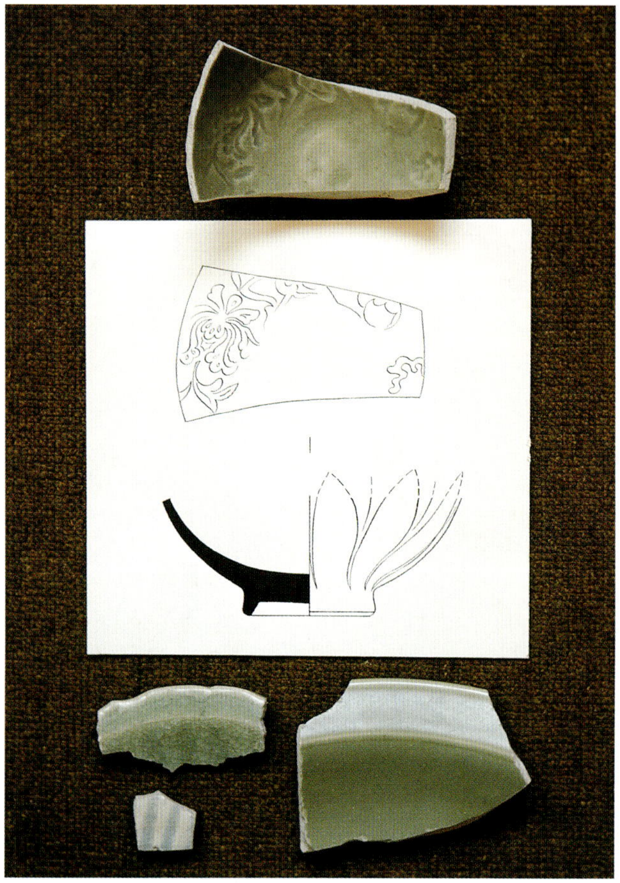

119 A group of celadon sherds from Male, Maldive Islands. Yuan dynasty, 13th/14th century.

120 a, b, c Celadon dish, from Syria. Ming dynasty. *D. 34 cm.* On the unglazed base are six characters: 'xinyou Kuan made / had it made…' (*xinyou* is a cyclical date, most probably 1381, but could be 60 years later).

already been mentioned. Another broken dish, found in Damascus and now in a private collection in Aleppo, is of special interest, for it bears a Chinese cyclical date written in black ink on the wide unglazed ring on the base **[120]**. This has been read as '*xinyou* Kuan made/had it made…', *xinyou* being the date, for which the most likely interpretation, on stylistic grounds, is 1381. Oddest of all is a celadon dish in the National Museum in Damascus. This dish has a ring of curious characters pecked in the glaze. No one has so far been able to identify what these might be, or whether they are simply some kind of nonsensical cabbalistic decoration **[121]**.[16]

121 a, b Celadon dish with pecked inscription. 14th/15th century.

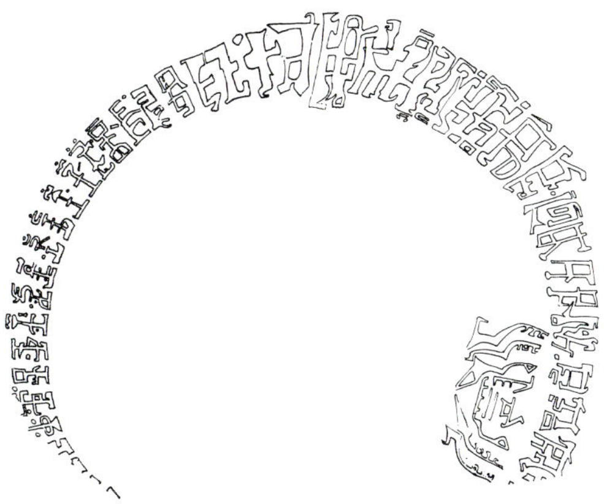

122 a, b Celadon bowl, with a moulded plaque at the centre and a carved scroll in the cavetto. Yuan dynasty, 14th century. *D. 42 cm.*

OPPOSITE

123 Celadon vase. Yuan dynasty, 14th century. *H. 69.5 cm.*

124 Celadon double-gourd vase, with Ottoman gilt mounts. Yuan dynasty, 14th century. *H. 45 cm.*

Whilst all the celadon listed so far serves to mark the export trail from China to the West, it is the Topkapi Saray collection which is the richest source of information. Consisting of 1,350 pieces of celadon – almost an eighth of the entire porcelain collection – it forms an unparalleled corpus. Although the Sinan celadons far outnumber the collection, they represent only a particular moment in time (*c.*1323), whereas in Istanbul one can study two centuries of development, to the end of the fifteenth century. The Topkapi Saray collection was published by Regina Krahl and her introductory essay is the most succinct account so far of the history of the Longquan kilns and their products.[17]

The first fixed point for such a study is a vase in the Percival David Foundation, which is dated 1327. With its impressive form and strongly moulded decoration, this piece represents Yuan celadon at its finest. However, the earliest piece in Istanbul is the lotus bowl (TKS 15/235), accompanied by a handful of others which might possibly be of late thirteenth-/early fourteenth-century date. All of the fourteenth-century celadons are crisply designed, combining freely carved decoration with moulded designs; radiating lotus petals and fluting are common features, as are the decorative plaques designed to cover the hole in the base of many large bowls. A feature in common with contemporary blue and white from Jingdezhen is the use of applied rosettes on the rim, either glazed or left so that they fire orange-red – like the dragon and flaming pearl on one spectacular dish. Besides dishes and bowls there are a series of noble vases, plain and with moulded decoration, and double-gourd vases with floral decoration in relief. There are also *guan* jars with wavy rimmed lids, both plain and ribbed.

As with the blue and white, the transition from Yuan to Ming is hazy, and it is not until the end of the fourteenth century that a new, consistent style emerges. Here the designs on bowls, ewers and dishes have an affinity with similar designs on Hongwu blue and white and copper red vessels. This continues into the fifteenth century, and under Xuande (1426–35) the emergent domestic taste for blue and white of imperial standard meant that celadon received a boost, filling the gap as far as the export market was concerned. Throughout the rest of the century there is a detectable decline in quality; with moulded and carved designs often incoherently combined. Two more dated vases in the Percival David collection demonstrate this neatly: one of 1432 with its clumsy profile, and an ill-proportioned vase of 1454. Falling in the middle of the Interregnum, the latter displays the same kind of all-over patterning as the Chicago blue and white *guan* of 1437.

LEFT

125 Celadon ewer with a silver-gilt Ottoman cover and coral finial. Ming dynasty, *c.*1400. *H. (with cover) 42 cm.*

ABOVE, FROM TOP

126 Celadon dish. Ming dynasty, *c.*1400. *D. 45.5 cm.*

127 a, b Celadon bowl. Ming dynasty, early 15th century. *D. 39.5 cm.*

128 Celadon ewer, with Ottoman silver-gilt mounts surmounted by a crescent. Qing dynasty, 17th/18th century. *H. 31.5 cm.*

129 Celadon dish with bunch of grapes design. Early 15th century. *D. 50.5 cm.*

Towards the end of the century, as blue and white increased in popularity as a viable export ware, celadon fell out of favour until there was no longer enough demand to support the industry. By the sixteenth century it had virtually ceased to exist. Later celadon with a white porcelain body was produced at Jingdezhen in the Qing dynasty, and modern imitations are currently made today.

Finally, the relationship between the forms and decoration of celadon and those of both Yuan and early Ming blue and white has already been remarked upon. Stem cups, spouted bowls and ewers are all forms that are found both in celadon and blue and white, as is the use of sprigged decoration. In the early fifteenth century the disposition of floral elements in the cavetto is common to both. This might imply that the potters were responding to a similar demand – the export market for both these wares. Patterns such as the three bunches of grapes are identical in painted dishes and incised celadon. But what remains unexplained is the link between the potters at Jingdezhen in Jiangxi and celadon production in Zhejiang, and the mechanics of just how this came about.

Porcelain decorated in underglaze copper red also has a symbiotic relation with blue and white. Although there was none of the latter on the Sinan wreck, there was a single oval saucer dish with two leaves faintly tinged and painted with a red inscription, evidence that the technique was in use at least as early as cobalt blue.[18]

Large fourteenth-century jars (*guan*) combine both underglaze blue and copper red on the same vessel. The body is broken up with four cut-out panels filled with a tracery of sprigged flowers and leaves, with *qingbai* beaded frames, very much in the manner of the Fonthill vase **[201]**. One of these jars is in the Percival David Foundation **[130]**,[19] and a second, finer example, which has its lid, is in the Palace Museum, Beijing. Apart from the underglaze blue cloud collars, lotus panels and knobbed scrolls, these bizarre medallions are decorated in blue with copper red accents. The red has a distinct tendency to diffuse and is only contained by the reliefs to which it is applied; a single spot applied to the lion finial on the lid has run all over its body. These jars can be linked to a group of objects also decorated in blue and red, discovered in a tomb at Jingdezhen dated 1338. These include a *qingbai* covered jar and a model storehouse decorated in a smudgy copper red and greyish blue.[20]

On other Yuan pieces, such as bottles (*yuhuchun*) and jars (*guan*), the red often gets completely out of hand and virtually destroys the shape of the vessel by its unrestricted flow **[132]**. Among the sherds collected by John Pope in Beijing is a

130 Jar (*guan*) of blue and white porcelain with copper red details. Yuan dynasty, 14th century. *H. 33 cm.*

131 A figure of an acolyte decorated in underglaze copper red. Yuan dynasty, 14th century. *H. 36.8 cm.*

132 Two porcelain vases *(yuhuchun ping)* decorated in copper red. Yuan dynasty, 14th century. *H. 22 cm.*

part of a stem cup with a moulded goose inside and scarlet splotches on the exterior.[21] There is a marked contrast between the formal design of the flying bird and the irregular red splashes. A rare Yuan figure of an acolyte is decorated in copper red and here the pigment is under control [**131**]. This is also so on an unusual *meiping* vase where the sketchy, swirling phoenixes and cloud-collar and lotus panels all derive from more carefully drawn Yuan motifs [**133**].

This cursive technique is most successful when applied swiftly to execute simple designs and, whilst lacking the refinement of the more carefully painted blue and white, it is certainly decorative. There is a group of vases (*yuhuchun*) in this style, with highly simplified floral scrolls, dispersed in various collections throughout the world, including one in the Hohhot Museum in Inner Mongolia [**134a**].[22] The Hohhot example is particularly interesting, for in the same museum there is a silver vase of identical shape and size [**134b**], neatly proving the close affinity of the metal and porcelain forms. Eight fragments of a similar red-painted vase were found at Kharakhoto and are now in the Ethnographic Museum in Stockholm.[23] Much further afield, another copper red vase was excavated from the

Great Mosque at Gedi on the coast of East Africa. There are other examples of Yuan porcelain loosely painted in copper red, including a rectangular flask, *guan* vases, stem cups, jarlets and spouted bowls.[24] The spouted bowls combine freely painted motifs within a red ring incised with a wavy line; the wide red ring is carelessly painted and frequently runs. This whole group suggests experimentation, sometimes successful but more often than not producing disastrous results. A telling example is a covered jar with a dragon crudely outlined in red.[25] Below, the carved lotus panels are exactly like those on the Fonthill vase and, even more to the point, on a pair of *qingbai* vases from a tomb dated 1324.[26] This would argue that all these experimental copper red wares can be dated to the first quarter of the fourteenth century, and that they were quickly eclipsed by the more efficient technology of blue and white.

It is only in the post-Yuan period that the use of copper red seems to have been properly harnessed. Under Hongwu it was used as an alternative to cobalt

ABOVE, LEFT

133 Porcelain vase (*meiping*) decorated in copper red, the unglazed base fired buff. Yuan dynasty, 14th century. *H. 33 cm.*

ABOVE AND OPPOSITE

134 a, b Porcelain vase decorated in copper red and silver vase of almost identical profile. *Both 28 cm high.*

blue, and utilized a similar repertoire of forms and designs. Two dishes in the Art Institute of Chicago are almost identical in design, one painted in blue and the other in copper red.[27] A third copper red example was once in the Addis collection.[28] Sir John Addis, when he was British Ambassador to China, was in a unique position to study porcelain from Jingdezhen; he also formed an important collection of Ming copper red ware. This he generously bequeathed to the British Museum, and his fascination with the group led him to become the first scholar to study it in depth. Whilst he changed his mind about the date of the Hongwu pieces over the years, initially ascribing them to the Yuan period, he was the first to describe their unique characteristics.[39]

But firing copper red was not without its own problems – not so much the diffusion of the colour in the glaze, but its transformation to a blue-grey as a result of uneven kiln temperature and poor control of the reduction process. The style of painting in the early Ming period is quite different from the haphazard use of copper red in the Yuan wares. A cup stand with a recessed centre **[135]** is a classic

RIGHT
135 Porcelain cup stand decorated in copper red, which has misfired grey-brown; the moulded cavetto with eight bracketed panels has a sunken centre. Ming dynasty, Hongwu period (1368–99). *D. 19.6 cm.*

example of a type which John Pope tentatively dated to the Hongwu period in his study of the Ardebil material.[30] It has a foliate rim whose profile is carried through into the moulded cavetto and painted with lotus sprays, a pomegranate scroll and four *ruyi* motifs in the form of a cross. Two bowls are related to the cup stand in the formal treatment of the floral designs, the petals outlined with a thin line and the elements symmetrically arranged [**105**, **136**]. One is the Sursock bowl from Beirut, where the copper red has misfired to a greyish colour.[31] The two bowls are very similar to each other in every respect. They have almost identical profiles, and whereas one has a chrysanthemum spray at the centre with a peony wreath in the cavetto, and more chrysanthemums on the outside, on the other the sequence is reversed. Both have key-fret rings at the centre and on the narrow foot ring. Both also have thinly outlined lotus panels indented at the top, with rosettes inside.

The design of the copper red ewers, vases, dishes and bowls is very similar to the blue and white wares being produced at that time, deriving from earlier prototypes but with a new freedom of approach [**137**]. This is particularly noticeable in the landscape friezes that are so often the main subject of the ewers and vases, with a lower margin of rocky outcrops from which spring flowering prunus, stands of bamboo, pine trees and plantains. The trees often rise behind the upper margin, which creates the impression of looking at a landscape through a window. This is even true on some of the bowls and dishes, where the feeling is as if one is contemplating the outside world through an ogival frame. During the same period copper red was also used successfully as a monochrome glaze, often over moulded designs that show through the pooled glaze. It is sometimes combined with blue; for instance, a stem cup in the British Museum has a moulded dragon inside under monochrome blue and is completely glazed red on the exterior.[32]

In the early fifteenth century control of the copper red became increasingly sophisticated, and in the Yongle period dragons are reserved on a flawless red ground. Under Xuande the monochromes reached a technical perfection never again to be equalled until the Qing dynasty. The copper red was also used as a silhouette, for a pomegranate, a peach and a persimmon on the sides of a white stem cup; on the interior is a Xuande mark inside double rings, in underglaze blue [**138**].

This striking use of red continues into the Chenghua period as an enamel; a cup with three red fish and a blue reign mark was found among the material from

136 a, b Porcelain bowl decorated in copper red, fired silver-pink. Hongwu period (1368–99). *D. 42 cm.*

138 Porcelain stem cup decorated in copper red with a pomegranate, a persimmon and a peach, with an underglaze cobalt blue mark inside. Xuande mark and period (1426–35). *H. 11.7 cm.*

LEFT
137 Porcelain ewer decorated in copper red. Hongwu period (1368–99). *H. 33 cm.*

139 a, b Porcelain dish decorated in iron red and inscribed in Arabic. The reign mark is phonetically transcribed. Zhengde mark and period (1506–21). *D. 19.7 cm.*

At the centre the inscription reads 'Allah be praised for all His blessings', encircled by 'the truly thankful never sin against the Lord even when affluent' in four parts.

On the reverse, the *hadith* (saying of the Prophet) reads:
'The Messenger of God (may His peace be upon him) said:
The body achieves repose by eating little
The tongue achieves repose by speaking little
The heart achieves repose by detachment from care
The soul achieves repose by sinning less.'

On the base, inside double concentric rings, *Da Ming Zhengde Nian Zhi* is written in Arabic.

the Zhushan excavations at Jingdezhen.[33] Also from Zhushan was an unfinished tricolour tripod bowl, as well as a complete example; this revealed that the colours – underglaze blue, overglaze green and red enamels – were applied during three separate firings.[34] Iron red enamel continued to be used throughout the Ming dynasty. A rare saucer of the Zhengde period is painted in iron red with pious Arabic phrases and *hadith* [**139**]. It also has the reign mark *Da Ming Zhengde Nian Zhi* on the underside, phonetically transcribed into Arabic! The social and religious questions this poses belong to the next chapter, in which a group of Zhengde blue and white with Arabic and Persian inscriptions are discussed.

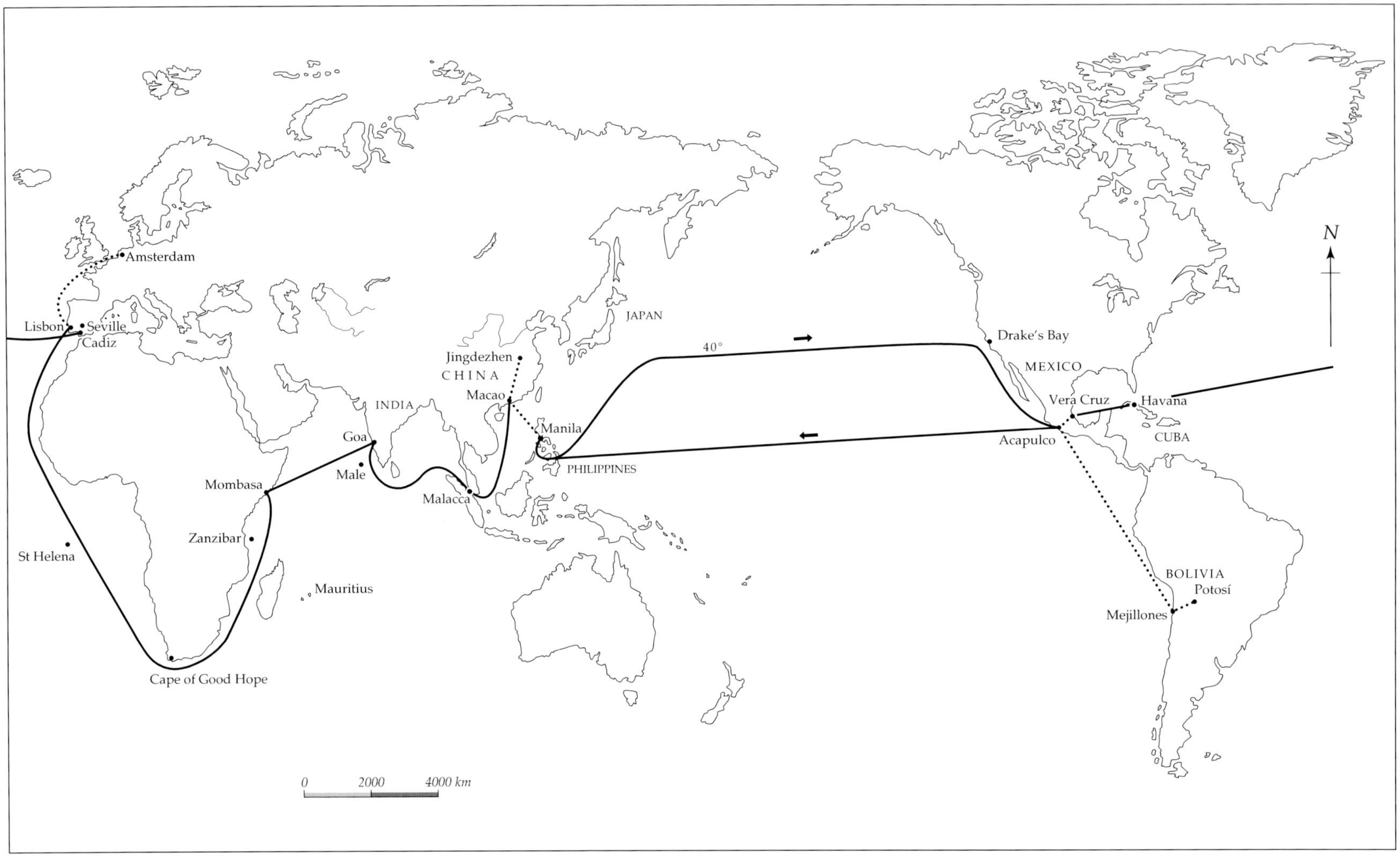

140 Around the world in the sixteenth century
By the end of the sixteenth century, Chinese porcelain was being carried right round the world to Europe, in two different directions:

First, by the Portuguese, who arrived in India in 1498 and established a base in Macao in 1514. From there blue and white was carried westwards via the Straits of Malacca, Goa, East Africa and round the Cape to Lisbon. From here much of it was trans-shipped to northern Europe, including Amsterdam.

Second, by the Spanish, who conquered Mexico in the early sixteenth century and sailed as far as the Philippines on Magellan's epic voyage of 1519–22. From the 1560s onwards the yearly Manila Galleon sailed across the Pacific carrying silver, and back from the Philippines laden with products from the Far East, including porcelain. The return voyage was as far north as 40° latitude, to take advantage of the prevailing westerlies. Sailing down the coast of California, the galleons finally reached Acapulco, where much of the porcelain was transported across Mexico to Vera Cruz, to be shipped across the Atlantic via Havana to Seville.

A major export from Bolivia was silver, mined in Potosi since 1545 and carried from Mejillones to Acapulco. Other goods shipped from Acapulco across the Pacific included cochineal, harvested from the prickly pear in Oaxaca, as well as cacao, wine, oil and woollen cloth from Spain.

6 EMPIRES

Portuguese and Spaniards, sultans and shahs

The end of the fifteenth century saw a Western interest in China that sharply changed China's perception of itself and led to what Jingdezhen thought was a fitting response. If the overland caravan routes were no longer such a dynamic force in trans-Asiatic trade, their maritime counterparts took on a new dimension. Here, unlike Zheng He's exploratory voyages earlier in the century, the stimulus came not from China but from the other direction. The Arabs had controlled much of the sea trade for more than a millennium, and, with their collective knowledge of routes, shipping, navigation and international commerce, were the keystone. They made one fatal mistake that cost them their virtual monopoly, which was to reveal the way to navigate across the ocean directly from the coast of Africa to India.

In the late fifteenth century the Portuguese began to explore the world. Like the Spaniards in America, they had realized that there were untold riches in the Orient, if only they could find their way there. Unlike the Spaniards, who sailed west across the Atlantic, from the 1440s onwards the Portuguese worked their way down the coast of Africa, reaching the Cape of Good Hope by 1488 in the search for a new way to the East. On Vasco da Gama's first voyage, in 1498 his stroke of good fortune was to encounter an Arab, by tradition Ahmad ibn Majid, who instructed him how to sail directly to India using the monsoon winds.[1] The secret was to set out to sea north of Malindi, whence the winds would take them directly to south India. Vasco da Gama reached Calicut in May 1458 and the Portuguese proceeded to colonize the Malabar coast, though not without opposition from the local population. Once this had finally been subdued, in 1510 Affonso de Albuquerque, now Viceroy of India, established a Portuguese colony at Goa.

In the centuries to come, Goa was to play a pivotal role in maritime relations between Portugal and the Far East. For a century or so, until the Dutch arrived on the scene, the Portuguese were the major players in the Indian Ocean and beyond. In the wake of the merchants came the Catholic Church, with opportunities to proselytize further East.[2] By 1509 they had reached Malacca, where they encountered Chinese junks, and Albuquerque secured Malacca for the Portuguese in 1511. In a letter to Manuel I a year later he extolled the potential benefits of direct trade with China, pointing out the wide variety of commodities available in exchange for pepper, which included silk and porcelain. Pepper could be bought in southern India easily and cheaply, and it was calculated that there was greater profit to be had by trading it with China than by sending it back to Portugal. The Portuguese made direct contact with China in 1513, when Jorge Alvares landed at Tongmen, an island near Canton. He established amicable relations with the Chinese and returned in triumph to Malacca in 1514 with a large cargo. But after this initial success the Portuguese suffered a reverse and their relationship with the Chinese deteriorated to such an extent that by 1521 their ships were forbidden to land on the China coast.

However, surreptitious trade with China continued through the use of intermediaries, and meanwhile the Portuguese were expanding further into Southeast Asia. By 1531 they had got as far as Manila in the Philippines, and in 1542–3 they arrived in Japan for the first time. In 1557 they were finally established at Macau. Here it should be pointed out that the link to Portugal was by now far extended; it took anything from eight to ten months to sail from Lisbon to Malacca. On the other hand, it was only twenty days further on to the China coast. Two points emerge: first, the Portuguese administrators were to a large extent autonomous because of the time it took to refer back decisions to Lisbon, and second, the merchant-entrepreneurs realized that as much profit could be made from the shorter trip between China and Malacca as between Malacca and Europe. In this way Malacca , like Goa, played a key role in the whole trading enterprise, just as Manila was to do a few years later for the Spanish.

When the Portuguese explorer Vasco da Gama returned from his first voyage to India in 1499, amongst the gifts he presented to King Manuel I (1495–1521) was porcelain, which he had purchased at Calicut. Pedro Álvares Cabral also gave the King porcelain, having taken it from a ship sailing from Cambay to Mecca.[3] The Frenchman Pyrard de Laval, who was shipwrecked in the Maldives in the early seventeenth century and lived to write about his experiences, mentioned that all the crockery used in the Royal Hospital at Goa was of Chinese porcelain. According to an old map, this establishment was close to the Dogana, the customs house.[4] During a survey conducted in 1974 masses of fragments of fine Wan Li blue and white were recovered from a coconut grove between the site of the Dogana and the river bank. They must have been broken pieces discarded when cargoes from the Far East were unpacked. A collection of these sherds is now in the Department of Eastern Art at the Ashmolean Museum.[5]

141 Coconut grove north of the Dogana (old Portuguese Customs House) in Goa, on the banks of the river.

There are numerous references to Chinese porcelain in the Portuguese archives, the oldest of which dates to 1499.[6] The monarch himself stimulated European taste for blue and white, both through his own acquisition of the ware and through its exchange with the other courts as diplomatic presents. An interesting illustration of this is in the Spanish archives of 1505 describing the present of a large bowl from the Queen of Portugal to Violante de Albion, lady-in-waiting to Queen Isabella. There are also Portuguese records of Manuel I's gift to the Monastery of St Jeronimos in Lisbon of twelve pieces of porcelain in 1512. Between 1511 and 1514 there are records of 692 pieces of porcelain entering the Royal Treasury in Lisbon. Inspired by Manuel I's own taste for Chinese blue and white, what began as a trickle at the beginning of the sixteenth century quickly grew into a flood. Relations between Portugal and Spain and the other royal courts of Europe created a sort of domino effect; the exchange of blue and white as presents engendered a thirst amongst the recipients for more, and Philip II is reputed to have owned over three thousand pieces.[7] At the same time, large quantities of porcelain arriving in Lisbon were trans-shipped to northern Europe, and to Holland in particular.

It might be argued that the growth of these private collections led to some of them simply becoming too large, leading to the creation of rooms specially designed to house specimens to be admired en masse rather than for any individual aesthetic merit. Examples of this phenomenon can be cited all the way from the Ardebil shrine on the shores of the Caspian Sea to the royal courts of Europe. In Portugal, the example par excellence is a unique room in the De Santos Palace in Lisbon, now the French Embassy [**142**]. Inside the pyramid vault the four triangular sides are covered with over 260 pieces of blue and white, the earliest dating from *c.*1500 and the latest from the middle of the seventeenth century.[8] One's initial impression is simply to gasp; it is almost impossible to take in the qualities of each piece. One cannot help but detect a certain sort of acquisitive madness. Unlike the blue and white at the Ottoman court, where we know that much of it was actually used, when this porcelain reached Europe it became largely disfunctional and simply a decorative adjunct. Be that as it may, the De Santos collection provides a marvellous catalogue of what did in fact arrive in Portugal from the sixteenth century onwards.

What was happening in China, and in particular at Jingdezhen, immediately before the advent of the Portuguese? Here much of the evidence is to be found in the Middle East and Southeast Asia as well as in China itself. From the late

fifteenth century onwards, corresponding to the reign of Hongzhi (1488–1505), vast quantities of blue and white were produced for export, in a style strongly reminiscent of earlier Yuan wares. It is almost as if the potters were trying to recollect what had been popular abroad in earlier days; otherwise it is difficult to explain this divergence from the sophistication of Chenghua wares to these all-over designs and the dense patterning in sub-Yuan style. The question is, what did they copy? The implication is that enough examples of Yuan blue and white remained in China to be imitated, whether in the hands of Moslem traders or the potters themselves.

Once again the lotus pond design makes its appearance, along with peonies, chrysanthemums and peacocks perched on rocks **[143, 144]**. The bowls and dishes are large in scale, some of the latter as much as 52 cm in diameter. The painting is swiftly executed, often to the point of crudity. And many of the shapes, such as fitted pen boxes and angular ewers, hint at a Moslem market **[150]**. Over two hundred of these vessels have been found in Syria alone, including both a pen box and a ewer. The group is well represented in Topkapi Saray, where another pen box was chosen to be set with jewels and sumptuously fitted out with gold inkwells, and may well have been used by Sultan Suleyman himself **[149]**.[9] Although there are only a handful of pieces from Ardebil, the type is commonly found throughout Southeast Asia.[10] The shipwreck of the Lena junk (*c.*1500) discovered off the Philippines contained quantities of it.[11] Although there are analogies between the group and the temple vase dated 1496 in the David collection, they are not striking, for the decoration on the vase is quite precisely, if rather clumsily, painted and has none of the fluency of this style. Nothing is

OPPOSITE
142 The pyramid ceiling of the De Santos Palace in Lisbon.

ABOVE, FROM TOP
143 Bowl of blue and white porcelain, from Syria. Hongzhi period, *c.*1500. *D. 33 cm.*

144 Dish of blue and white porcelain, from Syria. Hongzhi period, *c.*1500. *D. 32 cm.*

RIGHT
145 Covered box of blue and white porcelain, from Syria. Hongzhi period, *c.*1500. *L. 27 cm, H. 12.5 cm.*

marked and the whole group cannot be precisely dated, except that there is at least a *terminus ante quem*, which provides a substantial clue. This is from a very unexpected source: Giovanni Bellini's last masterpiece, *The Feast of the Gods*, in the National Gallery in Washington, D.C. [**148**].

The subject is Ovid's story of how Cybele invites the Gods to a feast, and whilst the nymphs and satyrs engage in drunken revelry, an incident of thwarted love occurs. This takes place in a landscape (not actually by Bellini, but a later addition by no less a master than Titian himself) and there are various artefacts: a silver cup, glasses and a jug, pottery, and three pieces of blue and white – two bowls and a dish. The bowls find exact parallels among the Syrian [**146**, **147**] and Istanbul material. The dish is more of a problem, for the pattern below the rim is not Chinese, and more reminiscent of an Islamic, perhaps Syrian, copy of a blue and white dish. The painting is signed by Giovanni Bellini and dated 1514. How the blue and white came to be included in Bellini's painting has been hypothetically attributed to his elder brother Gentile Bellini, who spent a year as Sultan Mehmed II's guest in Istanbul in 1479–80.[12]

Thus this whole group, which is certainly not in Zhengde style, can be placed at around 1500, or perhaps even earlier. This date is further reinforced by a covered box found in Damascus, whose decoration of lotuses, other floral designs and classic scrolls is in exactly this style [**145**]. More to the point, the form precisely copies a piece of late Mamluk fifteenth-century metalwork.[13] It should be noted that wares of this type have also been found all over Southeast Asia. Similar blue and white dishes and bowls were acquired by the Portuguese and are included among the pieces set in the pyramid ceiling of the De Santos Palace in Lisbon.

ABOVE, FROM LEFT

146 Bowl of blue and white porcelain with rounded profile, from Syria. Hongzhi period, *c.*1500. *D. 31.4 cm.*

147 Bowl of blue and white porcelain with everted rim, from Syria. Hongzhi period, *c.*1500. *D. 33 cm.*

OPPOSITE

148 Giovanni Bellini, *The Feast of the Gods* (detail), 1514.

149 a, b Pen box of blue and white porcelain, based on an Islamic metal prototype. With Ottoman gold hinges and fittings inset with rubies and other jewels, and gold leaf decoration inside the cover. Hongzhi period, *c.*1500. *L. 27.5 cm, W. 7.7 cm.*

150 Ewer of blue and white porcelain, copying an Islamic metal shape. Hongzhi period, *c.*1500. *H. 25 cm.*

OPPOSITE

151 Ewer of blue and white porcelain, with armillary sphere, the emblem of Manuel I. Xuande mark, but Zhengde period, *c.*1519–21. *H. 26.4 cm.*

152 Jar of blue and white porcelain, with a cross and IHS, the device of the Jesuit order. Ming dynasty, *c.*1620–44. *H. 32.9 cm.*

153 Bowl of blue and white porcelain, with inverted arms of Manuel I and armillary sphere, IHS, and inscribed AVE MARIA GRATIA PLENA (Hail Mary Full of Grace). Jiajing period, *c.*1540–50. *D. 25.5 cm.*

Right from the very beginning the Portuguese addiction to Chinese porcelain led to a direct involvement in its design and production. By the 1520s, by means that are still not exactly clear, the Chinese potters were producing blue and white specifically designed for the Portuguese market. The earliest known example is a ewer in Lisbon with an apocryphal Xuande mark but of the Zhengde period (1506–21) **[151]**.[14] It is decorated with an armillary sphere, Manuel I's own device. This ewer was probably an indirect result of the Portuguese diplomatic mission of Tome Pires (1517–21). The Portuguese were the first Europeans to establish close relations with the Chinese. By the reign of Jiajing (1522–66) the continuing Portuguese connection was evident in the production of porcelain still bearing Manuel I's coat of arms, although he had already been dead for two decades. These pieces are inscribed inside the rim with the names of Portuguese officials – such as a bowl inscribed on the inner rim with EN TEMPO DE PERO DE FARIA DE 1541 (Pedro de Faria was captain of Malacca in 1528, and again in 1539–43) – or simply with pious phrases, such as AVE MARIA GRATIA PLENA ('Hail Mary, Full of Grace'). The religious connection is evident, for many pieces are marked IHS (*Iesus Hominum Salvator*).[15]

At least one bowl and two IHS dishes meant for the Portuguese market got sidetracked and are now in the Topkapi Saray collection (TKS 15/2254; 1969, 3329). The bowl is again inscribed for Pedro de Faria and dated 1541; it inspired a

TEMPO EPER

Moderata durant

OPPOSITE

154 Bowl of blue and white porcelain, inscribed AVER [AVE] AMARIA [MARIA] GRACIA PLENA DOMINUM (Hail Mary Full of the Grace of God). Xuande mark, but Jiajing period, *c.*1540–50. *D. 24 cm.*

155 a, b Bowl of blue and white porcelain, with armillary sphere and arms of Manuel I, inscribed PEM TEMPO DE PERO DE FARIA DE 1541 (from the times of Pedro de Faria, in 1541). Xuande mark, but dated 1541. *D. 25 cm.*

156 Large dish of buff pottery decorated in blue under a bluish glaze. Inscribed in the cavetto 'Moderata.durant' (moderation endures). Late 17th century. *D. 44.2 cm.*

whole group of dishes made at Iznik, where Manuel I's armillary sphere and coat of arms were wildly misunderstood.[16] An Iznik interpretation of one of these bowls even turned up in Damascus in the 1970s. Finally, a large plate in the Cleveland Museum, of European blue and white faience, has a central design of an elaborate armillary sphere and Masonic motifs **[156]**. Two landscape vignettes on the rim depict clusters of buildings and a pair of hooded monks, one clutching a rosary and the other a censer, approaching a chapel. Could this be Macao, the Portuguese colony on the China coast, handed back only very recently to the mainland Chinese?

The fashion for personalized dishes with coats of arms persisted throughout the sixteenth century, and one series of dishes was decorated with that of Matias de Albuquerque, who was both captain of Malacca and Hormuz (1577–82) and Viceroy of India (1591–97) **[158]**.[17] Indeed, the whole concept of armorial porcelain for the West, which was to dominate the production of enamelled wares in China in the eighteenth century and later, would appear to have had its origin in the earlier wares manufactured specially for the Portuguese. A later example is a jug bearing the arms of the Pinto, Pereira, Guedes and Pimentel families; José Pinto Pereira was a captain in India from 1620 to 1645 **[168]**. In the middle of the seventeenth century, jars and flasks of square section (inspired by gin bottles, Dutch glass prototypes) were decorated with IHS and other motifs such as the Cross and Resurrection, alluding to the Jesuit missions.[18] These combine Christian iconography with Chinese themes, such as watery landscapes with a pagoda **[157]**.

157 Square bottle of blue and white porcelain, with motifs of Christ's death and resurrection, and a Chinese landscape. Ming dynasty, *c.*1620–44. *H. 39.2 cm.*

158 Dish of blue and white porcelain painted with arms attributed to Matias de Albuquerque, Captain of Malacca and Hormuz (1577–82), Viceroy of India (1591–7). Ming dynasty, late 16th century. *D. 26 cm.*

Whilst the Chinese potters were catering for the Portuguese market from the early sixteenth century, they also had other clients in mind. A group of blue and white from late Hongzhi onwards and the reign of Zhengde (1506–21) has Arabic or Persian inscriptions as a specific feature of its decoration.[19] This has been attributed to the powerful control that the Moslem eunuchs exercised at court at that time, reflected in the production of these exceptional pieces at Jingdezhen. A number of them bear the emperor's reign mark as well as the inscriptions. They include dishes, bowls, brush-holders, hat stands, plaques, covered boxes and tripod incense burners. It is likely that they were made for the local Moslem population rather than for export, though there are two examples in the Ardebil collection, and four more in Istanbul. The Ardebil examples are a large dish with a Zhengde mark and a bowl with an apocryphal Xuande *nien hao* (29.313, 29.346). The Topkapi Saray pieces are a dish and three bowls (TKS 15/2270, 2663, 10407, 4386); the cursive script is characterized by its linear style and exaggerated vertical strokes, and the inscriptions have Shi'ah overtones. There is a similar, slightly larger dish with a Hongzhi mark (1488–1505).[20]

In spite of these seven pieces, which travelled abroad, the likelihood that these Arabic/Persian pieces were originally intended for local Chinese Moslems is substantiated by a fragmentary bowl found by John Pope in Beijing in 1945–6, which has an Arabic inscription reading 'Thanks for his favours' and a Persian one: 'May the good fortune and power of the prince which is daily on the increase be eternal.' There is a Zhengde mark on the base inside two rings. The fragmentary inscription can be reconstructed by the existence of an identical complete bowl in the Freer Gallery.[21] The eulogistic nature of the inscriptions and the Beijing provenance of the bowl discovered by Pope would strongly reinforce the argument that these pieces were made primarily for Moslems in China. There is, of course, nothing to have prevented the export of some of them for the use of co-religionists abroad.

Three inscribed tripod incense burners present a further problem.[22] Two of them are decorated in underglaze blue and the third, a plain one, is carved. A porcelain incense burner in the Benaki Museum is inscribed 'He who gets close to a perfume seller he acquires a share of his own scent' **[161]**. A second one, in the British Museum, of taller form is inscribed in Arabic in six cartouches: 'I am the tender-hearted / so seek Me [and] / thou shalt find Me / ... (?) to Me / Thou shalt not desire / [anyone] but Me' **[162]**. The plain white censer in the Ashmolean Museum is carved in three cartouches with: 'The best confessional invocation [is]

159 Brush rest of blue and white porcelain with two Persian inscriptions, reading together 'pen rest'. Zhengde mark and period (1506–21). *L. 22.8 cm.*

160 a, b Dish of blue and white porcelain, inscribed in Arabic. The roundel at the centre reads 'The Prophet [Muhammad] said'; on the underside are five more roundels, one of which reads 'he said'. Zhengde mark and period (1506–21). *D. 28.6 cm.*

大明正德年製

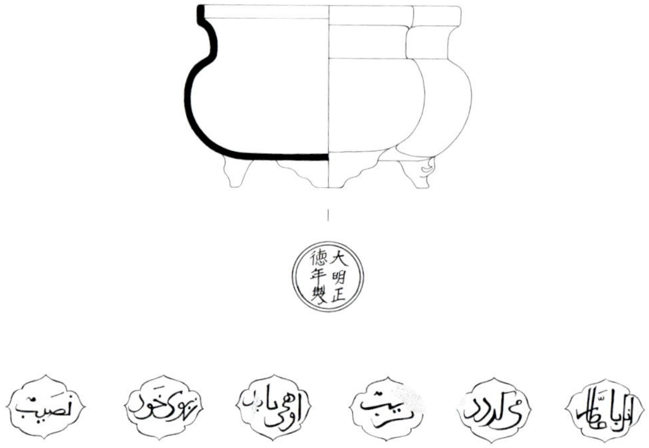

161 Tripod censer of blue and white porcelain with Persian inscriptions in six cartouches reading: *an keh ba 'attar / migardad / qarib / u hami yabad / ze bu-ye khod / nasib* ('He who gets close to a perfume seller he acquires a share of his own scent'). Zhengde mark and period (1506–21). *H. 10.3 cm.*

162 Tripod censer of blue and white porcelain, with an Arabic inscription in six roundels reading: *ana l-hannan / fa-utlubni / tajiduni / sulh(?) ilayya / la taqsud / siwaya* ('I am the Tender-hearted / so seek Me [and] / thou shalt find Me / …[?] to Me / Thou shalt not desire / [anyone] but Me'). Zhengde mark and period (1506–21). *H. 12.4 cm.*

163 Bowl of blue and white porcelain, with Koranic inscriptions. At the centre is the *Surat al-Ikhlas,* in the cavetto and on the rim the *Ayat al-Kursi.* Ming dynasty, third quarter of 16th century. *D. 37 cm.*

There is no God but God. Mohammed is the apostle of God.' All the tripods are based on bronze prototypes, of which at least three in turn also have Arabic inscriptions and probably apocryphal Xuande marks. It seems likely that the whole group, porcelain and bronzes alike, belongs to the early sixteenth century.

The decorative motifs, including floral designs and interlocking and arabesque scrolls of Islamic origin, are all typical of wares of the Zhengde period and link these unusual pieces to the general output of the kilns at that time. Indeed, the interlocking scrolls also make their appearance on the group made for the Portuguese market. As for the Arabic/Persian inscriptions, the calligraphic style is certainly the work of someone not particularly well versed in the finer points of the script in Western Islamic terms, though entirely within the canon of Arabic script in China. The wedge-shaped alifs can be found on any Chinese Moslem restaurant sign to this day.

The Spanish involvement with China was rather different from that of the Portuguese, as they literally approached the Far East from a totally different direction, across the Pacific from Mexico and South America. This began with Magellan's famous voyage round the world in 1521, opening up a new route via Cape Horn. He also annexed the island of Tidore, off the west coast of the Moluccas, the centre of the spice trade and much coveted by the Spanish.[23]

The conquest of the Americas in the early sixteenth century and the subjugation of the indigenous Indian population brought immense rewards to Spain, particularly an unimaginable wealth of Mexican and Bolivian silver.[24] Much of this came back to Europe, but a large quantity was reinvested in trade with the Far East. Each year, from 1573 onwards, a Spanish galleon would sail from Acapulco directly across the Pacific to Manila. The Manila Galleon (*Não de China*, also known as the Silver Galleon) would then invest its cargo in desirable commodities from the Far East, returning to Mexico by a slightly longer northern route. The goods were later sold at great profit at an annual fair in Acapulco. However, what is very little known is that alongside silver there was another export almost as valuable in the Far East. This was the cochineal beetle (L. *coccinus scarlet*) **[164]**. The beetle is a parasite that grows on the paddles of the prickly pear (nopal cactus), which is indigenous to Mexico and Guatemala. It appears as a cluster of dusty white spots, and the beetles are collected by prising them off the prickly pears and drying them out in sieves. When they are crushed they produce a vivid permanent crimson dye. As the only source of this colour for textiles in Europe and the Far East, it was greatly prized; indeed, it was not until

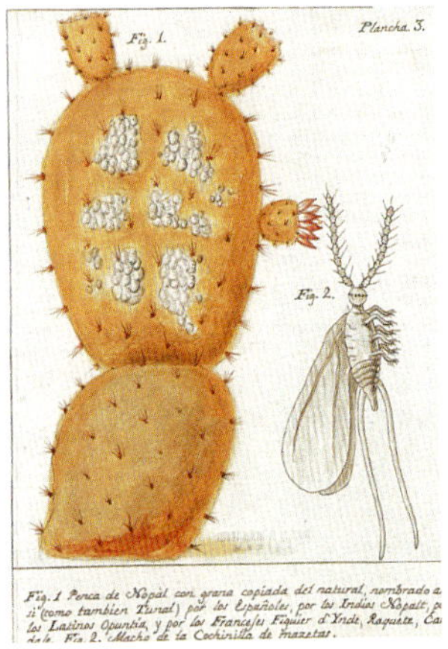

164 Gathering the cochineal beetle from the prickly pear. From the *Alzate Codex*, 1777.

the middle of the nineteenth century and the invention of industrial aniline dyes that this natural product was superseded.[25]

Among the commodities most sought after by the Spanish, such as silk and ivory, was Chinese porcelain. Upon its arrival in Acapulco, the porcelain was transported overland to Vera Cruz and onwards to Spain. But some remained in Mexico itself and inspired the local production of blue and white. Most of this was made at Puebla, southeast of Mexico city, on the route to the Atlantic. The exuberant Puebla ware, including both tiles and pottery, is an eclectic mix of misunderstood Chinese, Aztec and Spanish motifs **[166]**. Almost lunatic in style, this Mexican *chinoiserie* nevertheless has its own amusing vitality.[26]

Less is known about the porcelain that inspired these Mexican imitations.

165 *The Walsingham Bowl:* Blue and white porcelain, with Elizabethan silver-gilt mounts. Wanli period (1573–1620), the mounts *c.*1580–1600. *D. 21.5 cm.* By tradition, this bowl was given by Queen Elizabeth to her godchild Sir Thomas Walsingham (1568–1630), whose granddaughter gave it to the eighth Earl of Exeter in 1731. It has been at Burghley House, Stamford, ever since.

OPPOSITE

166 Jar of Mexican blue and white pottery. With four panels painted with a fisherman, buildings of various kinds, towers, trees, birds, cranes, fish and a rabbit. *c.*1625–50. *H. 46.9 cm.*

167 Flask of blue and white porcelain, with the arms of Philip II of Spain (1556–98). Wanli period, *c.*1585–95. *H. 30.5 cm.*

When Sir Francis Drake was in the Pacific, in 1596 he captured one of the Spanish galleons; after throwing overboard the broken pieces of Chinese porcelain, he brought some of the intact ware back to England. In 1584 he presented one piece to Queen Elizabeth I, who in turn gave it to her godchild Thomas Walsingham; it is now at Burghley House.[27] With Elizabethan silver-gilt mounts, it is a typical Wanli (1573–1620) bowl with floral sprays and a ring of horses galloping through waves below the rim, with pagodas and pavilions within a landscape frieze **[165]**. More material has been found from excavations at Point Reys on the Californian coast, including sherds; some blue and white was even cut down to make drilled discs, beads found in Indian graves.

The oldest piece known to have been made for the Spanish market is a Wanli jar, *c.*1575, with the double-headed Hapsburg eagle surmounted by a strange elongated building.[28] Philip II (1585–95) granted the use of the Hapsburg eagle to the Augustinian order in the Philippines, and the jar may have been commissioned by them when they made one of their first expeditions to China itself. A second piece of blue and white is a circular flask with a tall neck bearing Philip II's own coat of arms,[29] painted within a beaded frame and probably copied from a Mexican coin **[167]**. The Mexican coins were of poorer quality than those minted in Spain and the copy shows the characteristics of the cruder prototype. Indeed, a coin from the *San Diego* wreck of 1600, off the coast of the Philippines, is of just such a type, the beading copying the rough milling of the edge. The porcelain arrived in Manila by Chinese junks, and it is recorded that forty such vessels came in 1580 alone.

Considering the Spanish involvement in the China trade, it is surprising that so little blue and white has been documented in Spain itself, compared with its neighbour Portugal. In both countries it influenced the design of the local glazed earthenware, and in Spain there is the now familiar situation, encountered in various parts of the world, whereby the imitations exist without the originals. This is also true in Mexico, which had a much longer tradition of local *chinoiserie* ware, over two centuries. In these cases, as elsewhere, it may simply be that nobody has searched for the originals, and if they exist in private hands, no one has recognized them for their historical importance. The case of Syria springs once more to mind.

Turning to the Ottoman empire, the domination of the Indian Ocean by the Portuguese had immediate repercussions on the Turkish naval presence, and access to the merchandise that would normally flow from the Far East to the Persian Gulf and Red Sea. This had a knock-on effect in the Mediterranean, for

instance in Venice, where the price of pepper rose steeply at the turn of the sixteenth century as a result of the shortage of supplies from the traditional markets of the eastern Mediterranean. This left the Venetians with a dilemma as to whether they should turn to Lisbon instead.[30] However, the Portuguese were unable to stop the Red Sea trade completely and had to rely on an annual blockade. Albuquerque's grand plan to control the Red Sea and conquer Egypt came to nothing. His attack on Aden failed and he died in 1515 on his way back to Goa, after establishing a Portuguese presence in Hormuz.

From then on the skirmishes between the Turks and the Portuguese did little to affect the flow of trade into the Ottoman empire, and the conquest of Syria and Egypt in 1517 must have even facilitated the swift passage of goods from the Far East to Istanbul. The Topkapi Saray collection reflects this, for there is plenty of porcelain of the reign of the emperor Jiajing (1522–66) of almost exactly the same duration as that of Sultan Suleyman (1520–66). But such were the demands of the Ottoman court at its zenith for fine wares, let alone glazed tiles that were not a Chinese export, that the indigenous Iznik industry which began about 1480 went into full-scale production during Suleyman's reign.

The impact of Chinese blue and white had already been felt before the conquest of Constantinople in 1453, as can been seen in the Chinese-inspired tiles in the Murad II mosque at Edirne of 1435, which show the influence of almost contemporary fifteenth-century Chinese wares alongside Yuan motifs.[31] There is no direct link between these tiles and the emergent Iznik industry, but there is a common interest in Chinese blue and white adapted for purely Ottoman purposes. An early Iznik example is a blue and white candlestick – like the Yongle and Xuande porcelain candlesticks copying an Islamic metal form – of about 1480, where the Chinese floral motifs are metamorphosed into something much more indigenous and into which is woven an illegible Arabic/Turkish inscription **[170]**.[32] Like the Edirne tiles, it also shows an awareness of the blue and white/white on blue syndrome that is such a feature of Yuan porcelain. In the same vein is a hanging lamp, now in the British Museum, that once hung in the tomb of Bayezid II, who died in 1512 **[169]**.[33] This again mixes Turkish *chinoiserie* with inscriptions and motifs drawn from Balkan silver and is noteworthy above all for its successful integration of all these very different sources. One of the great achievements of the Iznik potters was to take the Chinese models and through their interpretation produce something vital and original in its own right. Indeed, Gerald Reitlinger once remarked that aesthetically a fine piece of Iznik far outstrips the Chinese prototype.

OPPOSITE
168 Jug of blue and white porcelain, with the arms of the Pinto, Pereira, Guedes and Pimentel families (the strap handle is on the opposite side). Chongzhen period (1628–44). *H. 33 cm.*

BELOW
169 Iznik hanging lamp of blue and white pottery; the decoration is influenced both by Balkan silver and by Chinese sources. One of five lamps believed to have come from the *turbe* of Sultan Bayezid II (1481–1512). Iznik, *c.*1510. *H. 22.7 cm.*

The later influence of Chinese blue and white on Turkish pottery is well documented, and the only question is how did the potters have access to the models they interpreted? The vigorous treatment of early fifteenth-century designs such as the bunch of grapes motif can hardly have been transmitted through the sketches of a court artist, but can only have evolved through close observation of an original dish. Iznik is more than a hundred kilometres from Istanbul, so this presupposes that the artist-potters travelled at least two days to the capital and there had access either to the Treasury and the kitchens of the royal palace or to other sources. A splendid example of Chinese inspiration and Iznik interpretation is a lion dish of which the Chinese blue and white prototype is in Limoges **[171]** and the Iznik polychrome interpretation was once in the Lagonikos collection **[172]**.[34] There are several Chinese examples of this fantastic beast **[46]**, this being the finest, though he no longer exists at Topkapi Saray.[35] But the stance and the tilt of the head are identical in the Iznik version, and the chevron-like stripe on the Chinese animal's forefront becomes a chain. In the background the rocks survive but the bamboo and lotuses are transformed into tulips and carnations. Unlike most Timurid blue and white, which slavishly attempts to copy the Chinese originals, this Iznik dish is the epitome of inspiration and originality.

The eclecticism of the four great blue and turquoise panels on the front of the Sunnet Odasi in Topkapi Saray suggests an intimate acquaintance with the Yuan porcelain in the palace collection **[173]**. The white on blue cloud scrolls in the spandrels are certainly taken from a Yuan example such as the dragon dish (TKS 15/1417), where the flaming clouds float on a blue ground, and so too are the emphatic white and blue borders. The pheasants and the flowers are elaborate creations also stemming from Yuan sources. Admittedly, these extraordinary panels – over a metre high and probably the largest underglaze panels successfully fired in the whole of ceramic history – were almost certainly designed and painted by Sahkkulu, the head of the *nakkashane*, or court designers.[36] But besides his own imaginative genius there is an underlying awareness of the contrapuntal subtleties of Chinese blue and white. These tiles were not made at Iznik but almost certainly in kilns close to the palace, so in this case the Chinese influence is more easily explicable.

In Persia in the seventeenth century the situation is completely different. Shah Abbas I's porcelain collection entered the Ardebil shrine on the shores of the Caspian in 1611 and was therefore unavailable to the Safavid potters. Their influences must have come from the day-to-day Chinese porcelain in his capital,

170 Iznik candlestick of blue and white pottery, the truncated neck with a silver mount. The inscription in *kufic* and *thuluth* is illegible. Iznik, *c.*1480. *H. 25 cm.*

171 Dish of blue and white porcelain. Yuan dynasty, 14th century. *D. 47.5 cm.*

172 Iznik pottery dish, painted in underglaze colours. Iznik, *c.*1575. From the Lagonikos collection, Alexandria.

173 Ottoman blue and turquoise glazed tiles, on the façade of the Sunnet Odasi (Circumcision Chamber), Topkapi Saray, Istanbul. Istanbul, *c.*1527–8. *Large panel, bottom right: H. 125 cm.*

established at Isfahan in 1598, and the other great cities of Persia. For instance, Chinese blue and white vases feature in the Safavid tiles which line the walls of the churches in New Djulfa, the Armenian suburb of Isfahan.[37] The Church of St Sargis, founded *c.*1608 and restored a century later, has a tile panel depicting a blue and white vase decorated with a pair of deer and a rocky landscape, filled with stylized peonies and lotuses [**174**]. Whizzing around in the background are pairs of peacocks, with cloud scrolls and more Chinese-inspired flowers.

The quarter of New Djulfa was created after Shah Abbas had captured Erevan in 1604 and moved the Armenian population of the old town of Djulfa on the River Araxes to Isfahan. The Armenians were merchants and, realizing their potential, Shah Abbas gave them the monopoly of the silk trade with Europe. In the next few years they became immensely wealthy and reinforced their position in Isfahan by providing interpreters for foreign ambassadors, who were usually lodged with them in this Christian quarter. With agents abroad all the way from Spain and Amsterdam to India, they played a leading role in international trade. And surprisingly, this included maritime trade with the Far East, for there are Dutch records of Armenian captains of vessels plying to the Far East.[38] This, then, is one probable route by which porcelain would have flowed into Persia.

The impact is fascinating, for the Persian potters at Shiraz, Kirman, Meshed, Yezd, Zarand and other centres were working with a white body decorated with a deep underglaze cobalt blue, of fine enough quality that in the mid-seventeenth century it was being exported by the Dutch to Europe, where it was infiltrated into shipments of Chinese porcelain.[39] From 1552 they also exported Persian pottery to India, Ceylon and the Far East, where it filled the gap created by the temporary suspension of supplies of porcelain from the kilns at Jingdezhen, following the collapse of the Ming dynasty in 1644. This eastern trade in Persian pottery reached its peak between 1675 and 1682. Specific confirmation of this comes from a group of modest Persian dishes excavated in Male in the Maldive Islands in 1972, some of which clearly imitate Chinese Transitional patterns [**175**].[40]

But the finer Persian products are often extraordinary in their total incomprehension of the Chinese Jiajing and Wanli patterns. Unlike the Iznik potters, who used the porcelain as a *point de départ* for their inspiration, the Persians created a total fantasy world with their own unique brand of *chinoiserie*. The results can be unintentionally hilarious, in a way not dissimilar to that of eighteenth-century Chinese misinterpretations of European subjects. An exception is a dish in the Ashmolean Museum, which is sensitively painted with a pair of

174 Detail of a *cuerda seca* tile panel in the Church of St Sargis, New Djulfa, Isfahan, depicting a Chinese blue and white vase. Safavid, 17th century.

birds perched on a skilfully drawn ground of lotuses, flowers and cloud scrolls [**176**]. The eight-pointed cloud-collar frame with thick and thin blue outlines and its extension to an eight-pointed star with pointed floral panels between suggest that, in this instance, the potter had access to a Yuan dish, such as one in the Ardebil collection (29.46). For once, the artist was in control and knew exactly what he was doing.

175 Dish of Persian blue and white pottery, from Male in the Maldive Islands. Persian, second half of 17th century. *D. 18 cm.*

176 Large dish of Persian blue and white pottery. The design may well have been inspired by a 14th-century Chinese dish, such as one in the Ardebil collection (29.46) with a similar 8-pointed medallion, but phoenixes instead of pheasants. Persia, 17th century. *D. 58.2 cm.*

177 Covered jar of blue and white porcelain. Korea, 15th century. *H. 16.5 cm.*

7 IMITATION AND RIVALRY

Korea and Japan

It was not only in Central Asia and the West that local potters felt the impact of blue and white porcelain. Whilst the Timurid, Persian, Syrian, Egyptian and, later, European potters were obliged to find ways of replicating porcelain in humble earthenware, the artisans of the Far East, closer to the Chinese stoneware tradition, were able to come up with more convincing imitations. Korea and Japan represent two instances of this technological transfer.

In Korea, imports of ceramics from China begin at least as early as the Tang dynasty; sherds of Tongguan ware from Changsha, exported to Japan, Southeast Asia and much further afield to the West, have also been found in Korea.[1] In the Song dynasty imports included *qingbai*, Ding, Cizhou and celadon wares, and the Korean potters of the Koryo dynasty (918–1392) manufactured ceramics influenced by these Chinese wares.[2] The celadons are of extreme refinement of shape and design, making Chinese Longquan celadons look clumsy by comparison. Their great innovation was a new decorative technique, *sanggam*, which consisted of inlaying the green-glazed body with designs in white or black clay.[3] A famous celadon ewer, produced in the mid-thirteenth century, is painted in underglaze copper red [**178**]. This is almost a century before copper red began to be commonly used in China.[4]

178 Celadon ewer decorated in copper red. Koryo dynasty, mid-13th century. *H. 32.5 cm.*

179 Celadon bowl, inlaid in sanggam. Koryo dynasty, mid-12th century. *H. 5.6 cm.*

180 Bottle vase of blue and white porcelain. Korea, late 18th century. *H. 35 cm.*

On the other hand, blue and white was a late starter in Korea compared with China, for the government-controlled kilns (*punwon*) producing fine white wares did not begin to operate until the second half of the fifteenth century, although white porcelain was produced in the Koryo period, as early as the twelfth century. The kilns were in Kwangju district, near Seoul.[5] These white wares were sometimes inlaid in black; bowls and *yuhuchun* vases have a sparse decoration of highly simplified lotus and other trailing lines, not unreminiscent of Yuan copper-red specimens. The blue and white decoration is largely confined to painterly interpretations of pine, prunus and bamboo, the latter so freely painted that it would have almost been more appropriate on a scroll than a pot. A superlative example is a jar unearthed in Seoul [**181**]; like the copper-red celadon ewer, it is

181 Jar of blue and white porcelain.
Korea, Choson dynasty, mid-15th century. *H. 41 cm.*

one of the treasures of the Ho-am Art Museum.[6] Another jar (*guan*) in the National Museum is painted with two chattering magpies on a flowering prunus branch – a design that can only derive from an early fifteenth-century Chinese dish.[7] A key piece is a vase (*meiping*) in the Dongkuk University Museum **[183]**, painted with bamboo and a pine tree enveloping the vase from foot to rim, almost as if the same motifs on one of the Chinese vases of the late fourteenth century had crossed their boundaries and sprung free.[8] This vase is important, as it is inscribed inside the rim 'Hong-ch'i second year' – that is, 1489 ('Hong-ch'i' being the Korean version of Hongzhi, 1488–1505). Many Korean pots had Chinese reign marks because Korea was a vassal kingdom of China. After the sack of Korea by the Japanese at the end of the sixteenth century there was a hiatus, the potters being all taken to Japan, and it was not until the eighteenth century that a new style of blue and white emerged, with dragons and flowers of an almost childlike simplicity **[182]**.[9]

In Japan there was a similar symbiotic relationship with China, and individual pieces of greenware and *sancai* from the early Tang dynasty have been found in Japan; *sancai* was extensively copied during the Nara period (645–805). In the Heian period (806–1184) regular trade with China was initiated, and this included ceramics, celadon, white wares, northern celadon and brown-glazed *temmoku*. By the twelfth century imports included Yue and Guan ware, *qingbai* porcelain and Longquan celadon. Whilst a number of pieces have been excavated, many of the intact examples of these wares, known as *densei-hin*, have survived in Japanese temples or within families, having been passed down from one generation to the next.[10]

The Sinan cargo, most probably destined for Japan, gives a wide perspective of the wares that were popular in the early fourteenth century. The absence of blue and white from this shipment has already been remarked upon; and it should be noted that Yuan blue and white is rarely found on Japanese sites, exceptions being at Kasai castle, and at Katsuren castle, far south on the island of Okinawa.[11] This seeming lack of interest continues through the Ming dynasty, although a number of Ming *densei* pieces have survived in families since the Edo period (1615–1868) and excavations in Japan show that pedestrian examples of blue and white found a utilitarian market throughout the fifteenth and sixteenth centuries. Japanese taste in Chinese ceramics was inextricably mixed up with fulfilling the demands of the tea ceremony, which was originally an aristocratic ritual but later became universally popular. In the sixteenth century the fashion for the simple ceremony

182 Jar of blue and white porcelain. Korea, 18th century. *H. 17.2 cm.*

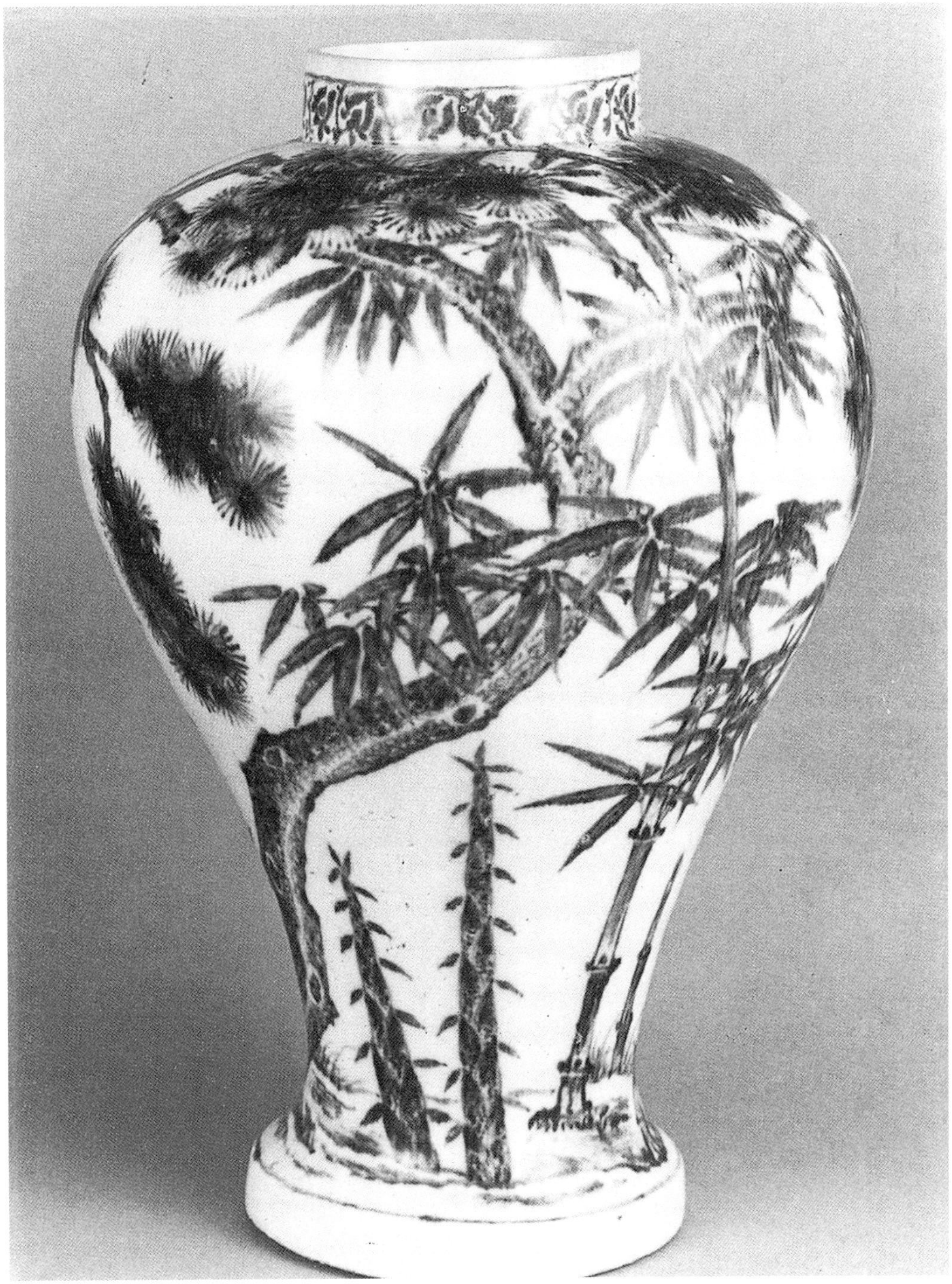

183 Vase of blue and white porcelain. Korea, dated AD 1489. *H. 48.7 cm.*

of the *wabi* style led to the use of roughly made Korean stoneware tea bowls, admired for their rustic simplicity and even their imperfections. Chinese imports played no great part in this movement.

This was to change in the seventeenth century, when masses of Swatow and other wares, known as *Ko-sometsuke* ('old blue and white') and *Shonzui* (*Shunzhi*) ware, were ordered by the tea masters from the mainland. There was also a great vogue for *kinrande* ('gold brocade style') porcelain with gilt decoration on a red, green, turquoise or white ground sometimes combined with underglaze blue designs. Of the Jiajing period (1522–66) it is estimated that the largest number of surviving *kinrande* pieces are in Japanese collections;[12] although there are more than thirty in Topkapi Saray, they are very rare elsewhere. The gold leaf decoration must have appealed greatly to Ottoman taste, for they made use of the same technique, for instance on the interior of the famous bejewelled blue and white pen case **[149b]**. That this was inspired by the imported *kinrande* would seem a distinct possibility, although there are early sixteenth-century Turkish tiles and pottery with gilded patterns on a white ground, which are an integral part of the design of the underglaze blue panels. A large polychrome Iznik flask of *c.*1675 (which later belonged to Enrico Caruso) has additional gilt decoration, and it was commonly used to enhance seventeenth-century Iznik dishes, whose quality was otherwise in decline.[13]

Two pieces of *kinrande* were acquired in Turkey in 1583 by Count Eberhardt von Manderscheidt and later transformed in Germany into stem cups with silver-gilt mounts.[14] One of the pair is now in the Victoria and Albert Museum and the other has remained in the family. The Victoria and Albert example has an inscription engraved on the mount which records its history **[185]**. Other *kinrande* bowls are in Schloss Ambras in Austria. According to an inventory of 1596 referring to '66 deep little porcelain bowls, some of them decorated [*geschmelzt*] in gold, all the others blue and white [*plau und weisz*]', these must have arrived in the sixteenth century. Another one from Turkey that got away (its pair is in the Topkapi Saray museum) is now in the British Museum **[186]**. It was presented in 1877 by Sultan Abdulhamid II (1876–1909) to the British Ambassador, Sir Henry Layard, and his niece, Lady Charlotte Scheiber, gave it in turn to the museum. Finally, a similar bejewelled bowl (it has lost its gems but the incisions for the mounts remain) is in the Sadberk Hanim Museum at Buyukdere in Istanbul.[15]

The 1616 inventory of a shogun's effects lists hundreds of repetitive pieces of various designs and shapes, suggesting sets of vessels intended for practical use.[16]

184 *Kinrande* octagonal double-gourd vase, of red enamelled porcelain decorated in gold. Ming dynasty, 16th century. *H. 37.5 cm.*

185 *Kinrande* bowl of blue and white porcelain, decorated on the outside in gold on red enamelled ground, mounted on a silver-gilt stand. Ming dynasty, 16th century; the European mount datable to 1583.

186 *Kinrande* bowl with four turquoise enamel medallions, with gold filigree and bejewelled decoration. Ming dynasty, 16th century. *D. 12 cm.*

187 Dish of blue and white porcelain. *Ko-sometsuke* made for the Japanese market. Tianqi reign mark (1621–7). *D. 21.4 cm.*

188 Dish of Japanese blue and white porcelain in *Kraak* style. Arita, 17th century.

Vietnamese and Swatow wares were also imported. The situation changed radically in the seventeenth century with the establishment of the Japanese porcelain factories at Arita in the 1620s, building on an existing stoneware tradition, itself stemming from Korea. A decade later, responding to the threat imposed by the indigenous industry, the Chinese and Dutch (who had been in Japan since the beginning of the century) began importing masses of porcelain from the mainland. The Chinese potters manufactured *Ko-sometsuke* dishes and other vessels with the Japanese market specifically in mind, thus acquiring a new market to fill the vacuum caused by the lack of imperial patronage following the death of Wanli in 1620.[17] Many *Ko-sometsuke* pieces **[187]** carry a Tianqi reign mark (1621–7), and the style lasted into the Chongzhen period (1628–44). The designs are quite unlike anything previously produced at Jingdezhen, with an emphasis on asymmetrical patterns and motifs in the Japanese manner. Besides dishes, there were vessels of unusual shape, some even moulded as horses or fish, and incense burners in the form of lions and birds. Characteristic of all of them is a simple and often wittily executed style of decoration.[18]

The designs from Arita reflect an awareness of the Chinese imports, whilst at the same time the Chinese artists were sensitive to the taste of the new Japanese clients. Who copied what, it is almost impossible to tell. With the collapse of the Ming dynasty, the Arita potters got their chance and swiftly engaged in the export market. This was ably managed by the Dutch traders, who placed large orders for Arita blue and white. The most salient characteristics of this ware are the use of a deep-toned dark blue, a freer style of execution and loose interpretation of the *Kraak* panel style. The inclusion in many of the compositions of the VOC monogram *(Vereenigde Oostindische Compagnie,* United East India Company) was an obvious reference to Dutch patronage and control of the export industry. Dutch records testify to the volume and extent of this trade in Japanese porcelain.[19] Numerous specimens have been found throughout Southeast Asia, and in Sri Lanka there are a number of Japanese blue and white dishes in the reserve collection of the National Museum in Colombo **[188]**. In the Near East, Japanese blue and white is well represented in the Topkapi Saray collection and also among the blue and white porcelain from Syria.

By the second half of the seventeenth century the Japanese potters were producing vast quantities of export ware, with the Dutch ordering porcelain to be manufactured specifically for the European market. Designs were often supplied in the form of wooden models and a common shape was the apothecary's bottle,

189 Dish of Japanese blue and white porcelain in *Kraak* style. Arita, 17th century.

190 a, b Dish of Japanese blue and white porcelain in *Kraak* style. Arita, 17th century.

based on a Dutch glass prototype with a spherical body and double rim. Another popular form was a bottle of square section with a rounded shoulder and cylindrical neck. This, too, was copied from a Dutch glass original, of exactly the kind excavated at Dhlo-Dhlo near Zimbabwe (see p. 91). Initials painted on many of the pieces of Japanese blue and white indicate that they were specially made for officials of the Dutch East India Company.

During the Edo period much Japanese porcelain was produced for the home market, and this was quite different in form and decoration from the export ware. But that it never travelled abroad is not the case, for an extraordinary collection of Edo porcelain was discovered a few years ago in England, among the contents of Burghley House.[20] The Cecil family have owned Burghley since it was built more than four hundred years ago by William Cecil, Lord Treasurer to Queen

191 Dish of Japanese blue and white porcelain. Edo period, second half of 17th century. *D. 38.4 cm.*

Elizabeth I. Five famous pieces of Chinese blue and white porcelain, embellished with Elizabethan silver-gilt mounts, were sold by the 4th Marquis of Exeter in 1888. Passing through the hands of Agnew's and then J. Pierpont Morgan, they were finally acquired by The Metropolitan Museum of Art in New York in 1944. Lord Burghley himself presented Elizabeth I with a white porcelain bowl mounted in gold on New Year's Day 1587.[21]

But how a unique collection of Japanese porcelain – strikingly different in style from the Chinese Wanli blue and white that was in vogue in Elizabethan times – came to be in Burghley House is a total mystery. This collection is of particular interest, for it can be tied to an inventory of Burghley dated 1688, and a second of 1690. The first inventory lists the house's contents room by room, often referring to porcelain as 'china over ye chimney', but with brief and succinct descriptions that can be equated with surviving examples. The second list, known as the Devonshire Schedule and dated 18 April 1690, records works of art in trust for the Duchess of Devonshire's daughter, Anne. Besides paintings, furniture, jewellery and other *objets d'art* it includes over 150 pieces of china, classified as 'plain', 'guilt and enameld' or 'garnisht with silver guilt' – that is, furnished with European silver-gilt mounts, like the Walsingham bowl **[165]** and other pieces referred to above. Lady Victoria Leatham recounts her excitement when cataloguing the porcelain collection after the death of her father, the 6th Marquess of Exeter, in 1982. She and Gordon Lang realized that a number of Japanese pieces had survived which were actually mentioned in these two seventeenth-century inventories. To quote one particular instance, a *blanc de Chine* figure of Budai, god of good fortune, found in her mother's bathroom, was identified as the piece described in the 1688 inventory as 'one balld fryor sitting [in] My Ladye's Dressing room'.[22]

It is the very Japanese style of so many of the pieces at Burghley that is so intriguing, leading one to speculate how this particular variant of mainstream Chinese blue and white ever found its way to Europe. The inventories also usefully furnish a *terminus ante quem* for the date of the porcelain's production in Japan. One remarkable piece is an Arita dish shaped like a crane **[192]**. Of dynamic form, it is elegantly and brilliantly painted in a simple, direct manner. A large jar is decorated with stiff and meticulously shaded sprays of flowers interspersed with vertical panels, the general effect derived from Chinese *Kraak* porcelain **[194]**. More Japanese in form is a bucket based on a wooden Japanese prototype, of a type used for *sake* **[195]**. The landscape on this example is very similar to the

192 Dish of Japanese blue and white porcelain in the form of a crane. Arita, Edo period, *c.*1660–80. *11.5 cm × 9 cm.*

193 Hexagonal covered box of Japanese blue and white porcelain with a hare. Arita, Edo period, late 17th century. *D. 7 cm.*

194 Cylindrical vase of Japanese blue and white porcelain, with peonies and chrysanthemums. Arita, Edo period, *c.*1690. *H. 30.2 cm.*

195 Bucket-shaped vessel of Japanese blue and white porcelain, copying the form of a wooden *sake* bucket. Arita, Edo period, *c.*1670–90. *H. 27.2 cm.*

mountainous scene on the dish in the Boston Museum of Fine Arts [**191**]. A hexagonal box has a cover painted with a lively hare dashing through a tuft of leaves and bamboo [**193**]. Although there are other examples of Japanese porcelain in English country houses such as Welbeck Abbey and Drayton House, the Burghley collection is unique. So, too, are its inventories, as they are the earliest of their kind in Europe where the descriptions can actually be matched with the surviving pieces.

If Korean and Japanese porcelain took off in different directions in the sixteenth century, what was happening in China itself? The sixteenth century can truly be said to be the moment when Jingdezhen became an industry on a grand scale, motivated by the massive demands made upon it by the export market, stimulated by the Portuguese and Dutch traders and the unquenchable European thirst for porcelain.

Asia still constituted a large market, by no means diminished by Western demands. This is exemplified once more by the Topkapi Saray collection, which contains a wide selection of late Ming wares. It is an interesting coincidence that the reigns of the Emperor Jiajing (1522–66) and Sultan Suleyman the Magnificent (1520–66) almost mirror each other, and certainly in the case of Suleyman vast quantities of Chinese porcelain entered the treasury. With a few exceptions, the designs of the blue and white bowls, dishes and ewers are standard Chinese patterns, including dragons and phoenixes, deer, hares, monkeys, flying horses, lions, elephants and other beasts, as well as white cranes, peacocks, butterflies and insects, often in a landscape setting. Pine, prunus and bamboo and other floral motifs and fruit sprays are popular. On some of the larger dishes the cavetto is left plain, contrasting an elaborate central panel with a different repetitive border design on the rim.[23]

Many of the dishes are finely painted with an idyllic garden, with a pavilion and a tree, pairs of pheasants and other birds, rocks and shrubbery, sometimes even with a monkey perched on a branch.[24] Others depict a watery landscape, with vertiginous rocks, islets swathed in misty clouds, pagodas, thatched huts and banners, fishing boats, two figures crossing a bridge, and a ceremonial barge with a canopy approaching the gateway of a city wall.[25] Yet more dishes have as their subject spotted deer gambolling in a rocky landscape with the moon above and a waterfall splashing into a pool in which paddles a turtle.[26] The rims of these dishes are frequently painted with a continuous watery landscape with clumps of reeds and lotuses, amongst which sail little fishing boats. These are depicted

196 Bowl of blue and white porcelain, with Daoist trigrams and symbols inside, and a lion on a pillar between pagodas on the outside. Ming dynasty, third quarter of 16th century. *D. 36 cm.*

197 Ewer of blue and white porcelain with a fountain design. Jiajing mark and period (1522–66). *H. 33 cm.*

198 *Kendi* in the form of an elephant, the pierced tusks forming a spout. Ottoman silver-gilt mount with ring. Ming dynasty, late 16th century. *H. 19.5 cm.*

with a light touch and on at least two examples a fisherman dives into the water displaying his bare bottom and legs.[27] On other dishes the watery scene is used as a backdrop for a procession of white cranes; this is the type that acquired Elizabethan silver mounts and ended up at Burghley House.

There are some unusual pieces amongst the typical mid-sixteenth century wares. A bowl in Istanbul has a central motif of alternating blue and white discs, an abstract Daoist symbol of Yin and Yang.[28] On the inner rim are eight trigrams alternating with waves and cloud-scrolls. On the outside are pagodas and lions perched on pillars **[196]**. Another bowl has similar pagodas on the exterior, this time including buffaloes with boys standing or seated on their backs flying kites.[29] In the same category is a bowl with grotesque masks on the exterior with glaring eyes **[16]**. It has been conjectured that these motifs stem from Italian Renaissance designs, perhaps transmitted by European engravings.

A whole series of tall ewers are painted with elaborate fountains, with water splashing into a basin supported by *qilins* or lions **[197]**.[30] As long ago as 1952 Sir Percival David speculated on these fountains, suggesting that they might represent the fountain constructed by the French goldsmith Guillaume Bouchier for Mangu Khan at Karakorum in 1295. John Pope more convincingly argued that they were, in fact, again based on Italian Renaissance prototypes, though by what means such a design may have been transmitted remains obscure. He also sensibly points out that it would be remarkable if the memory of a thirteenth-century fountain made for the Mongols survived in the collective memory of the Ming dynasty for three centuries.[31]

Yet another novelty are the *kendis* in the the shape of elephants, of which a whole platoon can be found in Topkapi Saray **[198]**.[32] These have cylindrical spouts, with the elephant's trunk coiled back to its body and a spout between the tusks. They all have an elaborate saddle-cloth and beaded trappings. Besides conventional *kendis* with mammiform spouts there are also two more odd ones in the form of frogs.

Some time towards the end of the sixteenth century, during the Wanli period, came the advent of the *Kraak* style, named after the Portuguese carracks – the merchant vessels that shipped so much of the blue and white to the West. This style is epitomized by the division of the rim and much of the cavetto into a series of radial panels, filled with fruit, flowers, auspicious emblems and other motifs, with narrower decorative panels in between.[33] The central design is often a landscape, sometimes with figures, in an elaborated scalloped frame of different kinds of diaper pattern. The most frequent design is of birds or deer within a landscape, but also to be found are dishes depicting interiors that contain furniture and vases filled with flowers. Nor was the *Kraak* style confined only to dishes; there are also bowls, vases and flasks with the same panelling and repertoire of motifs.

With the end of the Ming dynasty and the Wanli era, there is an interlude which in the history of blue and white has been christened the Transitional period. Some of the porcelain produced in the mid-seventeenth century is of outstanding quality and workmanship and Gerald Reitlinger was one of the first to collect this period in earnest; all of it was bequeathed by him, along with the rest of his collections, to the Ashmolean Museum.[34] I remember visiting him years ago when he still lived in his elegant Georgian house at Beckley near Rye, and, during the ritual progression through the house which all *cognoscenti* were obliged to make, coming to the spare bedroom that contained most of his Transitional blue and white. His daughter had spent the night before in the room and Gerald stopped dead in his tracks when he saw that she had looped her silk stocking to dry through the handle of one of his prize pieces.

The defining feature of Transitional ware is the painting, in intense shades of cobalt blue with graded washes finely fading out into the white background. At its best it is superlative. There is also a lesser quality, more primitively painted, much of which found its way to the Middle East. The vestiges of the panel style are still there and the dishes are populated with quaintly drawn figures.[35] What remains is the use of graduated washes of blue in exaggerated form, and it is this type which seems to have inspired the Safavid potters in Persia to imitation. One should also note that a common motif on Transitional ware, particularly on the tall necks of blue and white flasks with a toros moulding, is a symmetrical floral design with wing-like leaves and a tulip-like flower. It has been pointed out by other scholars that the shape itself is very Ottoman, whereas in Iznik ware and Turkish metalwork this would be a *surahi* or water-bottle.[36] This presents the intriguing possibility of the export of Turkish wares to the Far East and their influence on Chinese designs. Reinforcing this argument is the introduction of slip-painted patterns on Swatow wares, which would seem to have been inspired by Iznik slipware, almost certainly pre-dating the appearance of this technique in China.[37]

This is a subject about which we know absolutely nothing, and it is a fitting conclusion to this chapter, which has been concerned with the effect that

Jingdezhen had on the outside world, and its reciprocal response to external influences.

During the Qing dynasty (1644–1911) the production of blue and white becomes another story. Not only did the Chinese potters furnish European and American clients with orders executed to specific demands, but the Europeans themselves discovered the true secret of the manufacture of porcelain. From now onwards it is altogether a different game.

8 SURVIVAL

Shipwrecks, China and the West

Nothing in chronology is so satisfying as a wreck, for here a whole period is encapsulated, often accompanied by a precise terminal date provided by historical records. Even without such a date, a shipwreck – as a sort of sunken tomb – can provide a detailed record of a certain moment. In addition it can tell much about the ship's structure, and the human factor is supplied by the recovery of artefacts used by the sailors, independent of the cargo carried. Also, where the shipwreck occurred can be indicative of the vessel's ultimate destination, and can reveal much about the international economy and maritime routes of the medieval world. In addition, even the timber of the wreck, thanks to the science of dendrochronology, can provide further evidence of the date of the vessel's construction. One of the advantages of working in a particular historical period is that the material can be weighed against what is already known from other sources, often corroborating them but sometimes providing conflicting and intriguing evidence. For instance, some seventeenth-century wrecks have altered the traditional view of the kind and variety of porcelain exported during that period.

In the early medieval period valuable evidence for the export of porcelain of the *qingbai* type – which was to become the basic ware at Jingdezhen for decoration in underglaze cobalt blue – is provided by thousands of sherds from a tiny island at the northeastern tip of Sri Lanka. Not exactly a wreck, it appears to have been rather an abandoned cargo. The exact circumstances of the discovery of over five hundred vessels of the early twelfth century merits being documented in detail. In 1976 I was awarded a grant by the Oriental Ceramic Society to make a survey along the coast of India and Sri Lanka of ports mentioned in Arabic and Chinese sources, to search for evidence in the form of broken pottery and to decide which sites might be propitious for future excavation. In India I visited fifty-four ports in all, from Cambay in the north to Cape Comorin in the south, and several more on the Coromandel coast as far as Madras. In Sri Lanka I made an almost complete circuit of the island. At the last moment I was thwarted in this as the jeep I had been loaned by the Archaeological Commissioner to travel to the north was requisitioned for a political rally. Left to my own devices, I proceeded

199 The excavations at Allaippidy on Kayts Island, near Jaffna in northern Sri Lanka.

OPPOSITE
- **a** The section of the deposit, showing the ceramic level below a darker layer.
- **b** The ceramic fragments uncovered.

ABOVE
- **c** Large earthenware storage jar and small vessels.
- **d** Bowls of translucent *qingbai* porcelain.

by train to Jaffna, where I had been told by a young architect friend in Colombo that he had discovered some Chinese sherds on the little island of Allaippidy, where they were digging sand for building material. When I arrived it was to find to my chagrin that the whole area had by then been completely dug away.

Here fate played a lucky card. A bemused Tamil boy on a bicycle asked us what we were up to, and when he was told that we were looking for Chinese ceramics, he said he knew where there was plenty. With nothing to lose, we followed him in our battered car through the sand dunes, and finally, after nightfall, we arrived. Although there was nothing to see, we got out and, clambering around in the dark, I heard the unmistakable sound of pottery breaking beneath our feet. Grasping a handful of sherds, I suggested we turn back and look at them in the light of our hotel back in Jaffna.

When we examined them it was to discover to our excitement that they were fragments of the finest *qingbai* dishes. Returning next morning, we found out what had happened. Once more local labourers had been digging for building sand and while trenching across a sand dune had come across a whole cache of broken ceramics, which they had impatiently tossed up on the bank above. It was clear that there was much more, visible in the rough section of their trench. With the help of a rapidly recruited band of students from Jaffna University, we returned with basic tools to make an excavation [**199 a, b**]. This was carried out over the next few days, during which we recovered thousands of sherds. These we took to the Kings House, the Government rest-house in the old Dutch Fort in Jaffna that I had been given by the District Commissioner as accommodation.[1] Here, in order to wash the sherds, we filled a large bath four times and then spent many days trying to match them up. The students were fascinated by this gigantic jigsaw puzzle and I had great difficulty in making them go home at night.

In fact, we were able to reconstruct the remains of more than five hundred different vessels. But what were they doing in a sand dune, on an almost deserted island off the coast of the Jaffna peninsula? Even from our rudimentary excavation it was clear that they were not associated with any settlement. We recorded fragments from the same vessels spread over several metres, suggesting that the whole mass had been jumbled up and then either intentionally hidden or covered up by drifting sand over the centuries. The only conclusion we reached was that it must have been a ship's cargo, abandoned after it had been beached, and sifted through to retrieve any whole vessels that might have survived.

Whatever the real history of the deposit may have been, it has provided a unique corpus of Chinese porcelain on its way westward **[199 c, d]**. Indeed, the closest parallels are with the porcelain excavated at Fustat in Egypt and similar wares recovered from Tioman Island and elsewhere in Malaysia.[2] The fine white translucent *qingbai* included shallow dishes and bowls of various forms, often with freely incised floral and combed patterns, the bowls having stylized plantain leaves on the exterior. There were also vessels of similar design but lesser quality, the off-white ware covered with a creamish glaze. Curiosities were the remains of two spouted ewers and a sherd of a small bowl with moulded trefoils on the inside, of a well-known type of Northern Song greenware, probably from the Xicun kilns in Guangdong province.[3] A series of cups with scalloped rims were of greyish-olive greenware, as were a number of small bowls with rolled rims. There were more than fifty large platters, and a number of earthenware vessels including two *kendis* and large storage jars and containers.

What of the date of this group? With the evidence of the greenware sherd, and the fine *qingbai* bowls, around 1100 would seem about right. This is reinforced by an early twelfth-century Chinese text describing the organization and maritime trade of Guangzhou (Canton), through which port most of the foreign trade would have passed.[4] One passage describes the ships and relates how the merchants divided up the space among themselves, sleeping on top of their goods. As for the goods themselves: 'The greater part of the cargo consists of pottery, the small pieces packed in the larger, till there is not a crevice left.' This precisely describes the Allaippidy ceramics, with the finer wares tucked into the larger earthenware basin; thus the date would seem exactly right.

A recent survey of *qingbai* from Chinese tombs dated from 986 to 1338 shows how important this ware, made at the Jingdezhen kilns as well as at a number of provincial centres, was for more than three centuries.[5] *Qingbai* with its bluish-green tint, along with the more opaque *shufu* ware, played a major role in the evolution of blue and white porcelain. The superior quality of *qingbai* can be exemplified by the earliest recorded piece of Chinese porcelain known to have reached Europe. This is the famous Fonthill vase, now in the National Gallery in Dublin. Its existence was predicated by John Ayers in 1957, on the basis of an early eighteenth-century drawing by Gagnières in the Bibliothèque Nationale in Paris of a vase in European mounts [**201**].[6] It was Arthur Lane who discovered the actual vase, minus its silver-gilt and enamelled mounts, in Ireland, and he published a full account of its extraordinary history in 1961.[7] Gagnières's drawing showed that the vase had been converted by the mounts into a ewer, which was presented by Louis of Hungary (1326–82) to Charles III (d. 1386) after his capture of the Kingdom of Naples. The mounts were still on the vase when it was owned by the eccentric William Beckford of Fonthill Abbey and are mentioned in the catalogue of the sale of his effects in 1822, but they disappeared at some later stage, either before or after the vase crossed the Irish Sea.

200 Stem cup of *qingbai* porcelain. Yuan dynasty, 14th century. *H. 10 cm.*

The vase is itself a mongrel. It is of the *yuhuchun* type, of *qingbai* porcelain with loosely carved lotus panels, a lotus scroll, and a ring of plantains on the neck. Four quatrefoil panels have been cut into the body with complete disregard for the original decoration. These were filled with freely modelled floral sprays, with beaded frames and pointed panels above. A series of little *qingbai* cups of related type, including examples in Bristol and Cleveland, are more coherently conceived. A little stem cup in the Calouste Gulbenkian Museum in Lisbon has beaded decoration and four exquisitely carved cut-out panels of scholars amongst bamboo [**200**]. The beaded trails are carelessly applied and one wonders exactly what technical process was used to produce them; they look remarkably like slightly wonky cake decoration. The technique was already in vogue at the end of the thirteenth century, for there are a series of Buddhist statues with this kind of supplementary beaded decoration, including one in the Metropolitan Museum of Art, and a Bodhisattva in the Nelson-Atkins Gallery in Kansas. The latter is inscribed in ink on the unglazed foot and dated 1298/9.[8]

201 *The Fonthill Vase*
Of *qingbai* porcelain, the vase has loosely carved decoration including lotus panels, into which are cut four lobed panels filled with moulded flowers, with beaded borders and spiral panels above. The vase is the earliest recorded piece of Chinese porcelain to have reached Europe. Yuan dynasty, *c.*1300. *H. 28.1 cm.*

Pre-dating the Kansas Bodhisattva are four pairs of *qingbai* funerary urns with figures and other appliqué decoration from tombs dated 1206, 1209, 1211 and 1293 respectively.[9] A seated figure of Guanyin of 1251 with *qingbai* details would appear to be the first dated example of the use of rather crude beading for its necklace and a bracelet.[10] Although there are a number of cruder dated *qingbai* vessels throughout the thirteenth century, of special interest is a later pair of vases dated 1324, carved with dragons, lotus scrolls and lotus panels very similar in style to those on the Fonthill vase.[11] This is just the moment when underglaze blue decoration is surmised to have been introduced at Jingdezhen. The next dated pieces are a *guan* and a model of a granary, inscribed and dated 1338.[12] These two pieces continue the tradition of moulded figures, dragons and phoenix as well as featuring the beaded trails. But their particular interest is the use of underglaze copper red. This was not altogether successful, for it is somewhat smudgy in application and on the lengthy granary inscription has run in the glaze and fired grey in the middle of the text.

A similar imperfection can be observed on the large *guan* in the Percival David collection, which has four cut-out panels with modelled flowers and beaded frames in the style of the Fonthill vase [**130**]. Here copper red has been applied unevenly to the floral details, but more successful is the use of underglaze blue on the same jar – cloud-collar panels with floral sprays, triangular knobbed scrolls and lotus panels. By this stage the potters must have realized where the immediate future lay, in the development of underglaze blue rather than the elusive copper red for decoration. As already discussed, it was not until the early fifteenth century that the Chinese potters finally mastered the technical problems of copper red.

The Sinan wreck has already been cited for the fact that its cargo, dated by wooden tags to 1323, contained almost every type of southern wares *except* blue and white, even including a dish roughly inscribed in copper red.[13] Although numerous attempts have been made over the years to ascribe the origins of blue and white to the Song dynasty, no substantial evidence has so far come to light. The earliest dated piece is a funerary vase found in a tomb of 1319 near Jiujiang in Jiangxi province.[14] This unique piece has a cloud-collar panel on the shoulder, a freely painted peony scroll on the body and a ring of plantain leaves at the base. With a cover surmounted by a tall, pagoda-like finial and its sharply angled foot, the vase bears little relation to later Yuan blue and white, and would seem to have been a one-off experiment.

202 A group of celadon sherds from the Nilaveli wreck, Sri Lanka. Yuan dynasty, first quarter of 14th century.

If the Sinan wreck can only supply negative evidence for the date of full-scale production of blue and white at Jingdezhen, another recently discovered wreck in Sri Lanka with a very similar cargo of celadon would appear to corroborate it.[15] Presumably the ship was on its way westwards until it came to grief on the east coast of the island, and although it has proved impossible to excavate it in view of the prevailing political situation and the continuing civil war in the area, its location is known from local fishermen and divers. The ship foundered on an underwater reef just off the coast north of Trincomalee, near Nilaveli. Its presence became known from the quantities of water-worn sherds washed up onto the beach, of which a selection is now in the reserve collection of the Ashmolean Museum at Oxford. One theory is that the great volcanic explosion at Krakatoa in the Sundra Strait in 1883, which produced a worldwide tidal wave whose oscillations even reached the English Channel, scoured the wreck and deposited the sherds on land. The *Ceylon Examiner* for 27 August that year recorded the effects of the tidal wave on Sri Lanka. At Hambantota on the east coast the sea rose twelve feet above its normal level; there is, in fact, nothing between the Straits of Malacca and the island. And there is also the possibility that the cyclones common to the Indian Ocean could have had a similar effect. Again, like Allaippidy, the sherds were scattered over a wide area and there is no evidence of any settlement with which they could have been associated.

As noted in chapter 5, the parallels with the Sinan material are close, with similar loosely incised and moulded designs [**117**, **118**, **202**].[16] Part of a bowl with a moulded floral design can be matched with one in Istanbul and another found in Aleppo, and all three with a fourth from a Longquan kiln site near Anfu in China. So, even before excavation of the wreck (unlikely in the foreseeable future), these few sherds have provided provisional evidence of the provenance and possible destination of its cargo.

Amongst all these Longquan celadons were two problem pieces.[17] The first was a flat porcelain sherd painted in underglaze blue with a diamond diaper ring and part of a flaming cloud scroll at the centre. Superficially it looked like the centre of an eighteenth-century dish, but closer inspection led one to speculate whether it might not indeed have been a piece of early blue and white. The only possible comparison would seem to be with the lid of a Yuan cylindrical covered box, such as one excavated at the Zhushan site at Jingdezhen, which has a diamond diaper on the edge; similar cloud scrolls are found on a dish from Luomaqiao.[18] The second puzzle was an unglazed base sherd, with a very rough surface. This feature is common on early miniature vessels, and in particular on a fragment of a blue and white vase picked up by John Pope in Beijing in 1946, now in the Freer Gallery. It is decorated with a lotus and spiked lobed leaves.[19] If these two pieces really are Yuan, they could well be amongst the earliest known examples of blue and white.

If the argument for Yuan blue and white in Sri Lanka is slender, recently discovered material from a shipwreck in the Red Sea could hardly be more positive. Although the exact location of the wreck has yet to be determined, the finds so far are spectacular.[20] They include the remains of fourteen blue and white dishes, three bowls, two *guan* and a celadon bowl (see itemized list, pp. 189–91). The dishes range from 40 to 50 cm in diameter and are almost equally divided between those with foliate and those with plain rims. All have sharply cut V-shaped foot rings and unglazed bases. Painted with a whole repertoire of fourteenth-century motifs, they represent the first specific evidence of the passage of these large-scale wares as far as the Red Sea, almost within sight of their ultimate destination: the Yemen, Egypt and Syria.

Following once again in John Pope's footsteps, the designs on the dishes can be classified as follows:

Rims – foliate or plain; breaking serpentine waves (either to left or right), diamond diaper, floral wreath reserved on blue ground, concentric arcs, crapemyrtle and blackberry lily
Cavetto – lotus wreaths with plain, single or double spiked lobed leaves; a peony wreath, in one case moulded in relief on a blue ground; cloud-collar panels; lotus panels with auspicious emblems, fruit and flowers
Centre – compositions including the following: rocks, melons, vine leaves, tendrils, bamboo, plantain, peonies, breaking serpentine waves, concentric waves, whirlpools, pairs of phoenixes, chrysanthemum, lotus and spiked leaves, lotus pond, a duck, cloud-collar panels, *lingzhi* fungus, knobbed classic scroll
Outside – lotus wreath with single or double spiked lobed leaves; lotus panels

Besides the dishes, there are three bowls, two jars (*guan*) and a celadon bowl. The bowls resemble ones found in Syria, and similar sherds from Fustat, characterized by sturdy, sharply cut foot rings and thick base sections (see p. 27). On all three bowls the bottom of the foot ring and the base are unglazed and fired pale orange. The designs include classic scroll, lotus pond, lotus wreath with spiked lobed leaves, lotus panels, a duck, a fish, eelgrass.

The two *guan* are of different types. The first, with its broad toros moulding, is of a well-known variety that usually has a cover. The second is simpler, with a vertical neck; there is a complete example, painted with a peacock, in Ye Peilan's compilation of Yuan porcelain.[21]

The design motifs include hexagonal and diamond diaper bands, lotus wreath with one or two spiked lobed leaves, breaking serpentine waves, plantain, rocks, bamboo, a peacock.

The large celadon bowl is a well-known type, of which there are a number in the Topkapi Saray collection. It is over 40 cm in diameter, with a foliate rim and two parallel lines incised below the rim on the outside. It is carved inside and out with narrow radiating panels. The bowl appears to have been thrown and then a large hole cut at the centre, which was covered with a ceramic plaque before firing. The roughly shaped foot ring was applied later and not cut out of the mass of clay, as is the case with the blue and white bowls.

The most obvious parallels with the Red Sea material are to be found in the Topkapi Saray collection, and to a lesser extent in the porcelain from Syria and

203 a–u Sherds of blue and white porcelain and celadon from a wreck in the Red Sea. Yuan dynasty, 14th century.

a

b

c

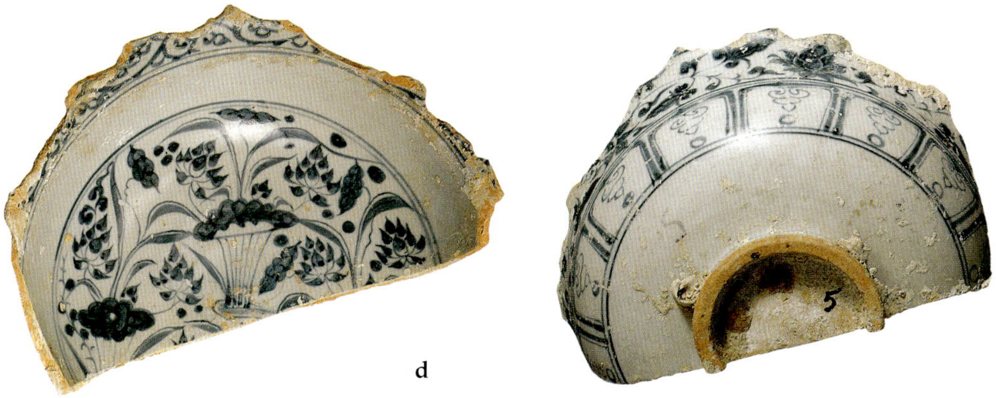

d

e

f

g

from the Ardebil Shrine. The vigorous swirling waves on the neck of *a* also decorate a *guan* in Istanbul of similar shape, with a plain toros moulding (TKS 15/1413), and the hexagonal diaper band is found on the two magnificent octagonal vases in Istanbul (TKS 15/1471, 1473). The second *guan* (*b*, *c*) has a plantain motif more commonly found on dishes, such as TKS 15/1418. The peacock motif occurs both on an Istanbul dish (TKS 15/1482) and on one of the octagonal vases (TKS 15/1471), where the leaves have incised veins, like the plantain. Two of the bowls (*d*, *e*), with their lotus pond designs, have parallels with pieces from Syria, and the form can be found in the Istanbul and Ardebil collections; the third bowl (*f*) has a fish swimming amongst eelgrass and other water plants, in the style of a *guan* in Istanbul (TKS 15/1411), which also has similar scalloped trefoils in the lotus panels.

The celadon bowl (*g*) is closest to a whole series in Topkapi Saray with foliate rims, fluted bodies, narrow foot rings and glazed plaques at the centre (TKS 15/1514 et seq.). Regina Krahl has commented on the function of these plaques, which cover a hole in the base, speculating whether they are simply decorative or were necessary for technical reasons when firing such large bowls. She notes that celadon bowls with the same feature are known from Fustat, Ardebil, East Africa and even from Japan, and that Egyptian potters copied it when imitating celadon.[22]

Of the fourteen dishes, whilst the interiors are decorated with a variety of different motifs, all of them are painted on the outside with a lotus wreath, with single or double spiked lobed leaves, which gives the group a certain homogeneity. One dish (*n*) is of particular interest in that the lotuses and spiked leaves in the cavetto, and forming a background to the central design of phoenixes, are unmistakably by the same hand, in this case arguing against the theory that there was a division of labour in executing various sections of the designs. The rims, whether foliate or plain, are decorated with a diamond diaper (*h*, *i*, *k*, *n*, *s*), serpentine waves breaking to the left (*j*, *p*, *u*) or right (*m*), crapemyrtle and blackberry lily (*q*, *r*), overlapping concentric arcs (*o*), and a moulded floral wreath reserved on a blue ground (*l*).

On the dishes where the cavetto is treated independently of the central area, the commonest design is a lotus wreath with spiked lobed leaves (*h*, *i*, *j*, *n*, *s*, *t*), and in one instance with atypical leaves (*k*). Next most common is a peony wreath (*o*), reserved on a blue ground (*m*), moulded, against waves (*l*), or with lotus panels (*p*), while *u* has lotus panels reserved on a blue ground.

h

i

j

k

l

m

The central designs vary considerably. Two are painted with lotus ponds (*o*, *t*) and two more with melons, leaves, tendrils and rocks (*h*, *u*). The rest of the dishes are all different; they are decorated with plantains, rocks, melons, tendrils and bamboo (*i*), plantains, bamboo, rocks and lotus (*s*), peonies reserved against swirling waves (*j*), two opposed phoenixes and chrysanthemum (*k*) or with lotus (*n*), lotus reserved on a blue ground (*l*), eight cloud-collar panels, rosettes and chrysanthemum reserved on a blue ground (*m*), cloud-collar panels with chrysanthemum and *lingzhi*, against waves, a ring of knobbed scroll and floral panel (*p*), cloud-collar panels against knobbed scrolls with a lotus pond and duck (*q*), and cloud-collar panels against serpentine waves with a pointed medallion at the centre with floral designs (*r*).

The lotus pond design is on three dishes in the Topkapi Saray collection (TKS 15/1427, 1428, 1429), three from Ardebil (29.38, 123, 129) and one from Damascus. The melons and rocks design with plantains and bamboo as a central motif is on two Istanbul dishes (TKS 15/1465, 1418) and three from Ardebil (29.39, 120, 121). Peonies against swirling waves are not in either collection. Pairs of phoenixes are on three Istanbul dishes (TKS 15/1467, 1434, 1466) and three from Ardebil (29.48, 127, 319), and one Red Sea dish (*n*) is almost identical to TKS 15/1466 and confirms the suggestion made above that a single artist was responsible for painting the whole dish, including the lotus wreath in the cavetto and the diamond diaper rim. The lotus reserved on a blue ground does not have an immediate parallel, but the moulded floral and peony wreaths on the rim and in the cavetto on this dish (*l*) are almost identical to one from Ardebil (29.128) and another from Delhi. The cloud-collar dish (*m*) also has very close affinities with three in Topkapi Saray (TKS 15/1383, 1382, 1434) with similar foliate rims, breaking serpentine waves and peonies reserved on a blue ground in the cavetto. Although the central designs are all different, they have very similar elements, featuring chrysanthemums with twisting, almost three-dimensional leaves. All four might well be by the same hand. Belonging to the same general design group is *p*, close in design to TKS 15/1383.

The dish *q* is in some ways the most intriguing of all. It has the remains of two cloud-collar panels (of which there would have been six originally), one filled with breaking serpentine waves. The ground between the panels is of knobbed spirals, and at the centre is part of a medallion with a lotus pond design and a single duck. The dish is closely related to one from Damascus, once in the Larsson collection, which is in turn linked to dishes from Topkapi (TKS 15/1480), Delhi,

n

o

p

q

r

s

t

u

Inner Mongolia and Jingdezhen itself. It is the perfect link between all of these sites, and nothing could better epitomize the universality of blue and white found from one end of Asia to the other in the Yuan period.[23] To the same family belongs *r*, a dish with similar elements and perhaps an even greater degree of sophistication. The cloud-collar panels, alternately larger and smaller in scale, are even more sharply delineated. Between them and the central medallion, instead of knobbed spirals there is a positively seething mass of breaking serpentine waves. As with so many pieces of Yuan blue and white, one detects the hand not of a simple craftsman, but of an artist of consummate skill and self-assurance. How strange that a fragment of his work should end up on an underwater coral reef, thousands of miles from its conception.

Apart from the earlier Sinan, Sri Lanka and Red Sea material, a whole series of wrecks from the sixteenth century onwards contain large quantities of porcelain. They illustrate the richness of material available for study, but also present some problems. The basic difficulty lies in the technology employed to rescue the remains. Underwater archaeology is a relatively new discipline and owes its origins to the development of the aqualung by Jacques Cousteau after the Second World War; although primarily intended for sporting purposes, it has begun to be used increasingly as an investigative tool.

In the late 1950s the first attempts were made to combine the recovery of artefacts from a wreck with careful planning *in situ* before lifting. The methods employed were the same as those used on land for recording a newly opened tomb. In fact, it was Honor Frost, an amateur diver and professional draughtsman who had worked on Kathleen Kenyon's excavations at Jericho, who made the imaginative connection between the two.[24] In 1957 she met a Turkish diver and his American colleague in Bodrum in southern Turkey, and together they planned and excavated a Byzantine wreck off the island of Yassi Ada. Over the following years recording techniques became increasingly sophisticated, and capable of surveying not only the disposition of the cargo on the ocean floor but also the structure of the ships themselves. What had started as an art quickly became a science, combining the skills of scientific archaeology with the equally impressive experience of professional divers. In this enterprise Honor Frost was not only a pioneer but subsequently played an important role in the development of scientific underwater archaeology.

Unfortunately, this new technology was infrequently applied to the category of wrecks discussed below, notable exceptions being that of the *San Diego* galleon

(1600) off Manila, and the *Witte Leeuw* (1613) off St Helena, both of which were carefully excavated and documented.[25] An element of plunder has often entered into the equation, for adventurous speculators realized that fortunes could be made if wrecks crammed with thousands of pieces of Chinese porcelain, along with other highly marketable commodities, could be located. The search still goes on.

A provisional list of wrecks particularly significant for the history of Chinese ceramics includes:

Lena junk	Philippines	*c.*1500
San Isidro junk	Philippines	*c.*1550
Royal Captain	Philippines	late 16th century
San Diego galleon	Manila	1600
Witte Leeuw	St Helena	1613
Banda	Mauritius	1615
San Gonçalo	Cape of Good Hope	1630
Concepción	Haiti	1641
'Hatcher' wreck	?South China Sea	1643–6
Vung Tau wreck	off Vietnam	1690
Geldermalsen	off Vietnam	1752

The first of these, the Lena junk, was pillaged by local fishermen before being excavated.[26] Apart from the ceramics – a collection of Chinese, Vietnamese, Thai and even Burmese material – the wreck was particularly interesting for its content of metalware, including lead and iron ingots, bronze cannons, bracelets, copper vessels, woks, needles, lacquer, spices and ivory tusks. The Chinese blue and white porcelain was the late fifteenth-/early sixteenth-century type commonly exported to Southeast Asia and to Syria and the Near East. For instance, out of more than six hundred pieces of blue and white found in Syria, more than a third are of this period and the type is well represented in Topkapi Saray. Characteristic is the loose style of painting, often freely interpreting earlier Yuan designs, such as the numerous large bowls with a lotus pond. As already noted (see p. 132), a *terminus ante quem* is provided by Giovanni Bellini's painting *The Feast of the Gods*, which is dated 1514 and includes two pieces of blue and white unmistakably of this type. The Lena junk, unlike ships moving westwards carrying porcelain, was apparently sailing towards the Philippines to supply a local market. So was the *San Isidro* junk, carrying crudely painted provincial Chinese blue and white of two basic types, again an instance of non-Eurocentric production.[27] Both junks were found on the west coast of the Philippines, their contents indicative of the general commerce of the South China Sea between the mainland and the islands. Although difficult to date with precision, the assignation of the *San Isidro* cargo to the mid-sixteenth century is convincing.

On 14 December 1600 the Spanish galleon *San Diego*, after unsuccessfully attacking the *Mauritius*, a Dutch marauder, sank off the coast of Manila with three-quarters of her crew of 450 and all her contents. By a diligent search through the Spanish archives, the excavator Franck Goddio not only learned the circumstances that led up to the disaster, but also formulated a pretty good idea of where the wreck must lie. Its location and excavation was a joint enterprise between the European Institute of Underwater Archaeology and the National Museum of the Philippines, financed by the Elf Foundation of the French petrol company. Over a thousand pieces of blue and white were recovered, mostly Wanli *kraak* porcelain but also some provincial wares and over five hundred storage jars. A large variety of Spanish and other artefacts, Mexican coins and even food remains were also found, and the careful recording of the ship itself showed that, although of Spanish design, it was actually locally built. The general impression is of everyday life on board a Spanish ship, with the blue and white just part of the everyday equipment of such a vessel. The date, however, is still important as a marker in the evolution of porcelain in the Wanli era (1573–1620).

The 'Hatcher' wreck (named after its discoverer and excavator, Captain Michael Hatcher) presents a massive corpus of material from the mid-seventeenth century. This was a ship that was indeed destined for the West and foundered *c.*1646 on a reef somewhere in the South China Sea. Over 23,000 pieces of Chinese porcelain were recovered, and their sale in Amsterdam between 1983 and 1986 provoked a sensation. A monograph on this wreck, and that of the *Geldermalsen* of 1752, also found by Captain Hatcher, and their significance for ceramic chronology was published in 1988.[28] The authors are somewhat coy about the exact location of the Hatcher wreck, and the circumstances of its excavation. In a carefully argued analysis of the porcelain it is made clear that the disaster occurred just at the end of the Ming dynasty, and the wreck contained blue and white that can be dated around 1643–6. What is particularly interesting is that there is evidence of the continuation in slightly modified form of a number of *kraak* designs familiar from the *Witte Leeuw* wreck of 1613,[29] and Van de Pijl-Ketel makes some telling comparisons. At the same time there are pieces that are the precursors of designs which, until now, would have been assigned to the late Transitional/early Kangxi period. Scrupulously noting the possibility that later material might have intruded onto the site, or even the unlikely event that this vast amount of porcelain could have been shipped at a later date, it is hard not to accept the authors' conclusion that the material is all contemporaneous – and it is necessary, in the light of this, to revise previous simplistic notions of what kind of decoration is to be associated with periods labelled *kraak*, 'Transitional' and of the Kangxi dynasty. The real conclusion is that, far from being a period when the Jingdezhen industry was only coasting along amid political upheaval, the mid-sixteenth century was actually one of great stylistic innovation and originality. The inclusion of a number of oddities such as celadon, Swatow and provincial wares only serves to increase the richness and diversity of the find.

The Vung Tau wreck of 1690 has a better documented history, and after its initial discovery by a fisherman off Con Dao island, a hundred miles south of Vung Tau on the southern coast of Vietnam, it came to the attention of the authorities.[30] The Vietnam Salvage Corporation entered into a joint-venture partnership with a Swedish diving expert to share expenses, proceeds from the sale of part of the cargo being used to install a representative collection in the appropriate Vietnamese museums. The site was gridded and the ship itself recorded. Burned to the water line, its fate appeared to have been the result of an accident on board rather than being wrecked on a reef. The vessel was almost certainly bound for Batavia, the major entrepot on the north coast of Java, where the representatives of the Dutch East India Company (VOC) would have purchased the cargo for re-export westwards. Only a few years after the revival of the Jingdezhen industry in 1683, the particular interest of the Vung Tau cargo is the evidence it provides for blue and white made specifically after European designs, often in the form of painted wooden models supplied to the Chinese artisans. As already discussed (see pp. 83–6), there is a much earlier instance of Chinese potters executing on command when, in the fifteenth century, Islamic metalware and glass were used as models for Chinese porcelain. The Vung Tau blue and white goblets, beakers, vases, teapots, pill boxes and mustard pots, decorated with an eclectic mix of Chinese and European motifs, were obviously destined for Europe.

They were the raw material for massed blue and white used in late seventeenth-century European interiors, on pedestals, fireplaces, on top of cupboards and doorways, in fact anywhere it could be imposed. What is quite evident is that what was required was a quantity of repetitive standard forms, rather than pieces of individual quality. The master of this new decorative style was Daniel Marot. Popular in Holland and Germany, the best example of his work in England is at Hampton Court, where the lavish use of porcelain owes much to Queen Mary II's personal predeliction for blue and white.[31] As she died in 1694, the Vung Tau wreck of 1690 is particularly relevant. At the same time the wreck's cargo contained a large quantity of provincial wares, plain or simply painted, intended for a more indigenous market. Unglazed pottery lamps, storage jars, charcoal-burners and two pestles, three mortars and a pair of millstones strike an even more humble note.

Colin Sheaf's account of the second wreck found by Captain Hatcher, the *Geldermalsen*, which sank in 1752, is instructive, for here the historical record is even more complete, thanks largely to a diligent search through the Dutch archives by Christiaan Jörg.[32] A great deal is known about the ship itself and its various voyages, and there are even details of how the disastrous wreck occurred from the testimony of the crew who survived. Moreover, Jörg was able to match the detailed record of the 223,303 pieces of porcelain that had been requested from Holland with what was actually loaded in Canton in 1751, revealing considerable discrepancy. This he explains by the length of time orders took to reach the Far East, often arriving too late to be fulfilled.

The *Geldermalsen* was one of six ships commissioned in 1746 by the VOC and left Holland on her first (and last) voyage to the Far East in August 1748. From Batavia the ship sailed to Japan, returned to Java, then went to Canton to collect a cargo destined for Surat in northwest India, returning to China in July 1751. Leaving with its new cargo on 18 December, just sixteen days later the ship struck a reef in the South China Sea, apparently due to a navigational error. Of the 112 people on board, only 32 survived.

Deposited on the reef, a mere four hundred years later most of the cargo was recovered. It consisted mainly of blue and white and enamelled wares of conventional design, mostly designed for the new fashion of drinking tea or coffee. There were also services consisting of dinner plates, butter dishes, sauce boats, milk jugs and teapots suitable for the European market. Again there were crudely painted provincial bowls and saucers, which can have been intended neither for Europe nor for a local market, as the ship was sailing direct from Canton and not stopping at Batavia. It is conjectured that they would have been unloaded at the Cape, for the use of the Dutch factory there. Other curiosities on

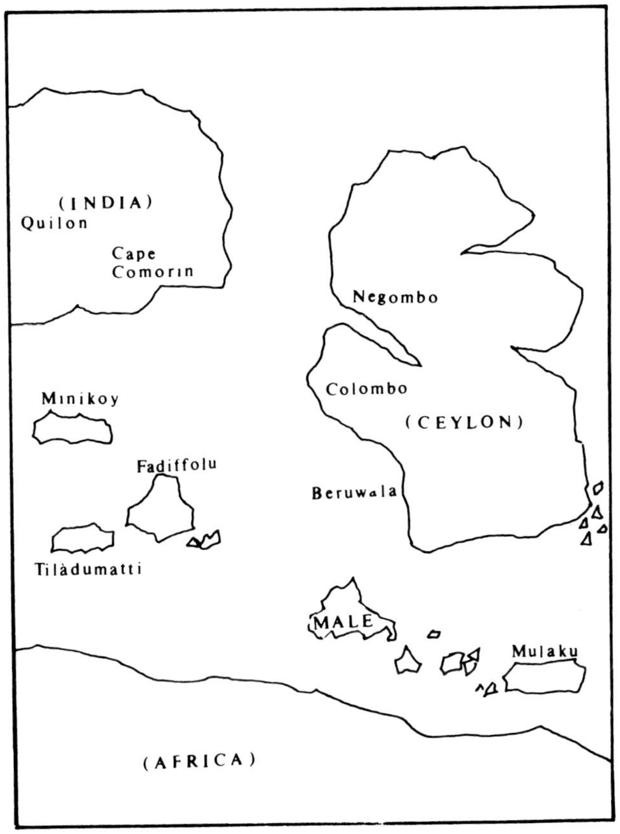

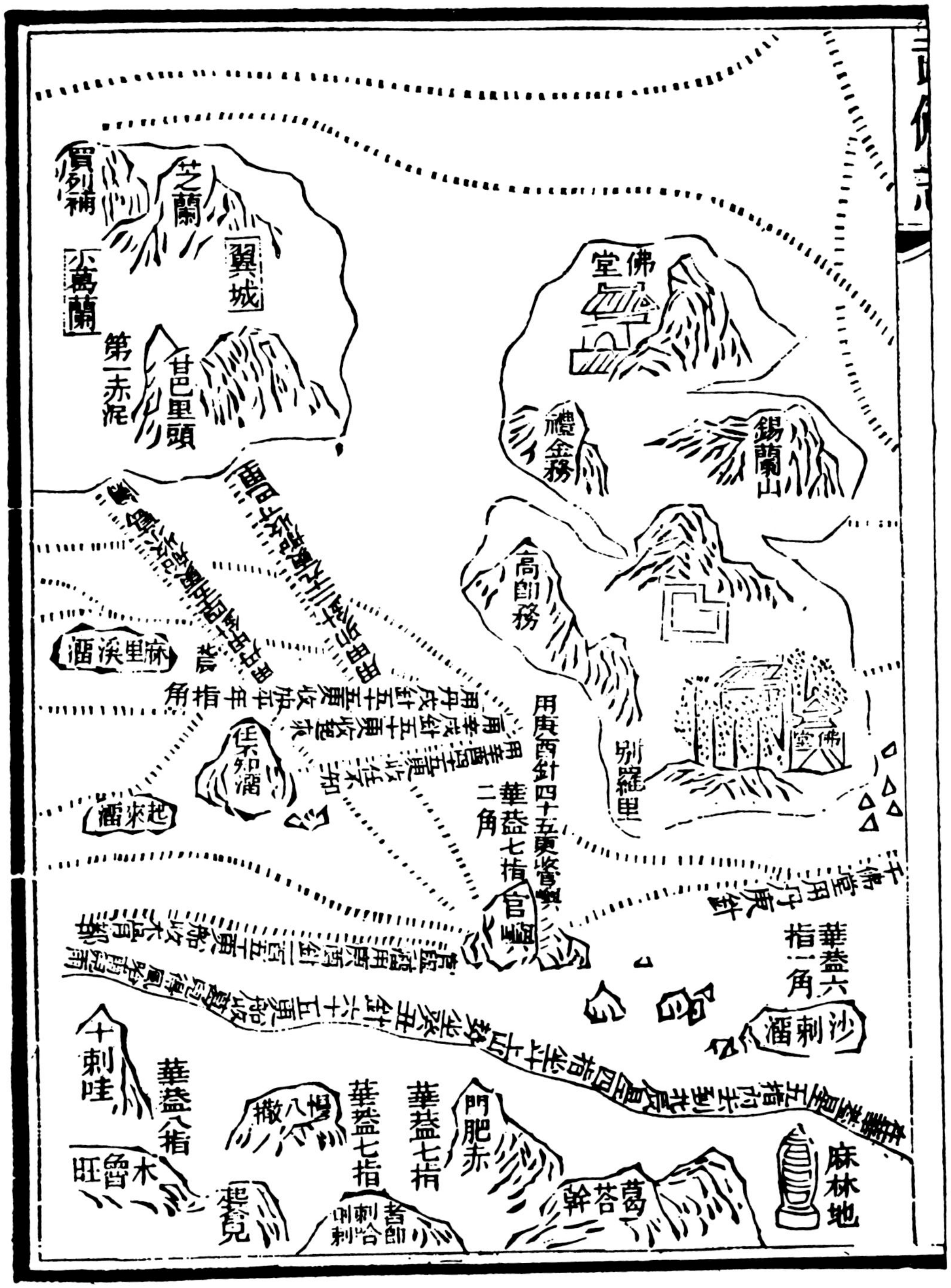

204 Portrait of the emperor Yongle.

205 a, b The Mao K'un map, folio 19v, showing India, Ceylon, the Maldive Islands and East Africa.

board consisted of four Yixing stoneware teapots and fifty-three *martaban* brown-glazed stoneware storage jars, used throughout the centuries for carrying water and other supplies on the voyage. Indeed, such *martaban* jars are still used for the same purpose to this day in the Maldives, tied down on the deck of the local *dhonies*. Glazed figurines copying European originals made at Meissen, as well as Chinese figures of Daoist immortals and other subjects, were also on board the *Geldermalsen*.

But perhaps the most spectacular success of Hatcher's expedition was the recovery of gold ingots from the wreck. Their loss had been a major concern when the Dutch authorities at Batavia carried out an enquiry into the circumstances of the wreck, based on the evidence of the survivors who arrived a week later in two of the ship's lifeboats. When the ship foundered, two seamen were ordered to bring up a weighty chest, but they only got it as far as the deck, from where it must have slithered into the sea when the ship struck the reef a second time and was finally lost. Hatcher found the ingots on the seabed just outside the remains of the hull.

It is clear even from this brief description of a variety of different wrecks that they are a potentially valuable source of information, not only for ceramic history but also for the types of vessels used across the centuries, and for life on board ship of the sailors who manned them. The caution is that the more careful the excavation, the greater the scientific result, but this is a difficult equation when the material rewards are so great. As for blue and white porcelain, one can only repeat Sir Mortimer Wheeler's perceptive comment years ago, about the importance of pottery for archaeology: 'It is easy to break – but difficult to destroy.' Even covered with concretions, shells and coral, the evidence is still there.

206 a–u Section drawings of blue and white porcelain and celadon recovered from the Red Sea wreck. *Dimensions are given in the accompanying descriptions.*

Jars (*guan*)

a The jar fragment is painted with a blue band on the moulded rim, with a hexagonal diaper band below; on the neck is a ring of breaking serpentine waves, the toros moulding is plain, and there is a lug handle on the shoulder. Below is a diamond diaper and a lotus wreath with pointed lobed leaves with either one or two spikes. *Diameter of neck: 18.6 cm.*

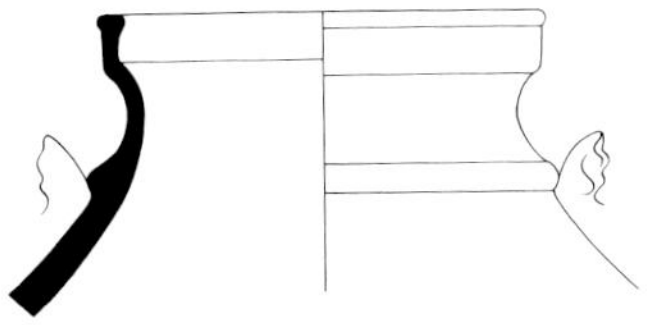

b, c The body and base are from the same vessel. On the upper section is a plantain with a central stalk springing from a rock; its leaves have incised veins. The plantain is surrounded by lotuses, a peony, bamboo and a leafy spray. The surviving lower part of the jar has similar floral designs and a peacock's tail, its body obscured by coral deposit. The slightly recessed base and bottom of the wide foot are unglazed and fired pale ochre. *Diameter of body: 34.6 cm.*

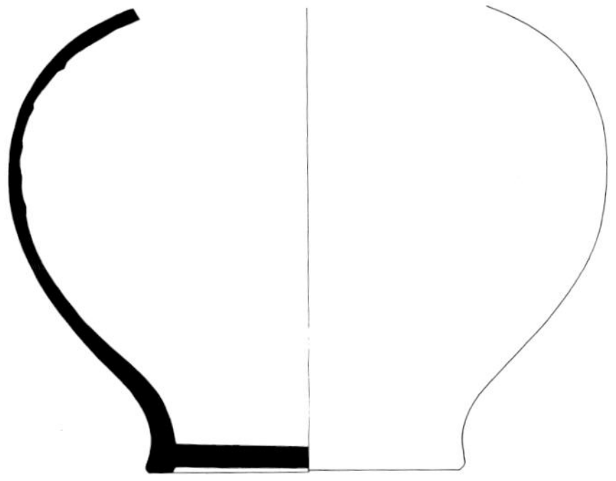

Bowls

d Inside, the remains of a broadly painted classic scroll just below the everted rim; at the centre, inside double rings, is a lotus pond design. Outside is a lotus wreath with single spiked lobed leaves, and lotus panels below. *Diameter of base: 11 cm.*

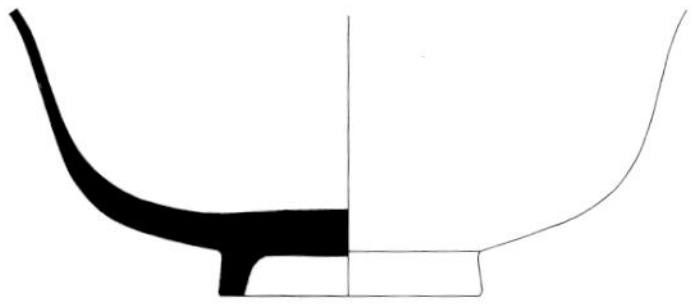

e Inside, part of a lotus pond, with duck looking backwards; outside, lotus panels. *Diameter of base: 10.4 cm.*

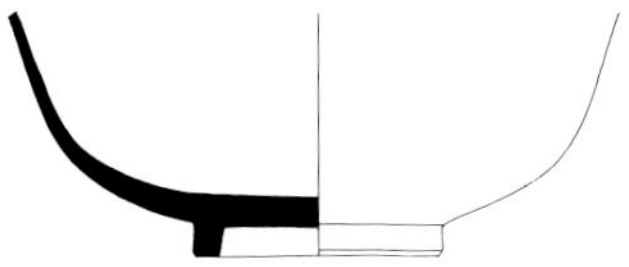

f Inside, a fish swims amongst water-weeds and eelgrass; outside, lotus panels. *Diameter of base: 9.8 cm.*

Celadon

g The large celadon bowl has a foliate rim, small foot, and below the rim outside, two incised lines. Both inside and out are moulded radiating panels. At the centre is a hole covered with a glazed plaque. *Diameter: 41.5 cm.*

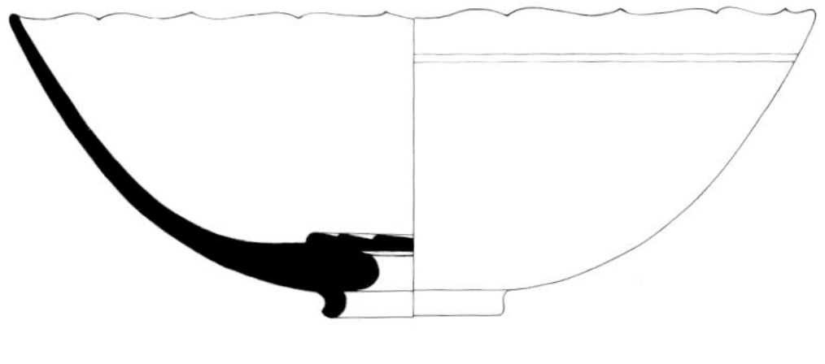

Dishes

h The flat sloping rim with diamond diaper pattern; in the cavetto, lotus wreath with double spiked lobed leaves; at the centre, part of a composition of melons, leaves and tendrils and a rock; outside, a lotus wreath with both single and double spiked lobed leaves; the unglazed base fired orange. *Diameter: 40.5 cm.*

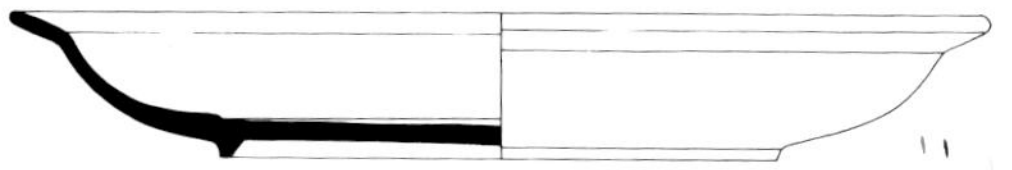

i The flat sloping rim with diaper pattern; in the cavetto, lotus wreath with single spiked lobed leaves; at the centre, a landscape with a plantain, a rocky outcrop with bamboo, melons and tendrils; outside, a ring of lotus panels. *Diameter: 42.2 cm.*

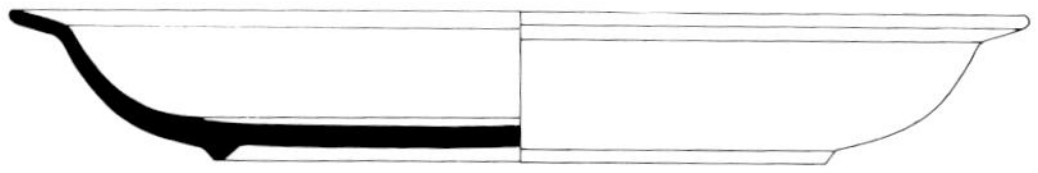

j The raised foliate rim with serpentine waves breaking to the left; in the cavetto, a lotus wreath with double spiked lobed leaves; at the centre, inside double foliate rings, part of a composition of peonies and leaves drawn in linear style and reserved against a ground of swirling waves; outside, a lotus wreath with double spiked leaves. *Diameter: 44.4 cm.*

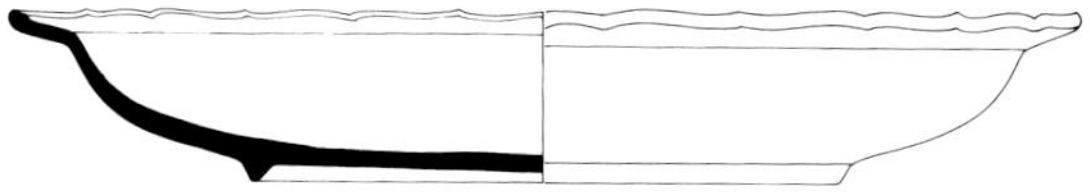

k The flat sloping rim with diamond diaper pattern; in the cavetto a lotus wreath with lobed leaves without spikes; at the centre, two opposed phoenixes, both with lobed spiral tails, with chrysanthemum with cross-hatched centres and spiralling leafy stems; outside, a lotus wreath with lobed spikeless leaves. *Diameter: 44.4 cm.*

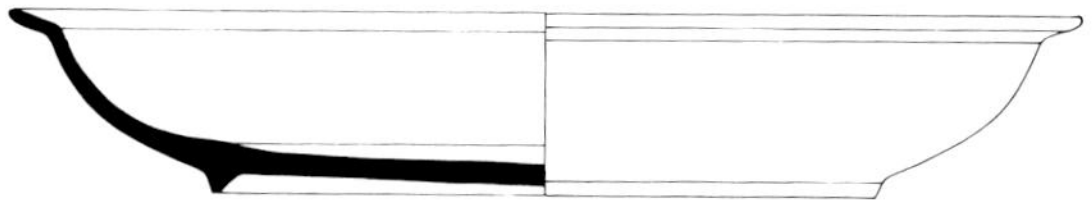

l The raised foliate rim moulded with a floral wreath reserved on a blue ground; in the cavetto, a moulded peony spray against waves; at the centre, part of a design of lotus and double-spiked lobed leaves against a blue ground; outside, a lotus wreath with single spiked lobed leaves. *Diameter: 45 cm.*

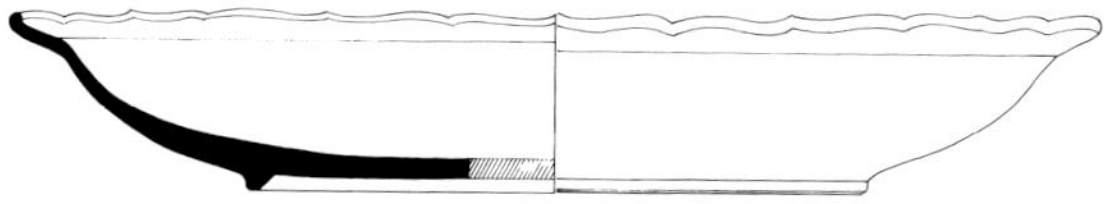

m The raised foliate rim with serpentine waves breaking to the right; in the cavetto, a peony wreath, some flowers in profile, and with buds, against a blue ground; at the centre, part of a design of eight cloud-collar panels with tiny panels and rosettes between their points; at the centre and extending into the panels, a composition of chrysanthemums with flowerets and leaves on spiralling stems all reserved on a blue ground; outside, a lotus wreath with single spiked lobed leaves and a pomegranate-like flower, the bottom of the foot ring and base fired orange. *Diameter 46 cm.*

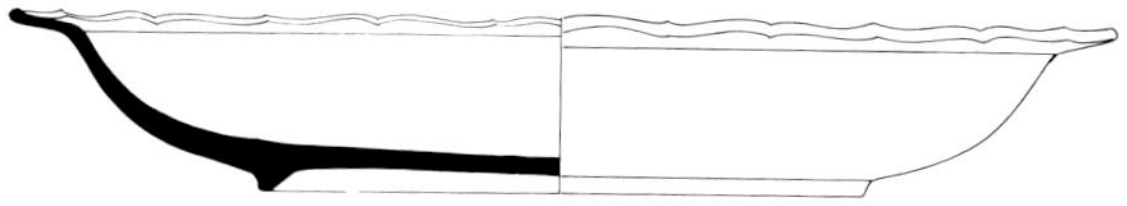

n The flat sloping rim with a diamond diaper pattern; in the cavetto, a lotus wreath with double spiked lobed leaves; at the centre, a composition of opposed phoenixes against a background of lotuses, single and double spiked leaves; outside, a lotus wreath with double spiked leaves. *Diameter: 47.5 cm.*

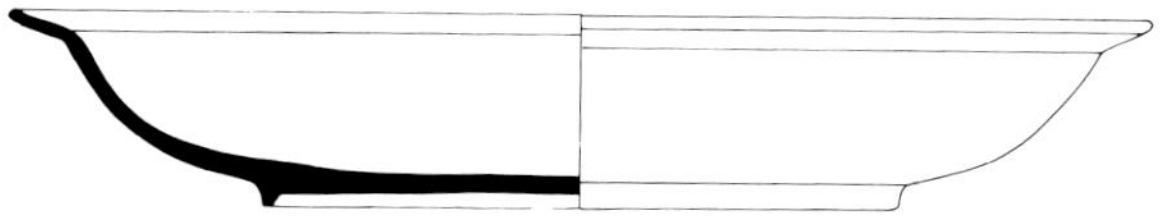

o The flat sloping rim with a band of overlapping concentric arcs; in the cavetto, a finely painted peony wreath with alternate flowers in profile; in the centre, a lotus pond; outside, a lotus wreath, one flower with a lobed centre, the leaves without spikes. *Diameter: 46 cm.*

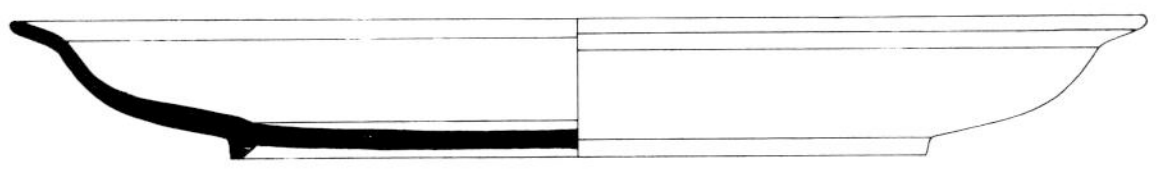

p On the rim, serpentine waves breaking to the left; in the cavetto, a peony wreath and a ring of twenty-six lotus panels with auspicious emblems, including books, coral, flaming pearls, cash, peaches and flowers, all reserved on a blue ground; at the centre, cloud-collar panels with chrysanthemum and *lingzhi* fungus on a ground of serpentine waves, a ring of knobbed classic scroll and a floral panel; outside, a lotus wreath with single spiked lobed leaves. *Diameter: approx. 47.5 cm.*

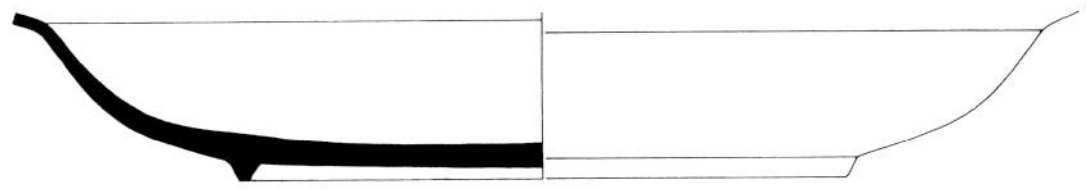

q The foliate rim with a raised edge and a wreath of crapemyrtle and blackberry lily; in the cavetto, six (?) cloud-collar panels, one filled with breaking waves and whirlpools, against a ground of knobbed scrolls; at the centre, a lotus pond with a duck; outside, a lotus wreath with single spiked lobed leaves. *Diameter: 47.5 cm.*

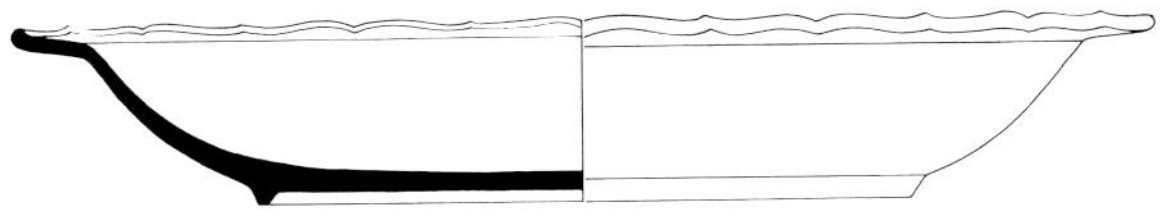

r The foliate rim with a crapemyrtle and blackberry lily wreath; in the cavetto, six cloud-collar panels, one with a lotus and scalloped spiralling leaves on a blue ground, two more with breaking and concentric waves against a background of serpentine waves; at the centre, a pointed medallion with a floral design; outside, a lotus wreath with single spiked lobed leaves. *Diameter: 48 cm.*

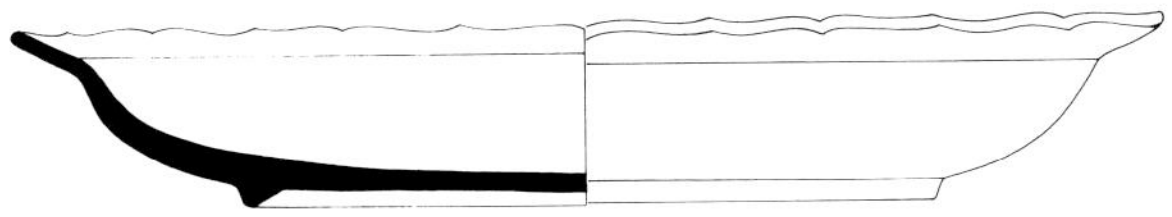

s The plain sloping rim with a diamond diaper band; in the cavetto, a lotus and pomegranate (?) with double spiked lobed leaves; at the centre, a spray of plantain and bamboo with rocky outcrops and a lotus spray curving downwards with spiked lobed leaves; outside, a lotus wreath with single spiked leaves. *Diameter: 48 cm.*

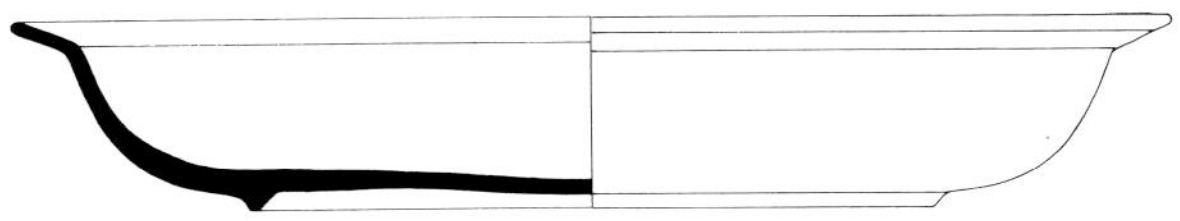

t The rim is missing; in the cavetto is a lotus wreath with single spiked lobed leaves, in the centre a lotus pond; on the outside is a lotus wreath. *Diameter: approx. 48 cm.*

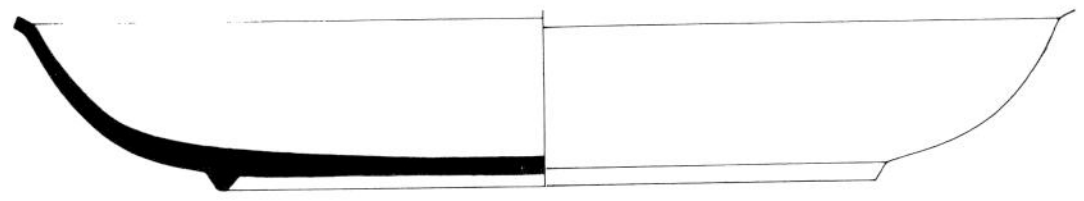

u The foliate rim has a raised edge painted blue on the outside, and serpentine waves breaking to the left; in the cavetto is a series of moulded lotus panels reserved on a blue ground, three of them with different floral designs; at the centre, part of a design of melons with vine-like leaves and tendrils; outside, a lotus wreath with single spiked lobed leaves. *Diameter: 50 cm.*

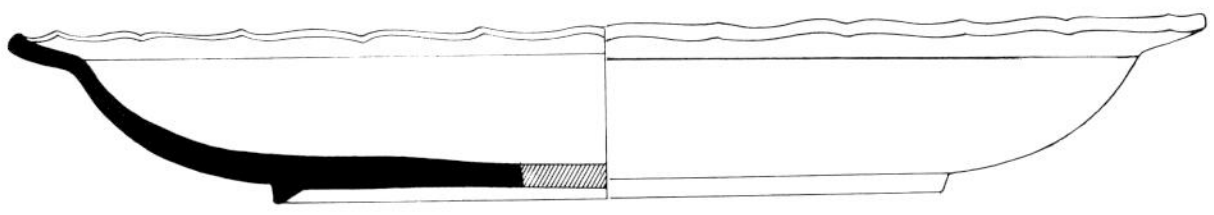

FROM TOP CENTRE, LEFT TO RIGHT
207 Chinese blue and white porcelain, 17th century; Vietnamese stoneware dish, 15th century; Syrian blue and white pottery, 15th century; Chinese blue and white porcelain (*c*.1500); Chinese blue and white porcelain sherds from Fustat, 14th century; Japanese blue and white porcelain dish, 17th century; Persian blue and white pottery, 17th century.

9 COLLECTORS AND EXCAVATORS

Collectors and *chinoiserie*, excavators and scholars

Perception is dangerous game, for, as has already been hinted, the observer is often not objective – and never perfect. One cannot study the history of blue and white without becoming aware of other researchers on the same trail, both past and present. There are big fish in the pond, and there are also minnows. Some are aware of the grand design, others concerned with minutiae. As in all fields of scholarship, passion and bias abound. The consolation is that knowledge consists of the sum total of all these parts, and can change direction from one moment to the next.

Awareness of the singular qualities of the blue and white phenomenon seems to have been around since the start, first of all amongst the Mongols and then very quickly spreading throughout Asia to the West. There had already been an appreciation of Chinese ceramics since at least as early as the Tang dynasty, so in a way the novelty of blue and white was only following a well-established track. It was the superior quality of the porcelain and its spectacular decoration in cobalt blue that swiftly established its reputation. The evidence for this lies not only in the fourteenth-century blue and white recovered from all over Asia and Africa, but also from the desperate attempts of potters worldwide to imitate it in more humble materials. The frustration lasted until the eighteenth century and the discovery of the true composition of porcelain, but in the meantime the process of imitation produced some interesting spin-offs. Whether it be Syrian, Turkish and Egyptian pottery, Italian Medici soft-paste porcelain, or German, French, Dutch, Iberian, English and Mexican blue and white, the results were often fascinating.

Collecting began early on, first of all within the royal courts of Turkey, Egypt and Persia, where blue and white porcelain was acquired for utilitarian purposes but still had a striking impact on indigenous taste. In Europe, amongst the ruling classes it was a symbol of distinction, suitable for massive displays and further embellishment with gold and silver mounts. For the wealthy middle classes also it was a mark of prestige – witness the slave boy's despair in Ibn Battuta's tale when he dropped his master's dish in the streets of Damascus. What is interesting in Syria is that over the centuries blue and white lost its identity and survived only in the form of family heirlooms. No one realized how old much of it was, because, apart from gaining a few scuff marks, Chinese porcelain (unlike pottery) does not visibly age. But this is not to say that it was not valued by its owners. I am reminded of a tale I heard in Douma, where an old mud-brick house had been pulled down and a false wall revealed in the main room. Behind it was a cache of blue and white. Why? Quite simply, when the heat of the city becomes too great in summertime, the Damascenes retreat to the relative cool of Bloudan in the mountains of the Anti-Lebanon. It was (and maybe still is) common practice to wall up your most valuable possessions for the summer months. In this case the family must have suffered some misfortune, perhaps the medieval equivalent of a traffic accident, and never returned.

Blue and white has a dual function of utility and display. The *cina-khaneh* at Ardebil in Safavid Iran finds its echo in the wall cabinets of the mud-brick houses of Douma. In Europe, the Santos Palace in Lisbon springs to mind, but there are numerous other examples in Germany, Sweden and England where the porcelain fulfils its function as superior wallpaper; pay and display is perhaps an apt epithet. For artists it has always been a useful studio prop. A bit of blue and white has served as an integral part of many a still life, setting off such objects as a scarlet lobster, a slice of lemon, a dish of oysters or a glass of wine. Even the less pedestrian painters – Bellini, Chardin, Monet and Matisse for instance – were susceptible. One has to remember that hundreds of thousands, possibly millions, of pieces of blue and white flooded into Europe from the sixteenth century onwards, becoming an accepted and normal attribute of everyday life, in the same manner as an oriental rug. Funnily enough, it was not until the nineteenth century that anyone started looking at blue and white for its intrinsic qualities. This was not simply a taste for *chinoiserie* but an attempt to nail down the strange qualities and appeal of this alien product. Again it was an artist – in this case an American, James McNeill Whistler – who first perceived its mysterious appeal.

Then came the scholars, collectors and dealers, who began to classify five hundred years' worth of blue and white porcelain, dividing into stylistic groups and establishing chronologies. This process has been going on ever since. Museums began to form serious collections of porcelain in the nineteenth century, and in the process of cataloguing them laid the foundations of modern scholarship. It was not only blue and white, but the whole range of Chinese ceramics which came in for scrutiny.

Certainly for most of the past century scholarship has been fundamentally the prerogative of the connoisseur, in which the handling and careful scrutiny of objects has played a leading part. This has been amplified by historical investigation and scientific analysis. Great private collections have been amassed, and public ones augmented and refined. Although archaeological finds of Chinese porcelain were noted in Egypt, the Indus valley and Zimbabwe (to name three instances at random), it was not until after the Second World War that the serious stratigraphic excavation of sites with Chinese material took place. The two leading sites have been Fustat / old Cairo in Egypt, and Siraf on the Persian Gulf. Even now the results from both sites are not definitively available. The archaeological record has been supplemented by numerous surveys of sites along the maritime and terrestial trade routes, and these have provided much evidence of cultural exchange and interaction throughout Asia. In China itself archaeologists have been particularly active, their excavations of kiln sites, tombs and urban contexts forming the basis of our knowledge of the evolution of Chinese ceramics. The most important have been the excavations at Jingdezhen, which have revolutionized our understanding of the development of Chinese blue and white.

With the advent of the new millennium, one might ask: What now? First of all, a fundamental misapprehension is to think that we now have in hand all the available evidence. The recent finds at Jingdezhen and others in China, India, Egypt and Syria, as well as the material from shipwrecks, indicate that there is still a wealth of material yet to be studied. Nor are the questions posed the same as those which might have been asked in the past. We now have a greater awareness of the social and economic factors that influenced the development of the porcelain industry, and the way in which blue and white has linked widely different social groups, of merchants and consumers, throughout the past six hundred years. Because of its sheer indestructibility, even when broken blue and white will not go away. I can think of no other commodity that can so perfectly illustrate the complexity of human relations in the past, and the interaction of civilizations at the opposite ends of Asia and indeed around the whole world.

NOTES

CHAPTER 1

1. Ibn Battuta 1853–9, IV, pp. 627–8, 630, 634; the French translation has a parallel Arabic text.
2. Gleeson 1996.
3. Carswell 1985*a*.
4. Larner 1999; see Appendix I, p. 114, for the Italianate/French text in the Bibliothèque Nationale (ms. fr.1116), first half of fourteenth century.
5. Carswell 1985*a*, pp. 13–14.
6. Hughes-Stanton & Kerr 1980, pp. 26–7. The modern name is Tong'an.
7. Père d'Entrecolles, in Bushell 1899.
8. Wood (in publication).
9. Allan 1973, pp. 111–20.
10. de Clavijo 1928.
11. Buell, in Amitai-Preiss & Morgan 1999, pp. 201–3.
12. Buell, Anderson & Perry 1998.
13. See chapter 8.
14. Smart 1977, p. 201, pls 72, 78b.
15. Père d'Entrecolles, in Bushell 1899, p. 339.
16. Krahl 1986, pp. 399, 496–7; Garner 1954, pl. 9a.
17. Lubo-Lesnichenko 1994; Sommarström 1956–8.
18. Carswell 1985*a*, p. 62, no. 10.
19. Bushell 1899, p. 186.
20. Addis 1977*b*, p. 34, pl. 18a (middle row, right).
21. Carswell 1985*a*, p. 60.

CHAPTER 2

1. Carswell 1995*a*, pp. 154–66.
2. Pope 1970.
3. Pope 1956, pp. 55–6; Carswell 1967, pp. 45–6, n.26.
4. Ayers 1951, pp. 134–41.
5. Beamish 1995, pp. 247–8, fig. 27.
6. Carswell 1967, n.27.
7. Lovell 1984, no. 112.
8. Jiang Qi, *Tao qi lue*, 1683 edition; Medley 1974, pp. 7–9.
9. Père d'Entrecolles, in Bushell 1899, pp. 332–58.
10. Père d'Entrecolles, in Bushell 1899, p. 337.
11. See Larner 1999 for a scrupulous examination of Marco Polo's texts and their historical validity.
12. Hughes-Stanton & Kerr 1980, nos 130–43; Carswell 1985*a*, p. 16.
13. Ibn Battuta 1853–9 (French trans.), 1958–94 (English trans.), 1963 (Arabic text).
14. Ibn Battuta 1958–94, I, pp. 143, 149.
15. Carswell 1967.

CHAPTER 3

1. Hourani 1995.
2. Begley & De Puma 1996.
3. Chu Yu 1975, p. 31.
4. Carswell 1999*b*, pp. 2–3, figs 1a, b.
5. Feng Xianming 1976, pp. 4–7.
6. Pope 1970, pl. 40.
7. Vainker 1991, pl. 99.
8. Guy 1990, pp. 45–58, 104–8. As the present work was going to press, the whole topic of Vietnamese stoneware was being revolutionized by the discovery of the Hoi An wreck, containing more than 150,000 vessels; see Butterfields 2000.
9. Guy 1990, pp. 26–7; Wong, in Yeo & Martin 1978.
10. Krahl 1986, pp. 527–8, TKS 15/1850, 2157, 2434; Chittick 1974, II, pls 140g, 146c, d.
11. Krahl 1986, pp. 527–8, TKS 15/1850. For further evidence of kiln sites in the Hanoi region and elsewhere in Vietnam, see Willetts 1971, pp. 9–11.
12. Krahl 1986, TKS 15/2157 (bottle), 15/2434 (*kendi*); one of the Kilwa sherds has the same pattern as the *kendi*, see Chittick 1974, II, pl. 140g.
13. Beamish 1995, figs 20, 23, 24, 26, 27, 29.
14. Wong 1978, to which one might tentatively add the following identifications: Patani (Moluccas), Tambralinga (Tambalan, Tambelan island, Borneo), Trenganu (Kuala Terenggan, east coast of Malaysia), Kelantan (Kelang, west coast of Malaysia), Su-luo-ga (Sulu Sea), Jai-li-na (Jailolo straits).
15. Karashima 1989, pp. 59–81.
16. Carswell 1978, p. 128, pl. 54b, fig. 3.
17. Willetts 1962, pp. 96–119.
18. Carswell 1978, p. 152, nos 134, 135, pl. 62c. The two 14th-century sherds are now in the study collection of the Ashmolean Museum, Oxford.
19. Chittick 1974; Kirkman 1954; Rougeulle 1996 gives a highly detailed survey of Chinese wares found west of the Indian subcontinent.
20. Chittick 1974, pl. 135a; Korea 1977, no. 125.
21. Wiesner 1979; Morgan 1991, pp. 67–83.
22. Kervran 1982, pp. 97–104, pls X, XI.
23. Hansman 1985; Sasaki 1990, pp. 111–125; Rougeulle 1996, pp. 174–5.
24. Hobson 1928.
25. Ibn Battuta 1958–94, I, p. 69.
26. Krahl 1986, pp. 99, 237, 272, no. 137 (TKS 15/234).
27. Rougeulle 1996, pp. 171–3.
28. Mikami 1982, with a useful bibliography of previous work at Fustat. The outstanding contribution has been George Scanlon's continuing excavations over many years.
29. Carswell 1985*a*, nos 7, 12a.
30. Carswell 1972*b*.
31. Carswell 1979*b*, pls I–V and 1985*a*, figs 2, 3.
32. Sotheby's, 14.12.82, lot 171. Personal communication from Julia Gonnella concerning the Aleppo sherds.
33. National Museum, Damascus, C917; Carswell 1985*a*, p. 69, no. 13b.
34. Riis & Poulsen 1957.
35. Carswell 1979*b*, p. 19, figs 12–15.
36. Carswell 1999*a*, fig. 1.
37. Carswell 1972*a*, pp. 100–101 and 1987, pp. 203–16.

38. Carswell 1998*a*, pp. 18–24.
39. al-Katibi, *Diwan*, *c.*1450–60. Topkapi Saray Library, Istanbul, R. 989.
40. Cao Zhao 1387; Pope 1956, pp. 43–4, where the precise Chinese passage is reproduced.
41. Liu Xinyuan 1993*a*; Addis 1977*a*.
42. Li Zhiyan 1989, p. 69.
43. Kessler 1993, figs 89, 90, 91, 92, 93.
44. Kozlov 1909 and 1925; Stein 1928; Warner 1926; Sommarström 1956–8.
45. Almalik/Huocheng 1979 and 1987; Carswell 1998*b* and 1999/2000.
46. Sommarström 1956–8.
47. Lubo-Lesnichenko 1994.
48. Stein 1928, pp. 429–506.
49. Pope 1956, pls 133, 134.
50. Almalik/Huocheng 1987, F2:1, p. 16 (the *guan* is illustrated upside down).
51. Carswell 1999/2000, pls 28, 30, figs 9, 14.
52. Ibid., pls 8, 12, 14.
53. Carswell 1985*a*, nos 10, 11a–e.
54. Almalik/Huocheng 1979.
55. Carswell 1999/2000, pls 1, 2.
56. Carswell 1995*b*, pp. 165–71, pls L, M, N.
57. Grube & Sims 1985.
58. Liu Xinyuan 1999, figs 9, 16b, 17b; Medley 1963, no. 683, pl. VI.
59. Carswell 1999/2000, fig. 1.

CHAPTER 4

1. Carswell 1966; Carswell 1985*a*, pp. 80–1; Gray 1977, p. 164.
2. Addis 1978, pp. 82–4, figs 35a, b.
3. Carswell 1985*a*, p. 81; Liu Xinyuan 1999, fig. 12b.
4. Krahl 1986, p. 622 (TKS 15/1426); Pope 1956, pls 54 (Isfahan) and 55 (29.439).
5. Pope 1959. The metal flask was previously in the G. Eumorfopoulos collection.
6. Liu Xinyuan 1999, figs 8, 9, 18a, b, c; Krahl 1986, pp. 612, 613, 616; Pope 1956, pl. 55 (29.458).
7. Krahl 1986, p. 612.
8. Ibid., p. 611.
9. Carswell 1985*a*, p. 84, no. 28.
10. Ma Huan [1433], trans. Mills, 1970.
11. Supplementary information is contained in the accounts of two other Chinese voyagers: Gong Zheng (7th expedition) and Fei Xin (3rd, 5th and 7th expeditions, and another independent of Zheng He in 1411–14); see Mills, in Ma Huan 1970, pp. 55–63.
12. The port for Champa was Quy Nhon, ten days' sailing south from the coast of China. Five kiln sites have recently been discovered in the area; see Diem 1999.
13. The Piccus Collection, Christie's 7.12.1984, lots 86, 94.
14. Van Orsoy de Flines 1969, pls 41 (dish), 38 (jar), 37 (ewer).
15. Duyvendak 1938, pp. 368–9, 372; Pelliot 1935, pp. 309–10.
16. Wiesner 1979, pls 6, 7.
17. Caton-Thompson 1931.
18. Pope 1956, p. 78.
19. Carswell 1970, pl. I.
20. Carswell 1995*b*, p. 170, pl. M.
21. Golombek, Mason & Bailey 1996.
22. Addis 1978, pp. 48–55, pls 30a–i; he states: 'In my opinion the best and greatest piece of blue-and-white in the world.'
23. Liu Xinyuan 1993*b*; Krahl *et al.* 1995.
24. Published by Julian Thompson for the first time in Krahl *et al.* 1995, p. 114, fig. 3.
25. Krahl *et al.* 1995, p. 102, no. 145.

CHAPTER 5

1. Yang Houli *et al.* 1998, p. 36.
2. Korea 1977; Youn Moo-byong & Chung Yang Mo 1983.
3. Jiang 1981, pl. 12, fig. 1.
4. Seizo 1977, nos 29, 30, 31.
5. Seizo 1977, no. 24.
6. Guy 1990, pp. 24–5; Van Orsoy de Flines 1969, pls 24–30, for celadon from Java and Borneo.
7. Carswell, in Hourani 1995, p. 145.
8. Smart 1977, pls 91a–e.
9. Gray 1967, pl. 21a.
10. Greensted & Hardie 1982, nos 1–15.
11. Carswell 1978, fig. 8, nos 71, 341, pl. 61.
12. Wiesner 1979, pls 2, 3; Morgan 1991.
13. Kirkman 1954; Chittick 1974; Sassoon 1975; Hansman 1985.
14. Gyllensvärd II, 1975.
15. Ibn Battuta 1958–94, IV, p. 916.
16. *Oriental Art*, XXII, 2, 1976, p. 217.
17. Krahl 1986, I, pp. 233–40.
18. Krahl 1987/8, frontispiece, fig. 2.
19. Medley 1974, colour plate B.
20. Yang Houli *et al.* 1998, pp. 84–5, nos 98, 99.
21. Carswell 1985*a*, p. 65, no. 11e.
22. Ayers 1957, figs 26, 28; Carswell 1999/2000, pl. 6a; Kirkman 1954, p. 129, fig. 32 (D).
23. Sommarström 1956–8, I, p. 124, (K.13717, 6–13), pl. 27, -1.
24. Ye Peilan 1998, nos 159–85.
25. Ayers 1957, fig. 29; Ye Peilan 1998, nos 173–5 (spouted bowls), 160 (vase).
26. Yang Houli *et al.* 1998, p. 83, no. 97.
27. Carswell 1985*a*, p. 70, 14a, b.
28. Medley 1974, pl. 55a.
29. Addis 1959.
30. Pope 1956, pp. 78–9.
31. Carswell 1970, pl. I.
32. Vainker 1991, pl. 135 (OA 1968.4-23.1).
33. Liu Xinyuan 1993*b*, pp. 132–3, B22.
34. Ibid., pp. 188–91, C50, C51.

CHAPTER 6

1. Tibbetts 1971, who as translator and editor of Ahmad ibn Majid's *Kitab al-Fawaid* examines the question of ibn Majid's actual role in detail, pp. 9–11.
2. Toussaint 1966; Chaudhuri 1985.
3. de Matos 1999.
4. Pietro della Valle 1892, p. 154.
5. Carswell 1979*a*, pp. 31–2.
6. de Matos 1999, p. 22.
7. de Rivera 1999*b*.
8. Lion-Goldschmidt 1984, 1986.
9. Krahl 1986, II, pp. 541–69.
10. Yeo & Martin 1978.
11. Crick 1999*a*; Goddio 1988 and 1997; Gotuaco, Tan & Diem 1997.
12. Carswell 1993.
13. Carswell 1979*b*, pl. XXIV, fig. 5; Allan 1971.
14. de Matos 1999, p. 22.

15. Ibid., figs 2, 3.
16. Carswell 1998*a*, pp. 95–8, pls 74–8.
17. de Matos 1999, p. 25, fig. 5.
18. Welsh 1999, pp. 16–17, no. 4; de Matos 1999, fig. 7.
19. Krahl 1986, II, pp. 534–6.
20. 1975, fig. 1.
21. Carswell 1985*a*, p. 31, fig. 8; p. 92, no. 36.
22. Ibid., pp. 93–7.
23. Toussaint 1966, p. 111.
24. Atwell 1982; de Maria y Campos *et al.* 1997; Querejazu 1997.
25. de Maria y Campos *et al.* 1997, pp. 18–20, 44–5.
26. Mudge 1985.
27. Leatham & Lang 1986, pp. 80–81, no. 5.
28. de Rivera 1999*a*, p. 38, fig. 1.
29. Ibid., fig. 2.
30. Chaudhuri 1985, p. 67 et seq.
31. Carswell 1998*a*, pp. 18–24.
32. Ibid., p. 16, pl. 16.
33. Ibid., p. 41, pl. 23.
34. Desroches 1987, pp. 82–4, no. 20.
35. Smart 1977, pls 82b, c.
36. Carswell 1998*a*, pp. 56–9, figs 31, 34.
37. Carswell 1968.
38. Volker 1954, pp. 113–16.
39. Lane 1971, pp. 68–111 – still the best general survey of the topic.
40. Carswell 1978, nos 767–74, pl. 68c.

CHAPTER 7

1. Gray 1984, pp. 186–7; Medley 1981, p. 92.
2. Kim & Gompertz 1961.
3. d'Argencé *et al.* 1979–80, nos 111–53; for analysis of *sanggam* and other Korean ceramic techniques, see Hughes & Joyner, in Portal, 2000, pp. 215–28.
4. Kim 1987/8, pp. 352–3, fig. 1.
5. d'Argencé *et al.* 1979–80, p. 52; Portal, 2000, pp. 137–40.
6. Kim 1987/8 p. 355, fig. 3 and cover illustration.
7. d'Argencé *et al.* 1979–80, no. 173, pl. XXX.
8. Ibid., no. 171, pp. 113, 173.
9. Garner 1954, pp. 58–9, nos 90, 91a, b.
10. Seizo, Trubner *et al.* 1977, pp. 82–3, nos 42A, B, C.
11. Seizo, Trubner *et al.* 1977; Impey 1999, p. 17, note 22.
12. Garner 1975, pp. 9–10, colour frontispiece and pl. 9a.
13. Carswell 1998*a*, p. 111, pl. 88.
14. Garner 1975, pp. 9–10, colour frontispiece and pl. 9a.
15. Carswell 1995*c*, p. 116, no. 141.
16. Impey 1999, p. 17, note 24.
17. Little 1982 (February).
18. Ibid., figs 14, 15, 19, 22, 28, 29.
19. Volker 1959.
20. Leatham & Lang 1986.
21. Carswell 1985*a*, p. 106.
22. Leatham & Lang 1986.
23. Krahl 1986, II, pp. 595–784.
24. Ibid., TKS 15/3448, colour plate, p. 451.
25. TKS 15/1904.
26. TKS 15/1824; see also Carswell 1995*a*.
27. TKS 15/1562; see also Carswell 1987, for a similar bowl from Syria.
28. TKS 15/1611.
29. Krahl 1986, II, TKS 15/1617, colour plate, p. 451.
30. TKS 15/1462, 1721, 1731, 1719.
31. Pope 1956, pp. 134–5.
32. Krahl 1986, II, colour plate, p. 460.
33. Ibid., pp. 758–73.
34. Oxford, Ashmolean Museum, *Eastern Ceramics and other works of art from the collection of Gerald Reitlinger,* London, 1981.
35. Krahl 1986, II, colour plates, pp. 466, 467.
36. Carswell 1985*a*, no. 63, p. 122; Mino & Robinson 1983, pp. 264–5.
37. Krahl 1986, II, colour plate, p. 479, of a brown Swatow ewer decorated with white slip.

CHAPTER 8

1. Carswell 1979*a*; for a complete record of the Allaippidy finds, see also 'Chinese ceramics from Allaippidy in Sri Lanka' in Lam *et al.* 1985, where much of the material is illustrated in colour.

   I found out later that a more distinguished visitor had once lived in the Kings House – Leonard Woolf. He recounts his youthful experiences as a political agent in Jaffna in the first volume of his autobiography, *Sowing*. More recently the building became the stronghold of the Tigers, the resurgent Tamil nationalists.
2. Gyllensvärd 1973; Lam *et al.* 1985.
3. Gyllensvärd 1973, I, pl. 3.1, for a similar sherd from Fustat.
4. Carswell, in Lam *et al.* 1985, p. 33.
5. Yang Houli *et al.* 1998.
6. Ayers 1957, pp. 78–9, fig. 20.
7. Lane 1961.
8. Lee & Ho 1968, cat. no. 26.
9. Yang Houli *et al.* 1998, nos 68, 70, 76, 94.
10. Ibid., no. 88.
11. Ibid., no. 97.
12. Ibid., nos 98, 99.
13. Krahl 1986, p. 483, citing John Ayers.
14. Ibid., p. 482, n.8.
15. Carswell 1995*b*.
16. Ibid., pls A–H.
17. Ibid., pls J, K.
18. Liu Xinyuan 1993*a*, pls 4, 7.
19. Carswell 1985*a*, p. 64, no. 11c.
20. The material recovered belongs to Sotheby's. I am deeply indebted to Julian Thompson, Colin Mackay and Henry Howard-Sneyd for most generously allowing me to publish the Red Sea wreck, and to Lucilla Phelps for meticulously photographing the sherds.
21. Ye Peilan 1998, p. 59, no. 76.
22. Krahl 1986, p. 236, n.20.
23. Carswell 1999/2000, pp. 24–5, pls 14, 16, 17.
24. Frost 1962.
25. Van de Pijl-Ketel 1971; Goddio 1994 (for a popular account of the discovery and sophisticated methods used to excavate the *San Diego*) and 1996.
26. Crick 1999*b*; Goddio 1988 and 1997; Goddio *et al.* 2000; Gotuaco, Tan & Diem 1997.
27. Crick 1999*b*, pp. 75–9.
28. Sheaf & Kilburn 1988.
29. Van de Pijl-Ketel 1971.
30. Jörg & Flecker 1999; Christie's 1992.
31. Lane 1952.
32. Jörg 1986; Sheaf & Kilburn 1988.

BIBLIOGRAPHY

The shortened bibliographical references given in the notes refer to the publications listed below. Where the list includes more than one work by a particular author (or authors) published in the same year, differentiation between those works is made by the insertion of a, b, *etc after the year of publication.*

ABBREVIATIONS: SOAS = School of Oriental and African Studies, University of London; *TOCS = Transactions of the Oriental Ceramic Society*

Addis, Sir John, 'A Group of Underglaze Red', *TOCS 1957–1958, 1958–1959*, vol. 31, 1959, pp. 15–37.

'A Visit to Ching-tê-chên', *TOCS 1975–1977*, vol. 41, 1977*a*, pp. 1–34.

'Hung-wu and Yung-lo White', *TOCS 1975–1977*, vol. 41, 1977*b*, pp. 35–59.

Chinese Ceramics from Datable Tombs, Sotheby Parke Bernet, London and New York, 1978.

'Porcelain-Stone and Kaolin: Late Yuan Developments at Hutian', *TOCS 1980–1981*, vol. 45, 1982, pp. 54–66.

Allan, James, 'Later Mamluk Metalwork, II. A Series of Lunch-boxes', *Oriental Art*, XVII, Summer 1971, pp. 156–64.

'Abū 'l-Qāsim's Treatise on Ceramics', *Iran* XI, 1973, pp. 111–20.

Almalik/Huocheng (in Chinese):

Xinjiang Bowuguan, 'Blue-and-White Porcelain and Other Cultural Relics of the Yuan Dynasty excavated at Huocheng County, Ili Prefecture, Xinjiang Province', *Wenwu* 8, 1979, pp. 26–31.

The Nei Monggol Institute of Archaeology and CPAM, Alashan Meng, 'Excavations at Heicheng in Nei Monggol', *Wenwu* 7, 1987, pp. 1–23.

Amitai-Preiss, Reuven & David Morgan (eds), *The Mongol Empire and its Legacy*, Brill, Leiden, 1999.

d'Argencé, René *et al.*, *5000 Years of Korean Art*, exhibition catalogue, USA, 1979/80.

Ashmolean Museum, Oxford, *Eastern Ceramics and Other Works of Art from the Collection of Gerald Reitlinger*, catalogue of the memorial exhibition, London, 1981.

Atwell, W.S., 'International Bullion Flows and the Chinese Economy circa 1530–1650', *Past and Present*, 95, 1982, pp. 68–90.

Ayers, John, 'Early Chinese Blue-and-White in the Museum of Eastern Art, Oxford', *Oriental Art*, III.4, London, 1951, pp. 134–41.

'Some Characteristic Wares of the Yüan Dynasty', *TOCS 1954–1955*, vol. 29, 1957, pp. 69–86.

Beamish, Jane, 'The Significance of Yuan Blue and White exported to South East Asia', in Scott & Guy (eds), *South East Asia & China…*, 1995, pp. 225–51.

Begley, Vimala & Richard D. De Puma (eds), *Rome and India: The Ancient Sea Trade*, University of Wisconsin Press, Madison, 1996.

Buell, Paul D., 'Mongol Empire and Turkicization: The Evidence of Foodways', in Amitai-Preiss & Morgan, *The Mongol Empire…*, 1999, pp. 200–223.

Buell, Paul D., Eugene Anderson & Charles Perry, *A Soup for the Qan: Chinese Dietary Medicine of the Mongol Era as Seen in Hu Szu-hui's 'Yin-shan Cheng-yao'*, Kogan Paul, London, 1998.

Bushell, S.W., *Oriental Ceramic Art*, Appleton, New York, 1899.

Butterfields, *Treasures from the Hoi An Hoard*, 2 vols, with contributions by Pham Quoc Quan, Mensum Bound & John Guy, San Francisco, 2000.

Cao Zhao, *Ge gu yao lun*, 1387; rev. & enl. by Wang Tso, 1459.

Carswell, John, 'An early Ming Porcelain Stand from Damascus', *Oriental Art*, New Series, XII, Autumn 1966, pp. 176–82.

'A Fourteenth-Century Chinese Porcelain Dish from Damascus', in F. Sarruf & S. Tuqan (eds), *American University of Beirut Festival Book (Festschrift), 1866–1966*, Beirut, 1967, pp. 39–58.

New Julfa: The Armenian Churches and Other Buildings, Clarendon Press, Oxford, 1968.

'Archaeology and the Study of Later Islamic Pottery', in D.S. Richards (ed.), *Islam and the Trade of Asia*, Bruno Cassirer, Oxford and University of Pennsylvania Press, Oxford, 1970, pp. 63–66.

'Six Tiles', in R. Ettinghausen (ed.), *Islamic Art in The Metropolitan Museum of Art*, The Metropolitan Museum of Art, New York, 1972*a*, pp. 99–124.

'China and the Near East: The Recent Discovery of Chinese Porcelain in Syria', in *The Westward Influence of the Chinese Arts from the 14th to the 18th Century*, Colloquies on Art and Archaeology in Asia, no. 3, Percival David Foundation of Chinese Art, SOAS, London, 1972*b*, pp. 20–25.

'China and Islam in the Maldive Islands', *TOCS 1975–1977*, vol. 41, 1978, pp. 121–98.

'China and Islam: A Survey of the Coast of India and Ceylon', *TOCS 1977–1978*, vol. 42, 1979*a*, Third George de Menasce Memorial Lecture, pp. 24–68.

'Sīn in Syria', *Iran*, XVII, 1979*b*, pp. 15–24.

Blue and White: Chinese Porcelain and Its Impact on the Western World, The David and Alfred Smart Gallery, The University of Chicago Press, Chicago, 1985*a*.

'Chinese Ceramics from Allaippidy in Sri Lanka', in Lam *et al.*, *A Ceramic Legacy…*, 1985*b*, pp. 31–47.

'Two Tiny Turkish Pots: Some Recent Discoveries in Syria', *Islamic Art*, 2, The Bruschettini Foundation, Genoa and The Islamic Art Foundation, New York, 1987, pp. 203–16.

'The Feast of the Gods: The Porcelain Trade between China, Istanbul and Venice', *Asian Affairs*, June 1993, pp. 180–85.

'White and Blue: Chinese Ceramics and the Albers Effect', *Asian Art*, Hali Annual 2, 1995*a*, pp. 154–66.

'From Chicago to Samarkand', *Asian Affairs*, June 1995*b*, pp. 165–71.

Chinese Ceramics in the Sadberk Hanım Museum, Sadberk Hanım Museum, Istanbul, 1995*c*.

Iznik Pottery, British Museum Press, London, 1998*a*.

'A Month in Mongolia: Kharakhoto Revisited', *Asian Affairs*, October 1998*b*, pp. 287–98.

'Beirut: The Future of the Past', *National Museum News*, London, Spring 1999*a*, pp. 19–22, 43.

'China and the Middle East', *Oriental Art*, XLV.1, 1999*b*, pp. 2–14.
'Kharakhoto and Recent Research in Inner Mongolia', *Oriental Art*, XLV.4, 1999–2000.
'Europe's first sight of blue and white?', *Cornucopia*, 28, vol. 5, 2003, pp. 10–11.
Caton-Thompson, Gertrude, *The Zimbabwe Culture*, Clarendon Press, Oxford, 1931.
Chaudhuri, K.N., *Trade and Civilisation in the Indian Ocean*, Cambridge University Press, 1985.
Chittick, Neville, *Kilwa, an Islamic Trading City on the East African Coast*, Nairobi, 2 vols, 1974.
Christie's, *The Vung Tao Cargo*, sale catalogue, Amsterdam, 7–8 April 1992.
Chu Yu, *P'ing-chou k'o t'an*, Taipei, Taiwan, 1975.
de Clavijo, Ruy Gonzales, *Embassy to Tamerlane, 1403-1406*, trans. G. Le Strange, Routledge, London, 1928.
Crick, Monique, 'Trade with France', *Oriental Art*, XLV.1, 1999*a*, pp. 52–9.
'Hongzhi (1488–1505) and Zhengde (1506–21) Ceramics found on Shipwrecks off the Coast of the Philippines', *TOCS 1997–1998*, vol. 62, 1999*b*, pp. 69–82.

Desroches, Jean-Paul, *Le Jardin des porcelaines*, Musée Guimet, Paris, 1987.
Diem, Allison I., 'Ceramics from Vijaya, Central Vietnam: Internal Motivations and External Influences (14th–late 15th century)', *Oriental Art*, XLV.3, 1999, pp. 55–64.
Donnelly, P. J., 'Chinese Porcelains with Inscriptions in the Arabic Script', *Connoisseur*, January 1975, pp. 7–13.
Duyvendak, J.J.L., 'The True Dates of the Chinese Maritime Expeditions in the Early Fifteenth Century', *T'oung Pao*, XXXIV, 1938, pp. 341–412.

d'Entrecolles, Père François Xavier, 'Letters from Ching-te-Chen' (*Lettres édifiantes et curieuses*), in Bushell, *Oriental Ceramic Art*, 1899, pp. 332–58.

Feng Xianming, 'Persian and Korean Ceramics Unearthed in China', *Orientations*, 17.5, Hong Kong, 1976, pp. 47–54.
Frost, Honor, *Under the Mediterranean*, Routledge & Kegan Paul, London, 1962.

Garner, Sir Harry, *Oriental Blue and White*, Faber & Faber, London, 1954.
'Chinese Export Art in Schloss Ambras', The Second Hills Gold Medal Lecture, Oriental Ceramic Society, London, 5 June 1975.
Gleeson, Janet, *The Arcanum*, Bantam Press, London, 1996.
Goddio, Franck, *Discovery and Archaeological Excavation of a 16th century Trading Vessel in the Philippines*, Manila, 1988.
'San Diego: An Account of Adventure, Deceit and Intrigue', *National Geographic*, July 1994, pp. 35–7.
Treasures of the San Diego, Paris, 1996.
Weisses Gold, Göttingen, 1997.
Goddio, Franck, Stacey Pierson & Monique Crick, *Sunken Treasures: Fifteenth century Chinese Ceramics from the Lena Cargo*, Periplus, London, 2000.
Golombek, Lisa, Robert B. Mason & Gauvin A. Bailey, *Tamerlane's Tableware: A New Approach to the Chinoiserie Ceramics of Fifteenth- and Sixteenth-Century Iran*, Royal Ontario Museum, Toronto, 1996.
Gompertz, G.M., *Chinese Celadon Wares*, rev. edn, Faber & Faber, London, 1980.
Gotuaco, L., R. Tan & A. Diem, *Chinese and Vietnamese Blue and White Wares found in the Philippines*, Bookmark, Makati City, 1997.
Gray, Basil, 'The Export of Chinese Porcelain to India', *TOCS 1964–1966*, vol. 36, 1967, pp. 21-37.
'Chinese Porcelain of the Fourteenth and Fifteenth Centuries and the John Addis Gift', *British Museum Yearbook* II, London, 1977, pp. 156–88.
Song Porcelain and Stoneware, Faber & Faber, London, 1984.
Greensted, Mary & Peter Hardie, *Chinese Ceramics: The Indian Connection*, Bristol Museum and Art Gallery, 1982.
Grube, Ernst & Eleanor Sims (eds), *Between China and Iran: Paintings from Four Istanbul Albums*, Colloquies on Art and Archaeology in Asia, no. 10, Percival David Foundation of Chinese Art, SOAS, London, 1985.
Guy, John, *Oriental Trade Ceramics in South-East Asia, Ninth to Sixteenth Centuries*, Oxford University Press, Singapore, 1990.
Gyllensvärd, Bo, 'Recent Finds of Chinese Ceramics at Fostat', *Bulletin of the Museum of Far Eastern Antiquities*, I, no. 45, Stockholm, 1973, pp. 91–171; II, no. 47, 1975, pp. 93–117.

Hansman, John, *Julfār, an Arabian Port: Its Settlement and Far Eastern Ceramic Trade from the 14th to the 18th Century*, Royal Asiatic Society, London, 1985.
Harrison-Hall, Jessica, *Catalogue of Late Yuan and Ming Ceramics in the British Museum*, British Museum Press, London, 2001.
Hobson, R.L., 'Chinese Porcelain Fragments from Aidhab, and some Bashpa Inscriptions', *TOCS 1926–1927*, 1928, pp. 19–22.
Hourani, George F., *Arab Seafaring in the Indian Ocean in Ancient and Medieval Times*, 2nd edn, rev. and exp. by J. Carswell, Princeton University Press, 1995.
Howard, David, 'The British East India Company's Trading to China in Porcelain', *Oriental Art*, XLV.1, 1999, pp. 45–51.
Hughes-Stanton, P. & R. Kerr, *Kiln Sites of Ancient China*, Oriental Ceramic Society, London, 1980.

Ibn Baṭṭūṭa, *Voyages d'Ibn Batoutah*, trans. C. Defrémery & B. Sanguinetti, with a parallel Arabic text, 4 vols, Paris, 1853–9.
The Travels of Ibn Baṭṭūṭa, A.D. 1325–1354, trans. H.A.R. Gibb & C.F. Beckingham, 4 vols, following the French format, Hakluyt Society, London, 1958–94.
Rihlāt Ibn Baṭṭūṭa (Arabic text), Dar Sadir & Dar Bayrut, Beirut, 1963.
Impey, Oliver, 'Chinese Porcelain exported to Japan', *Oriental Art*, XLV.1, 1999, pp. 15–21.

Jiang Qi, *Tao qi lue* ('Appendix to the Ceramic Records'), in *Fouliang xian zhi* (Gazetteer and History of Fouliang Xian), 1683 edn.
Jiang Zhongyi, 'Zhejiang Longquan xian Anfu Longquan yaozhi fajue Jianbao', *Kaogu*, 6, 1981, pp. 504–10.
Jörg, Christiaan J.A., *The Geldermalsen: History and Porcelain*, Kemper, Gröningen, 1986.
'Chinese Porcelain for the Dutch Market', *Oriental Art*, XLV.1, 1999*a*, pp. 30–37.
'The Inter-Asiatic Dutch Porcelain Trade', *Oriental Art*, XLV.1, 1999*b*, pp. 71–7.
Jörg, Christiaan J.A. & Michael Flecker, 'Porcelains from the Vung Tau Wreck', *Oriental Art*, XLV.1, 1999.

Karashima, N., 'Trade Relations between South India and China during the 13th and 14th Centuries', *Journal of East–West Maritime Relations*, I, Tokyo, 1989, pp. 59–81.

al-Katibi, *Diwan*, Topkapi Saray Library, R.989, Istanbul.

Kee Il Choi, Jr., 'Chinese Export Porcelains for America', *Oriental Art*, XLV.1, 1999, pp. 90–99.

Kervran, Monik, A. Negre & M. Pirazzoli t'Sertsevens, *Fouilles à Qal'at al-Bahrein*, 1ère partie, 1977–9, Ministry of Information, Directorate of Archaeology and Museums, Bahrain, 1982.

Kessler, Adam T., *Empires Beyond the Great Wall: The Heritage of Ghenghis Khan*, Natural History Museum of Los Angeles County, 1993.

Kim, Chewon & G.M. Gompertz, *The Ceramic Art of Korea*, London, 1961.

Kim, Madeleine, 'Introducing the Ho-am Art Museum, Seoul', *Oriental Art*, XXXIII.4, 1987/88, pp. 352–6.

Kirkman, James S., *The Arab City of Gedi: Excavations at the Great Mosque, Architecture and Finds*, Oxford University Press, 1954.

Korea, National Museum, *Special Exhibition of Cultural Relics found off Sinan Coast*, Samwha Publishing Co., Seoul, 1977.

Kozlov, P.K., 'The Mongolia-Sze-Chuan Expedition of the Imperial Russian Geographical Society', *Geographical Journal*, 34, October 1909, pp. 384–408.

Mongolei, Amdo und die Stadt Chara-Choto, Berlin, 1925.

Krahl, Regina, 'Plant Motifs of Chinese Porcelain: Examples from the Topkapi Saray Identified through the *Bencao Gangmu*' (in two parts), *Orientations*, May and June 1987.

'Relics salvaged from the seabed off Sinan', *Oriental Art*, XXXIII.4, 1987/88, pp. 399–401.

Krahl, Regina, in collaboration with Nurdan Erbahar, *Chinese Ceramics in the Topkapi Saray Museum, Istanbul*, ed. John Ayers, 3 vols, Sotheby's, London, 1986.

Krahl, Regina, Liu Xinyuan, Ts'ai Ho-pi & Julian Thompson, *The Emperor's Broken China: Reconstructing Chenghua Porcelain*, Sotheby's, London, 1995.

Lam, Peter, J. Carswell, T. Russell, M.M. bin Abu Bakr, K.K. Kwan & J. Martin, *A Ceramic Legacy of Asia's Maritime Trade*, Southeast Asian Ceramic Society, West Malaysian Chapter, Oxford University Press, Singapore, 1985.

Lane, Arthur, 'Queen Mary II's Porcelain Collection at Hampton Court', *TOCS 1949–1950*, vol. 25, 1952, pp. 21–31.

'The Gagnières-Fonthill Vase: A Chinese Porcelain of about 1300', *The Burlington Magazine*, CIII, April 1961, pp. 124–132.

Later Islamic Pottery, 2nd edn, Faber & Faber, London, 1971.

Larner, John, *Marco Polo and the Discovery of the World*, Yale University Press, New Haven, Conn., 1999.

Leatham, Lady Victoria, Gordon Lang *et al.*, *The Burghley Porcelains*, Japan House, New York, 1986.

Lee, Sherman E. & Wai-kam Ho, *Chinese Art Under the Mongols: The Yüan Dynasty (1279–1378)*, Cleveland Museum of Art, Cleveland, Ohio, 1968.

Li Zhiyan & Cheng Wen, *Chinese Pottery and Porcelain*, 2nd edn, Foreign Languages Press, Beijing, 1989.

Lion-Goldschmidt, Daisy, 'Les Porcelaines chinoises du Palais de Santos', *Arts Asiatiques*, XXXIX, 1984.

'Ming Porcelains in the Santos Palace Collection, Lisbon', *TOCS 1984–1985*, vol. 49, 1986, pp. 79–93.

Little, Stephen, 'Ko-sometsuke in the Asian Art Museum of San Francisco, *Orientations*, April 1982, pp. 16–19.

Liu Xinyuan, 'Yuan Dynasty Official Wares from Jingdezhen', in Rosemary Scott (ed.), *The Porcelains of Jingdezhen*, 1993*a*, pp. 33–46.

A Legacy of Chenghua: Imperial Porcelain of the Chenghua Reign excavated from Zhushan, Jingdezhen, Tsui Museum of Art, Hong Kong, 1993*b*.

'Imperial Export Porcelain from Late Yuan to Early Ming', *Oriental Art*, XLV.3, 1999, pp. 48–54 (illustrated).

Lovell, Hin-chueng (ed.), *Jingdezhen Wares: The Yuan Evolution*, Oriental Ceramic Society, Hong Kong, 1984.

Lubo-Lesnichenko, Evgeny, 'The Blue-and-White Porcelain of Yuan Period from Khara-Khoto', *International Symposium on Ancient Chinese Trade Ceramics*, National Museum of History, Taipei, 1994.

Ma Huan, *Ying-yai sheng-lan*, ('The Overall Survey of the Ocean's Shores'), [1433], trans. J.V.G. Mills, Hakluyt Society, Cambridge University Press, 1970.

de Maria y Campos, Alfonso *et al.*, *The Silver Galleons*, Instituto Cultural Mexicano, Houston, TX, 1997.

de Matos, Maria Antónia Pinto, 'The Portuguese Trade', *Oriental Art*, XLV.1, 1999, pp. 22–29.

Medley, Margaret, *Illustrated Catalogue of Porcelains decorated in Underglaze Blue and Copper Red in the Percival David Foundation of Chinese Art, Section 3*, SOAS, London, 1963.

Yuan Porcelain and Stoneware, Faber & Faber, 1974.

The Chinese Potter, 2nd edn, Phaidon, Oxford, 1976.

Tang Pottery and Porcelain, Faber & Faber, London, 1981.

Mikami, Tsugio, 'China and Egypt: Fustat', *TOCS 1980–1981*, vol. 45, 1982, pp. 67–89.

Mino, Yutaka & James Robinson, *Beauty and Tranquillity: The Eli Lilly Collection of Chinese Art*, Indianapolis Musem of Art, Indianapolis, 1983.

Morgan, Peter, 'New Thoughts on Old Hormuz: Chinese Ceramics in the Hormuz Region in the Thirteenth and Fourteenth Centuries', *Iran*, 31, 1991, pp. 67–83.

Moule, A.C. & Paul Pelliot, *Marco Polo: The Description of the World*, 2 vols, London, 1938.

Mudge, Jean McClure, 'Hispanic Blue-and-White Faience in the Chinese Style', in Carswell 1985*a*, pp. 43–54.

Pelliot, Paul, 'Notes additionnelles sur Tcheng Houo et sur ses voyages', *T'oung Pao*, XXXI, 1935, pp. 274–314.

Notes on Marco Polo, 3 vols, Paris, 1959–73.

Père d'Entrecolles – see under d'Entrecolles.

Pope, John A., *Chinese Porcelains from the Ardebil Shrine*, Freer Gallery of Art, The Smithsonian Institution, Washington, D.C., 1956.

'An Early Ming Porcelain in Muslim Style', in R. Ettinghausen (ed.), *Aus der Welt der Islamischen Kunst: Festschrift für Ernst Kühnel*, Berlin, 1959, pp. 357–75.

Fourteenth-Century Blue-and-White: A Group of Chinese Porcelains in the Topkapu Sarayi Müzesi, 2nd edn, Freer Gallery of Art Occasional Papers, 2, no. 1, Washington, D.C., 1970.
Portal, Jane, *Korea: Art and Archaeology*, British Museum Press, London, 2000.
Pyrard de Laval, *Voyage to The East Indies, The Maldives, The Moluccas and Brazil*, trans. and ed. by A. Gray & H.C.P. Bell, Hakluyt Society, London, 1887–90.

Querejazu, Pedro & Elizabeth Ferrer, *Potosí: Colonial Treasures and the Bolivian City of Silver*, Americas Society, New York, 1997.

Ray, H.P. & J.-F. Salles (eds), *Tradition and Archaeology: Early Maritime Contacts in the Indian Ocean*, Manohar, New Delhi, 1996.
Reichel, Friedrich, 'The German Trade', *Oriental Art*, XLV.1, 1999, pp. 66–70.
Riis, P.J. & Vagn Poulsen, *Hama: Fouilles et recherches de la Fondation Carlsberg 1931–38: les verreries et poteries médiévales*, Copenhagen, 1957.
de Rivera, Antonio Diez, 'The Spanish Market', *Oriental Art*, XLV.1, 1999, pp. 38–44.
'Chinese Export Porcelain for the Spanish Market', *The Legacy of Macao*, proceedings of a symposium held at the Calouste Gulbenkian Foundation, Lisbon, 22–24 November 1999 (in publication).
Rougeulle, Axelle, 'Medieval Trade Networks in the Western Indian Ocean (8–14th Centuries): Some Reflections from the Distribution Pattern of Chinese Imports in the Islamic World', in Ray & Salles 1996, pp. 159–80.

Sasaki, T., 'Excavations at A'ali, 1988–89', *Proceedings of the Seminar for Arabian Studies*, 20, 1990, pp. 111–125.
Sassoon, Caroline, *Chinese Porcelain in Fort Jesus*, National Museums of Kenya, Mombasa, 1975.
Scott, Rosemary E. (ed.), *The Porcelains of Jingdezhen*, Colloquies on Art and Archaeology in Asia, no. 16, Percival David Foundation of Chinese Art, SOAS, London, 1993.
Scott, Rosemary E. & John Guy (eds), *South East Asia & China: Art, Interaction & Commerce*, Colloquies on Art and Archaeology in Asia, no. 17, Percival David Foundation of Chinese Art, SOAS, London, 1995.
Seizo Hayashiya, Henry Trubner *et al.*, *Chinese Ceramics from Japanese Collections*, The Asia Society, New York, 1977.
Sheaf, Colin & Richard Kilburn, *The Hatcher Porcelain Cargoes: The Complete Record*, Phaidon-Christies, Oxford, 1988.
Smart, Ellen, 'Fourteenth Century Chinese Porcelain from a Tughlaq Palace in Delhi', *TOCS 1975–1977*, vol. 41, London, 1977.
Söderpalm, Kristina, 'The Swedish Trade', *Oriental Art*, XLV.1, 1999, pp. 80–89.
Sommarström, Bo, *Archaeological Researches in the Edsen-Gol Region, Inner Mongolia*, Parts I–II, Statens Etnografiska Museum, Stockholm, 1956–8.
Stein, Sir Aurel, *Innermost Asia*, 4 vols, Clarendon Press, Oxford, 1928.

Tibbetts, G.R., *Arab Navigation in the Indian Ocean before the Coming of the Portuguese*, Royal Asiatic Society, London, 1971.
Toussaint, Auguste, *History of the Indian Ocean*, trans. J. Guicharnaud, The University of Chicago Press, Chicago, 1966.

Vainker, S.J., *Chinese Pottery and Porcelain: From Prehistory to the Present*, British Museum Press, London, 1991.
Valenstein, Suzanne G., *A Handbook of Chinese Ceramics*, The Metropolitan Museum of New York, New York, 1989.
Valle, Pietro della, *The Travels of Pietro della Valle in India*, trans. G. Havers, ed. E. Grey, Hakluyt Society, London, 1892.
Van Orsoy de Flines, E.W., *Guide to the Ceramic Collection, Museum Pusat, Jakarta*, Jakarta, 1969.
Van de Pijl-Ketel, C.L., *The Ceramic Load of the Witte Leeuw (1613)*, Rijksmuseum voor Volkenkunde, Leiden, 1971.
Volker, T., *Porcelain and the Dutch East India Company as recorded in the Dagh-Registers of Batavia Castle, those of Hirada and Deshima and other Contemporary Papers, 1602–1682*, Rijksmuseum voor Volkenkunde, Leiden, 1954, pp. 113–16.

Warner, Langdon, *The Long Old Road to China*, Doubleday, Page and Company, New York, 1926.
Watt, James C.Y. & Anne E. Wardwell, *When Silk was Gold: Central Asian and Chinese Textiles*, The Metropolitan Museum of Art, New York, 1997.
Welsh, Jorge, *Important Collection of Chinese Export Porcelain / Importante Colecção de Porcelana Chinesa de Exportação*, London and Lisbon, 1999.
Wiesner, Ulrich, *Chinesische Keramik auf Hormoz*, Museum für Ostasiatische Kunst, Cologne, 1979.
Willetts, William, 'Ceylon and China', *Transactions of the Archaeological Society of South India, 1960–62*, Madras, 1962, pp. 96–119.
Ceramic Art of Southeast Asia, Southeast Asian Ceramic Society, Singapore, 1971.
Wong, Grace, 'Chinese Blue and White Porcelain and Its Place in the Maritime Trade of China', in Yeo & Martin, *Chinese Blue and White Ceramics*, 1978.
Wood, Nigel, 'China, Ceramic Country' and 'Kaolin Body Changes in Jingdezhen Porcelain in the Yuan Dynasty', in *Blue and White from the Near East to China*, Musée Cernuschi and SFECO, Paris, 22–23 October 1999 (in publication).

Yang Houli, Fan Fengmei & Rita C. Tan, *Dated Qingbai Wares of the Song and Yuan Dynasties* (ed. Peng Shifan), Ching Leng Foundation, Hong Kong, 1998.
Ye Peilan (in Chinese), *Yuandai Ciqi* ('Yuan Dynasty Porcelain'), 1998.
Yeo, S.T. & Jean Martin, *Chinese Blue and White Ceramics*, Southeast Asian Ceramic Society, Ars Orientalis, Singapore, 1978.
Youn Moo-byong & Chung Yang Mo, *The Sunken Treasures off the Sinan Coast*, The Chunichi Shimbun, Tokyo, 1983.

ILLUSTRATION CREDITS

ABBREVIATIONS:

BM OA = British Museum, Department of Asia (Oriental Antiquities), Photography and Imaging, © The Trustees of the British Museum; SL = Sotheby's London; SHK = Sotheby's Hong Kong; SNY = Sotheby's New York; TAS = Technical Art Services; TKS = Topkapi Saray, Istanbul. These are followed by the registration, photo reference or sale date/lot number.

1 BM OA 1947.7-12.231, Oppenheim Bequest
2 Museum of Turkish and Islamic Art, Istanbul; reserve collection; photo Ali Konyali, courtesy *Cornucopia*
3 BM OA 1972.6-20.1, Brooke Sewell Bequest
4 BM OA 1963.12-19.1; 1972.6-19.1; 1975.10-28.3; 1947.7-12.162; 1952.5-13.2; 1954.4-20.3; 1939.5-23.1
5 SNY 9.12.87/256
6 Courtesy Museum of Fine Arts, Boston, 50.2053, Hoyt Collection (reproduced with permission); © 2000 Museum of Fine Arts, Boston; All Rights Reserved
7 TKS 15/1481
8 TKS 15/1422
9 SHK 26.10.93
10 TAS
11 Author
12 Courtesy Museum of Fine Arts, Boston, 37.296, Clara Bertram Kimball Collection, by exchange, 1937 (reproduced with permission); © 2000 Museum of Fine Arts, Boston; All Rights Reserved
13 Author
14 Benaki Museum, Athens
15 TKS 15/1387
16 TKS 15/1512
17 TKS 15/4137
18 Courtesy Museum of Fine Arts, Boston, 14.649, Francis Bartlett Donation of 1912 and Picture Fund (reproduced with permission); © 2000 Museum of Fine Arts, Boston; All Rights Reserved
19 SL 9.12.86/188
20 SL 21.6.83/245
21 Author; ex-H. Pharaon Collection, Beirut
22 TKS 15/1471
23 TKS 15/1413
24 TKS 15/1379
25 TKS 15/1370
26 Courtesy Museum of Fine Arts, Boston, 37.292, Clara Bertram Kimball Collection (reproduced with permission); © 2000 Museum of Fine Arts, Boston; All Rights Reserved
27 SL 15.4.80/ 237
28 BM OA 1959.40-20.1
29 Sinan, 21
30 SL 18.11.98/861
31 TKS 15/1408
32 Indianapolis Museum of Art, 79.512, gift of Mr and Mrs Daniel Henkin
33 SHK 2.5.95/13
34 Private collection, London
35 The Cleveland Museum of Art, 53.122, anonymous gift
36 TKS 15/1480
37 Author
38 SHK 1.11.94
39 SHK 18.5.82/20
40 Percival David Foundation of Chinese Art, B613, B614
41 Author
42 TKS 15/7035
43 Author; ex-H. Pharaon Collection, Beirut
44 TKS 15/1420
45 SL 9.6.87/209
46 SHK 24.11.87/9
47 National Museum of Iran
48 Author
49 Courtesy Arthur M. Sackler Museum, Harvard University Art Museums, Gift of Richard B. Hobart, 1961.112, Photographic Services; © President and Fellows of Harvard College, Harvard University
50 SHK 30.4.91/8
51 TKS 15/1473
52 TKS 15/1391
53 SHK 17.5.88/16
54 Courtesy Åmells, Stockholm, *Paintings of the China Trade 1770–1870*, 1990
55 Private collection, Hong Kong
56 BM OA 1960.7-28.1, Brooke Sewell Bequest
57 The Metropolitan Museum of Art, 1991.456.13, Gift of Betty and John R. Menke, 1991
58 SL/CP.46935/205
59 SL/CP.46898/203
60 TKS 15/235
61 Author
62 Author
63 Author
64 Author
65 Author
66 SL 14.12.82
67 TKS R.989
68 Author
69 SHK 17.5.88/22
70 Author
71 TKS H.2153
72 Author; courtesy of *Oriental Art*
73 Author
74 Bibliothèque Nationale de France, Paris, RCB 18153
75 SHK 1.11.99/311
76 SL 6.12.94/149
77 SHK 30.4.91/10
78 Courtesy Åmells, Stockholm, *Paintings of the China Trade 1770–1870*, 1990
79 SHK 1.11.99/309
80 After Liu Xinyuan, *Oriental Art*, XLV.3
81 Author; ex-private collection, Damascus/BM OA 1966.12-15.1, Brooke Sewell Bequest
82 BM OA 1963.12-19.1
83 SHK/CP.42898/12
84 SHK 18.5.82/144
85 TKS 15/1403
86 Asian Art Museum, San Francisco, Avery Brundage Collection, B60 P33+
87 Author
88 Author
89 TKS 15/1374
90 Author
91 Kathleen Kenyon, after G. Caton-Thompson, 1931, pl. XLIV.1
92 SHK 21.5.84/50
93 TKS 15/9299
94 TKS 15/1371
95 Calouste Gulbenkian Foundation, Lisbon, 2374
96 TKS 15/1407
97 TKS 15/1372
98 TKS 15/1372
99 SL/CP.45301/199
100 TKS 15/1436
101 TKS 15/1456
102 TKS 15/1448
103 TKS 15/2944
104 Author; ex-Larsson Collection, London
105 Author
106 Author; ex-H. Pharaon Collection, Beirut
107 Author; private collection, Beirut
108 Author
109 Author
110 TAS
111 SL/CP.46743/213
112 Courtesy The Art Institute of Chicago, 1997.391, gift of Stanley Herzman in honour of Gladys Wolfson Herzman; © The Art Institute of Chicago; All Rights Reserved
113 TKS 15/239
114 Author
115 Author
116 TKS 15/143
117 Author; Ashmolean Museum, Oxford
118 Author
119 Author; Ashmolean Museum, Oxford
120 Author
121 Author; National Museum, Damascus
122 TKS 15/422
123 TKS 15/148
124 TKS 15/185
125 TKS 15/193
126 TKS 15/80
127 TKS 15/84
128 TKS 15/5608
129 TKS 15/248
130 Percival David Foundation of Chinese Art, B661
131 SHK 21.5.85/15
132 SHK 20.5.81/652
133 SHK 1.11.99/306
134 Author; Hohhot Musem, Inner Mongolia
135 SHK 21.4.93/34
136 SHK 16.5.89/8
137 SHK 16.5.89/9
138 SHK/CP.52962/10
139 SL 2.12.74/287
140 TAS
141 Author
142 French Embassy, Lisbon, photograph by Arnaldo Soares, Divisão de Documentação Fotográfica, Instituto Português de Museus
143 Author; private collection, London
144 Author; Larsson Collection, London
145 Author; private collection, London
146 Author; private collection, London
147 Author; private collection, London
148 Widener Collection, 1942.9.1; photograph © Board of Trustees, The National Gallery of Art, Washington, DC
149 TKS 15/2894
150 Author; ex-H. Pharaon Collection, Beirut
151 Fundação Medeiros e Almeida, Lisbon, 247, photograph by José Pessoa, Divisão de Documentação Fotográfica, Instituto Português de Museus
152 Casa-Museu Dr Anastácio Gonçalves, Lisbon, 118, photograph by José Pessoa, Divisão de Documentação Fotográfica, Instituto Português de Museus
153 Fundação Medeiros e Almeida, Lisbon, 241, photograph by Arnaldo Soares, Divisão de Documentação Fotográfica, Instituto Português de Museus
154 Jorge Welsh
155 TKS 15/2254
156 © The Cleveland Museum of Art, 2000, gift of R. Henry Norweb, 1966.221
157 Museu National de Arte Antiga, Lisbon, 7455, photograph by José Pessoa, Divisão de Documentação Fotográfica, Instituto Português de Museus
158 Museu National de Arte Antiga, Lisbon, 5489, photograph by José Pessoa, Divisão de Documentação Fotográfica, Instituto Português de Museus
159 Courtesy Museum of Fine Arts, Boston, Julia Bradford Huntington James Fund and gift of Mrs F.G. Macomber, 1913 (reproduced with permission); © 2000 Museum of Fine Arts; All Rights Reserved
160 SL/CP.45353/22
161 Author; Benaki Museum, Athens, 119.9.v.D20
162 BM OA 1973.7-26.367
163 TKS 15/3168
164 General National Archive, Mexico
165 Burghley House Collection
166 Courtesy The Art Institute of Chicago, 1923.1444, gift of Mrs Eva Lewis in memory of her husband, Herbert Pickering Lewis; © 2000 The Art Institute of Chicago; All Rights Reserved
167 BM F778+
168 Jorge Welsh
169 BM OA 1878.12-30.520, Henderson Bequest
170 SL (Islamic) 93187/NAHL/98
171 Musée Adrien Dubouché, Limoges, 7238; © Photo RMN/M. Beck-Coppola
172 SL (Islamic) 14.10.99/125
173 Author
174 Author
175 Author; private collection, London
176 Ashmolean Museum, Oxford
177 National Museum of Korea
178 Ho-am Art Museum, Yongin
179 National Museum of Korea
180 Hong Du-yong Collection, Korea
181 Ho-am Art Museum, Yongin
182 British Museum
183 Dongkuk University Museum, Korea
184 Private collection, Japan
185 Victoria and Albert Museum, London
186 British Museum
187 Asian Art Museum, San Francisco, Effie B. Allison Collection
188 Author; National Museum, Colombo
189 Author; private collection, Beirut
190 Author; private collection, Beirut
191 Courtesy Museum of Fine Arts, Boston, 62.357, John Ware Willard Fund, 1962 (reproduced with permission); © 2000 Museum of Fine Arts, Boston; All Rights Reserved
192 Burghley House Collection
193 Burghley House Collection
194 Burghley House Collection
195 Burghley House Collection
196 TKS 15/1611
197 TKS 15/1462
198 TKS 15/2426
199 Author
200 Calouste Gulbenkian Foundation, Lisbon, 2372
201 The National Museum of Ireland
202 Author; Ashmolean Museum, Oxford
203 Lucilla Phelps; Sotheby's, London
204 After Ma Huan, 1970, frontispiece
205 After Ma Huan, 1970, pp. 290–1
206 Author
207 The David and Alfred Smart Museum, Chicago

INDEX

An asterisk (*) after a page number denotes a direct reference to an illustration; † denotes a map. Otherwise, page numbers refer to the main text of the book, in which related illustrations are indicated in bold type within square brackets.